West Sussex Library Service

WITHDRAWN

For Sale

'All that I know most surely about morality and the obligations of men, I owe to football.'

Albert Camus

For Rachel, Mum, Danny, Lilly, Ray, Rod, Glynis, Billy and Stephen Smith and for my Dad.

The World's First
FOOTBALL SUPERSTAR
The Life of Stephen Smith

The World's First
FOOTBALL SUPERSTAR

The Life of Stephen Smith

OWEN ARTHUR

PEN & SWORD
HISTORY
AN IMPRINT OF PEN & SWORD BOOKS LTD.
YORKSHIRE – PHILADELPHIA

First published in Great Britain in 2022 by
PEN AND SWORD HISTORY
An imprint of
Pen & Sword Books Ltd
Yorkshire – Philadelphia

Copyright © Owen Arthur, 2022

ISBN 978 1 39908 348 5

The right of Owen Arthur to be identified as Author of
this work has been asserted by him in accordance with the Copyright,
Designs and Patents Act 1988.

A CIP catalogue record for this book is available from the British Library.

All rights reserved. No part of this book may be reproduced or transmitted in
any form or by any means, electronic or mechanical including photocopying,
recording or by any information storage and retrieval system, without permission
from the Publisher in writing.

Typeset in Times New Roman 11.5/14 by
SJmagic DESIGN SERVICES, India.
Printed and bound in the UK by CPI Group (UK) Ltd.

Pen & Sword Books Limited incorporates the imprints of Atlas, Archaeology,
Aviation, Discovery, Family History, Fiction, History, Maritime, Military, Military
Classics, Politics, Select, Transport, True Crime, Air World, Frontline Publishing,
Leo Cooper, Remember When, Seaforth Publishing, The Praetorian Press,
Wharncliffe Local History, Wharncliffe Transport, Wharncliffe True Crime and
White Owl.

For a complete list of Pen & Sword titles please contact
PEN & SWORD BOOKS LIMITED
47 Church Street, Barnsley, South Yorkshire, S70 2AS, England
E-mail: enquiries@pen-and-sword.co.uk
Website: www.pen-and-sword.co.uk

WEST SUSSEX LIBRARY SERVICE	
202160659	
Askews & Holts	18-Aug-2022
B SMI	

Contents

Acknowledgements — vi
Introduction — vii

Chapter 1   Abbots Bromley — 1
Chapter 2   Hazel Slade — 7
Chapter 3   Hednesford — 13
Chapter 4   Perry Barr — 37
Chapter 5   Culture Shock — 47
Chapter 6   The Team of All Talents — 61
Chapter 7   On the Sidelines — 69
Chapter 8   English Champion — 71
Chapter 9   Apotheosis — 83
Chapter 10   World Champion — 105
Chapter 11   'For Archie' — 119
Chapter 12   William Smith — 133
Chapter 13   Celebrity, Superstar, 'Double Winner' — 140
Chapter 14   Champion Again — 144
Chapter 15   Portsmouth — 159
Chapter 16   The Old Warrior's Return — 201
Chapter 17   Gillingham — 208
Chapter 18   Life After Football — 245

Postscript — 260
Addendum — 264
Endnotes — 266

Acknowledgements

There are many people to thank for help with this book and if not mentioned here then they are acknowledged in the post-script. In 2017, John Lerwill started me on this journey by giving me a first-hand account of how Stephen Smith signed for Aston Villa at the coal mine where he worked in 1893. Since I have been fascinated about finding out more about what happened to Smith after this almost mythical sounding event.

My mother's research through her ancestry.co.uk subscription threw more flesh on the bones of the story's skeleton before lifelong Aston Villa fan Brian Halls gave me access to his website that had an abundance of photographs from Steve's heyday that fuelled my research. My partner Rachel, a driving force in all aspects of research, was able to find crucial archival information about Wolverhampton Wanderers thanks to her colleague Carl Baldwin which helped greatly with evidence regarding Stephen's brother Billy who played for Wolves when Steve was at Villa.

My friend and neighbour Paul Taylor and his father Robert Taylor kept me furnished with statistics from throughout the history of Aston Villa. The Pompey Historical Association, guardians of Portsmouth FC's archives, were an almost 24/7 resource thanks to the quick work of Colin Farmery, Graham Dubber and Paul Boynton to answer my queries. Many first-hand accounts of the life and times of Billy Smith were bequeathed to me thanks to Ray Stubbington via his uncle Rod Cowan the grandson-in-law of Billy. Unfortunately, Rod passed away in April 2021, having been a vital source corroborating many events detailed in the book.

Others have played key parts in the writing of this book and their contributions appear in the post-script. I hope this book does Rod's memories of Billy and Steve justice as well as the efforts of all those involved in its creation. Thank you.

Introduction

Stephen Smith was born in Abbots Bromley, Staffordshire on 14 January, 1874 and died in Littlemore Hospital in the village of Benson, Oxfordshire, near to where he had retired, in May, 1935. He grew up in the village of Hazel Slade just yards from the wilds of Cannock Chase and worked underground in the mines of the Cannock and Rugeley Colliery, eventually graduating to the position of haulage machine operative, taking men and materials to and from the coal face.

Whilst working as a miner he played football for Hednesford Town after originally playing for his Colliery team. He was signed by Aston Villa Football Club Director, Fred Rinder, at the coalface, still on a shift. Steve continued to work down the mines whilst going on to gain five League Championship medals, an FA Cup medal and was part of the only the second football team in history to claim the League and Cup Double in 1897. He was denied a second FA Cup medal due to not being picked for the cup final side of 1897. With no substitutes allowed at that time, he could not play a part from the bench or claim a medal as surely he would have had modern football rules applied.

At Aston Villa he was playing for the best club in the land in the best and only fully professional league in the world. Villa could lay claim to being 'World Club Champions', they regularly beat Rangers and Celtic of the Scottish League, the only clubs from the only country that could lay claim to being superior in world football. Not only did Smith play for the best club in the world, in 1895 he played for England in the International Championship contested by the other British home nations. The only international team in world football at that time that could claim to match the mighty Scottish side of that period were the English.

In order to clinch the 1895 title, the English team needed to hold the traditionally stronger Scottish team to a draw to claim the title of 'International Champions'. A Stephen Smith inspired England blew

Scotland away in the first half and Smith confirmed victory with a screamer of a strike that made the score 3-0 on the stroke of half-time. Victory made England 'de facto' World Champions that year and was the starting point for the end of Scottish hegemony at the top of the world game.

Smith left Villa for Portsmouth in 1901 due to the Football League imposing a wage cap on players. Moving for the greater earning opportunities that were available in the ambitious but fledgling Southern League meant Smith no longer needed to work his second job as a miner, as he did every summer during pre-season. He was part of Portsmouth's first ever Southern League winning team during his first season with the club in 1901–02. Smith then left for New Brompton (who would eventually change their name to Gillingham) in 1906 and was player-manager, their first ever, in the modern sense of the word, before retiring from football in 1908. Smith made 187 appearances for Villa scoring 42 goals, 152 appearances for Pompey scoring 16 times and then playing 71 times for New Brompton scoring on 5 occasions.

He became a fishmonger on returning to Portsmouth until moving to Benson, Oxfordshire to run a local shop near there, Roke Stores. He died from a stroke on 19 May 1935, aged 61 years, and left a wife, Susan, sons Stephen and William and daughter, Irene.

The Smiths were a footballing family; his son Stephen Charles Smith carved out a career with West Ham and Charlton amongst other clubs in the 1920s. Steve's brother and best friend William 'Billy' Smith played for Wolverhampton Wanderers and against Stephen when he was at Aston Villa in the 1890s. Stephen eventually followed Billy to Pompey where they won the Southern League together in 1902. All three men were left footed, outside lefts.

Stephen Smith's exploits on the football field started nearly 130 years ago in the mists of the earliest professional footballing times. And yet Smith and football of the Victorian era, whilst looking a lot different to its modern-day counterpart, still resonated with the people in terms of its importance to the nation then as now. Smith was one of many local heroes that played for clubs close to where they grew up.

The idea of the local hero in football is one that is evocative of the zeitgeist of the Victorian era when professional football was in its embryonic stage. Much is still the same in 2022 as it was in the 1890s. The same teams that were dominant then may have changed slightly in terms of who is winning what, but the biggest and best supported teams

Introduction

from the industrial centres of England are the same now as they were then, with the exception of the London clubs who became prominent much later in professional football compared to their midland and northern counterparts.

But while the earliest giants of the game, Aston Villa, Sunderland, Newcastle and the two Liverpool clubs are still in the top ten best supported sides over 130 years since the Football League was set up, local heroes are at a premium.[1] Due to the large influx of foreign players, homegrown players that supporters see as 'one of their own', as modern parlance dictates, are more cherished than ever.

These homegrown players are the embodiment of local pride, a symbol of one of the supporters rising from the ranks, off the terraces of the club they grew up loving, and now performing feats to please the masses that identify more closely with them due to them walking the same streets, playing on the same football pitches and going to the same schools as the supporters. They are authentic in a way the foreign player or 'hired gun' from another club from a different part of England could never be.

Stephen Smith was one of the very first local heroes, representing his Colliery club, then the closest club to where he lived as a Hednesford Town player. Then he followed the long production line of players signed by Aston Villa from 'The Pitmen' that had started with Eli Davis who represented Hednesford and Villa in the 1880s. The Villa club has always been the West Midlands flagship side and the pride engendered both in Hazel Slade, Hednesford and Birmingham for the unprecedented success of a local son from this regional footballing production line was clear to see in an article entitled 'Viva Villa' as the Hednesford Town Centenary Book of 1980 explains:

> Long live Villa and long live Hednesford. For as long as the illustrious history of Aston Villa is remembered, so too will be the strong connection with Hednesford, who have supplied so many fine players to Villa Park. None more illustrious than the first 'big' name to move from Hednesford to Villa Park, Stephen Smith. Stephen came to Hednesford in 1892/93, playing mainly on the left on the old Anglesey Ground. Soon he was attracting attention with his speed and finishing power and the following season he moved to Villa and won a Division One championship medal.[2]

The only difference between Smith and the more recent local footballing heroes of the modern age is that he couldn't grow up on the terraces like Gary Shaw, Gabriel Agbonlahor or Jack Grealish (whose great great grandfather, Billy Garratty, was a teammate of Smith's) for when Stephen Smith was born in 1874, Aston Villa had not even been formed (it would be later that year in fact). Most football clubs were formed in the late 1870s or 1880s and the Football League itself and officially professional football did not start until 1888.

Stephen Smith's exploits require context based on comparison with players whose skills were recorded on camera and not just in the newspapers and in people's memories as was the case with Steve. His death in 1935 was big news and in all the papers, such was his fame and ability, despite not having played football professionally for over twenty years, nor played in the Football League with Aston Villa for over thirty years prior to his death.

His immortality lingered on until after the war, however, as articles 'and several more letters concerning Steve Smith the former Villa winger' were discussed concerning his achievements in the Birmingham football paper the *Sports Argus* as late as 1949, fully forty years after his retirement and over fifty-five years since his professional career had begun.[3]

Smith's contribution to the history of Aston Villa was also faithfully retold in Simon Page's 'Pinnacle of the Perry Barr Pets' which documented the double winning season of 1896/7 in 1997. Stephen's performances for Villa are also described extensively in John Lerwill's terrifically detailed two volume tome, *The Aston Villa Chronicles 1874–1924*. This was published in 2009 and Smith's career was further documented in 2010 in *Aston Villa – The Complete Record* published in 2010 which includes Smith in the section entitled 'A–Z of Villa Stars'.

So why is Stephen Smith so deserving of such praise and exultation in the annals of footballing history? Well, in my opinion this is relatively clear once you compare his achievements to modern day footballers that we all know and whose successes we understand. If we compare Smith to other players of both Villa and Portsmouth from the modern era we can understand the esteem in which I believe Smith deserves to be held. Stephen Smith was world champion at club and international level, a man with as many league title winning medals as Peter Schmeichel, John Terry and Wayne Rooney. A man with more league winner's medals than

Introduction

Eric Cantona, Sergio Aguero, David Silva, Dennis Bergkamp, Frank Lampard, Cristiano Ronaldo, Thierry Henry and Alan Shearer.

But what type of modern day footballer was he like? In terms of his instant impact as a footballer with Aston Villa and England he is akin to Gary Shaw. Shaw burst onto the scene with Villa in the early eighties as a young forward winning the League Championship in 1981 and the European Cup in 1982 and gaining a call up to the England preliminary squad for the World Cup later that same year – all by the age of 21. By the time Smith was 21 in 1895, he had won the League title with Villa in 1894, the FA Cup in 1895 and played for England. Like Shaw, though not to the same extent, he suffered with knee injuries picked up early in his career.

Stephen Smith was described as 'a player who rose to the big occasion'.[4] He consistently performed well in big matches at the top of Division One and also in the FA Cup as well, of course, for England and the Football League versus the Scottish League which was then seen as on a par with playing for England. Of course, the biggest matches for any supporter are the ones against their club's local rivals. They are huge occasions, intensely passionate and sometimes bitter occasions that players dared not lose. Victory was essential in order for players not to get dirty looks or disparaging comments from their own supporters who they lived and worked amongst in Smith's Day.

That the stakes in these games were high can be best illustrated by the behaviour of the fans at these matches even in the 1890s. A report on Villa's derby fixture away at West Bromwich in 1896 explained the atmosphere:

> It was time to make the short journey to the sloping pitch at Stoney Lane where the Lions took on their oldest and most bitter of rivals, West Bromwich Albion. At Stoney Lane matches against the Villa could turn very nasty indeed. Often the two sets of supporters would head to the ground with pockets full of stones to hurl at one another and the local constabulary were in a state of red alert whenever the fixture came around. Yes, hooliganism was around 100 years ago and, whilst it wasn't as widespread as certain eras have known it to be, some of the antics of 'Victorian Thug' would cause even the most crazed of 1980s hooligan to wince.[5]

Steve Smith made a name for himself against Villa's local rivals having scored key winners for Hednesford Town against Cannock Town on the non-league circuit. In local derbies Smith was regularly on the winning side against West Bromwich Albion and Wolverhampton and scored against both clubs. He was famously known for being part of the 1895 FA Cup winning team that pipped Albion to the trophy and enjoyed being in the Villa side that beat the Baggies 7-1 in 1899 that clinched the League title.

Victories over Wolves were particularly special for Stephen as his brother Billy was his direct opponent in the Wanderers forward line. Billy missed a late sitter that allowed Villa victory on the way to the double in the 1896/7 season. Whilst Wolves is more a regional rivalry than a bitter cross-city one as Albion and Birmingham City is, Steve Smith could well be relied on to put in a performance that would usually lead to victory.

In the Birmingham derby against Small Heath and then Birmingham City, Smith again earned much success against the blue half of the Second City. In fact, Smith scored Villa's first ever goal in the first ever Football League fixture between the two sides. He also scored direct from a corner in a 7-3 win over Small Heath in September 1895. But the 'goal' was disallowed as the ball had not touched another player before going over the line, a requirement in the rules of the game at the time.[6]

He was never on the losing side against the men from across the city. In modern terms, Steve Smith's consistent good form against Villa's nearest and dearest makes him a Victorian version of Gabriel Agbonlahor. Like Smith he made his international debut in his very early twenties, at just 22 years old. Agbonlahor is held in such high esteem by Villa fans due to his ridiculous goal scoring and personal win record against Birmingham City. From April 2006 until April 2017, Agbonlahor in eleven league matches against Blues was on the winning side seven times, losing just once and never losing a league fixture against the old enemy. He also hit five goals against them including three late winners, two of which were in front of the travelling Villa fans at St Andrew's.

Agbonlahor also scored goals and claimed victories regularly against Wolves and Albion during his career including one in a league victory against Albion that was followed a few days later by a cup quarter final victory that sent Villa to Wembley in 2015 and saw a pitch invasion where players and fans clashed as parochial bad blood continued between the two ancient rivals as it had since the Victorian era over a century before. Local hatred runs deep and lasts several lifetimes.

Introduction

Gabriel Agbonlahor is Aston Villa's record goal scorer in the Premier league era but it was his derby day heroics that have afforded him legendary status in the claret and blue half of Brum. Never underestimate the affection fans have for players who protect local bragging rights so effectively. Agbonlahor is one of the modern players famous for defending Villa's regional honour picking up a baton against Birmingham City that was first carried by Stephen Smith back in 1894.

Unlike many professional footballers today, Stephen did his time in non-league football, firstly with his Colliery team and then of course with Hednesford Town. It is thus more difficult to find a direct comparison to Smith. These days footballers are signed up before they are even teenagers to be hot housed in club academies. This would have been an alien concept to Victorian footballers, just as doing your time on the non-league circuit would be to a Premier League player in the 21st century.

The player that most mirrors Smith in the modern era in terms of his style of play, skill and sheer tenacity ,as well as career path and position on the pitch, is former Aston Villa captain Jack Grealish. The most used quote when describing Smith is one from the *The Villa News and Record* of 1 Sept. 1906. When describing Smith one could also be describing Grealish, the most fouled player in whichever league he was playing in, four years running from 2017– 2021:

> A particularly close dribbler, with a fine turn of speed, he was only robbed of the ball with difficulty, and with anything approaching a chance would centre most accurately. He often suffered from the lungeous opponent, and while with the Villa received more than his share of hard knocks. He proved a most unselfish partner and could always be relied upon to do his utmost.[7]

Smith's performances, like those of Grealish, sometimes suffered from trying to do too much for the cause. Smith, like Grealish, created many goals for his team mates as well as the ones he scored himself. In the past Grealish has been criticised for being too unselfish. When in 2020 he became more selfish in front of goal and added the knack of goal scoring to his repertoire in the way Smith had from an early age, Grealish too was able to follow Smith into the England team, although he was three years older than Smith when he finally made his debut.

Like Grealish, Smith was brave and resilient, constantly getting back up and driving at the opposition who could only stop him by hacking him down. Both Smith and Grealish suffered at times with injuries due to the wear and tear of being constantly kicked and clattered by less skilfull opponents. Grealish had been battle hardened in a League Two relegation fight on loan at Notts County in the way Smith and been during the tussles with the coal miner and factory worker opponents he faced playing for Hednesford Town – both brutal footballing crucibles.

When looking at written descriptions of Smith and Grealish's style of play it is impossible not to see the similarities. The Coaches' Voice Academy, which helps coaches at all levels to improve their game, Voice explains Grealish's way of playing:

> He is one of the best dribblers in the Premier League, with a low centre of gravity and technique that means he is perfectly balanced as he moves the ball with his right foot, and is therefore able to jink in either direction away from his marker. Sometimes it can seem he is moving too slowly and allowing opponents to recover into good defensive positions, but he does this to take advantage of his express change of pace. He waits for the opportune moment to quickly change direction and eliminate his direct opponent by bursting past them before delivering a pass or shot at goal.[8]

Stephen Smith was described during Villa's FA Cup semi-final victory of 1895 as follows. Grealish, like Smith, played a leading role in helping Villa win an FA Cup semi-final in 2015, both players were young, up and coming prospects on these occasions:

> The display of Steve Smith was one of the best I have ever seen. None of the Sunderland defenders seemed to be able to cope with him. He had one trick which he could do better than any man I have watched. He used to walk past an opponent from practically a stationary position, and rarely did he fail to get right clear. Smith each time planted the ball into the net with the most wonderful and skilful judgement, two of the finest goals ever scored by one player on the same afternoon.[9]

Introduction

Grealish had a free-role for Villa but roamed out to the left wing as much as possible. This was also Stephen Smith's preserve during his career. Grealish emulated Smith by winning with Villa at Wembley in 2019 albeit on the less grand scale of the Championship play-off final. And Grealish, by playing at Wembley, also emulated his own great great grandfather, Billy Garraty, a teammate of Smith's from Villa's glory years. Grealish like Smith left Villa at around 26 years of age for a nouveau riche club looking to challenge the traditional footballing hegemony (The Champions League in Man City's case and the Southern League in the case of Portsmouth). The Birmingham club was not able to match the wages on offer at City in 2021 nor Pompey in 1901.

There are so many contextual comparisons that can be made regarding Smith and ex-players who played for Villa and Portsmouth. Paul Merson left Aston Villa for Portsmouth and reinvigorated his career guiding Pompey back to the Premier League in 2002–3. This was like the way Smith won the Southern League in his first season on the South Coast. Merson like Smith then left Portsmouth and became a player-manager.

It is clear from this introduction that Stephen Smith was a man who could rub shoulders with the very best players in footballing history. But enough of comparisons, this is his own individual story.

Chapter 1

Abbots Bromley

The Staffordshire village of Abbots Bromley in January 1874 had changed little in the previous one hundred years. It consisted basically of one long main street and still hosted fairs and markets as it had since medieval times.[1] It was, and still is a place of old-fashioned countryside traditions. The hobby horse dance known as the 'Abbots Bromley Horn Dance' was observed here until the English Civil War and though it was discontinued has been resurrected in more recent times. Ten or twelve dancers would carry deers heads on their shoulders painted with the arms of Paget, Bagot and Welles, to whom the chief property of the town belonged.[2] It was a pagan ritual designed to ensure a plentiful catch each year, a tradition that survived into Christian times and gradually came to be seen as affirming the villagers' hunting rights.

There is a record of the hobby horse being used in Abbots Bromley as early as 1532, and it is possible that the horn dance component of the custom was also present at that time but not commented upon by the writer.[3] Abbots Bromley had fairs and markets since it had been granted permission in 1221, and close to its ancient surviving church was a butter cross which held a market every Tuesday including animals such as horses and horned cattle.[4]

The only other leisure activities for the local populace were the public houses of The Crown, The Goat's Head (where Dick Turpin once stayed the night after stealing a horse in Uttoxeter) and the Bagot's Arms named after the Lord of the Manor, Lord Bagot who resided at nearby Blithfield Hall.[5] These pubs survive to this very day showing their importance to the local community and want of any other modern leisure facilities. It was into this rural, still almost feudal, farming community that Stephen Smith was born on 7 January 1874.

The son of farm labourers who relied on casual, seasonal work to survive, Stephen was one of four children, the youngest, with three older siblings, John who was nine, Mary, aged five and Charles, aged two.

They lived in a farm labourer's cottage on the estate of Lord Bagot. The Bagots had been linked to Abbots Bromley for over 700 years by 1874 and their dominance over the local area gave it a medieval feel despite the Industrial Revolution turning Britain into the world's number one economy with massive urban sprawl now enveloping the country. Abbots Bromley, however, despite being close to England's second city, Birmingham, 'the city of a thousand trades', was still as rural and idyllic as can be. Almost feudal by comparison, with its Lord of the Manor, Bagot living at Blithfield Hall, an ancient mansion with embattled towers and walls, which gave it the air of a knight's fortress, looking over its serfs and peasant farmers, which was not far off the truth for a farm labourer in England, even in 1874.

The rights of a worker, rural or urban in England at this time were limited. When Stephen Smith was born, all adult males over the age of 21 who owned property had only had the vote for seven years. In 1866, all voters had to be male and own property. By the early 1860s around 1.43 million could vote out of a total population of 30 million. In 1867, the Conservative government introduced the Parliamentary Reform Act. This increased the electorate to almost 2.5 million.

The most important change was the granting of the vote to occupiers in the boroughs (people who rented properties rather than owning them) and, as a result, the electorate in some of the newer towns in England and Scotland increased dramatically. However, the Act did not alter the balance of political power in Britain. The middle classes still dominated the electorate in both towns and boroughs. Life was not about to change for the better any time soon for the people at the bottom of society. People like the family of Stephen Smith. Stephen and his brothers and sister would get no real education growing up in the countryside. Clarke's Free Grammar School during this time was a school just for girls and infants.[6] Anyway, Stephen and his siblings would be needed to work in the fields or help at home to keep the family out of the workhouse – or at least not in the Alms-houses that Abbots Bromley provided for its rural poor in times of extreme hardship.

Not for the Smith family, the newly set up private schools by Canon Nathaniel Woodard. Whilst this schooling was initially intended for boys, Woodard later developed a second system for girls, based on the teachings and practices of the Church of England.[7] In 1872 the first of two Woodard schools for girls opened in Abbots Bromley when the 'Big House' and its grounds in the High Street were purchased for the establishment of St Anne's school. In 1882, St Mary's school was founded at Bromley House in Uttoxeter Road to cater for the slightly less affluent gentlemen's daughters. The middle classes were headed for a better standard of education in Abbots Bromley. Stephen, when old enough, was headed for the farmer's fields.

Stephen's mother Elizabeth would have to make ends meet every week to make sure the budget would feed the family and it would take all her housekeeping skills to keep the Smith family afloat. Even as Stephen came to labouring age times would continue to be tough. On the meagre earnings mentioned above, Stephen's father endeavoured to support his wife and children. For two years after Stephen was born, Elizabeth was thrifty and Stephen did not take his money to the public house, so they managed to exist and keep a decent home on this pittance; but difficulties soon came, and debt at the village shop followed. The prices were too high for labouring families on only one or two wages. And the ultimate humiliation of putting one's wife and daughters in the field could become a greater possibility the more labourers slipped into debt.

In Abbots Bromley there were two village shops. One at each end of the mile long high street. In nearly every village are two or three of these establishments, where many articles are retailed at almost 100 per cent above their cost price. The villagers tended to accept the high prices and variable quality though, as the *Cornhill* agriculture magazine explained in an 1874 article on the subject:

> So long as ready money is paid the purchaser gets fairly good articles at such a shop, though the price is high. If the red herring be somewhat stronger than the bloater or sardine, it is more a smaller quantity of tea than in our own homes will serve to colour the water, so that there is no doubt that black tea has been sold; the bacon, when cooking, sends its fragrance far down the village street. All this, however, is as the purchaser would wish it to be.[8]

It was a struggle for survival, a hand to mouth existence for the Smith family. They dipped in and out of debt as Stephen grew up. They could rarely save when things such as new shoes for the children would cost a week's wages. Money would be lost when Stephen senior was sick, a couple of days off here and there would cost a third of a week's wages. Mercifully their father was very healthy and rarely ill but life was still on the bread line. Mr Smith only managed to keep his family out of debt and his wife out of the fields when John became six years of age and could go to work alongside his father in the fields. The Smiths emerged from debt when brother John was sent at far too early an age into the fields to earn his living instead of being kept at school. John could barely read or write.

We don't know the exact household income of the Smiths at this time but just after Stephen was born, the cost of bread to feed a family was just over 6 shillings a week.[9] If the Smith family was earning between the average of 9 and 15 shillings you can see that the chunk of money needed to pay for the main staple food in England was around half a worker's weekly wage, at best. More likely it was two thirds of a worker's weekly income. The Smiths were literally living just over the bread line.

John Smith's graduation to farm labourer was a source of much relief for the Smith family. However, John's services wouldn't always be called upon. Mechanisation during the Agricultural and Industrial revolutions of the eighteenth and nineteenth centuries meant that in Abbots Bromley there were three labourers for every two farmers. Machines were doing the work and only at harvest time was there a real shortage of labour for farm owners. However, there were some agricultural operations, such as turnip-hoeing, mowing, and reaping not done by machinery, trenching, clearing copses, and the like, which were almost invariably done by piece-work, and at these the labourer could earn from three to four shillings a week more than at the rest of his labour.[10]

There were still times when extra money could be earned by Stephen senior and his son, back-breaking though the work was, this money usually came in harvest time with 'harvest money' giving a better chance of survival in the countryside. Yet wherever Stephen senior and John tried to make money for the family it seemed that the farmers they toiled for would try and cut them out of any tiny profit they might achieve. This was because as farmers openly admitted, that as a man's wages were nine shillings, and that by employing two boys (instead of one man), at three and sixpence a week each, by employing two boys they saved two shillings and got a man's work for seven shillings a week. There were times when his father wasn't working at all, but John was. John didn't want to be in the fields. He wanted to sneak behind the Abbots Bromley girls school to its cricket pitches. There John could watch the cricket team that had been formed in 1881 and used the Anglesey Road Ground off Swan Lane that the gentlemen of the village rented from the school at a nominal rate.[11]

The cottage they lived in on Ashbrook Lane on the Newborough Road on the way to Burton and Lichfield was small and cramped for a family of five. Nearly all the houses in a village were let with the farms, and were sub-let by the farmers to the labourers, the rent being deducted from their weekly wages. Some cottages had a few pieces of garden, enough in a favourable year to grow potatoes for consumption by the family. The farmers Stephen and John worked for were not looking to give the Smiths a great deal if they could help it. In general they distrusted their labourers, and thought that their grain, their hay, and, still more, the time that is due to them, would be purloined if the labourer farmed ever so small a territory, and kept stock to however small an extent.

Things had to change, Stephen senior needed to get a better life for him and his family. The countryside could no longer, if it ever really had, support him and those he cared for. There were job opportunities to be had in the late 1800s, as the Industrial Revolution continued unchecked. The black gold currency that was coal had turned Britain into and then maintained it as the world's leading economy and empire.[12]

Coal mining in the north and the Midlands was booming and would continue to do so. And opportunities were about to come the Smiths' way. This was the catalyst that would see the family leave Abbots Bromley and join the urban work force like so many others of the lumpen proletariat. Six miles south of Abbots Bromley on the edge of Cannock Chase is the former mining town of Rugeley. On the other side of the Chase in the east are Hednesford and Cannock, again former mining towns. In the late nineteenth century, they were the perfect commuter towns for the workers of the many mines that had and were to be sunk under the forest.

The Industrial Revolution was going at full tilt and mining on Cannock Chase was exploding into life with secure jobs and regular wages for all men willing to toil in the pits. Regular wages, better wages meant Stephen's children could go to school instead of work until they really, really had to. It would be a new beginning. The Cannock Chase Colliery was set up in 1850. The Marquess of Anglesey anxious to cash in on the burgeoning midland coal industry. He opened the Uxbridge pit at Chasetown and then immediately leased it to the Cannock Chase Colliery Company in 1852.

Between 1860–1867 the Cannock Chase Colliery Company opened three more pits at Chase Terrace, Rawnsley and Heath Hayes. Rival mining company, Cannock and Rugeley Colliery sank one mining shaft at Cannock Wood Colliery as the coal industry on Cannock Chase began to really take off. Cannock Chase Colliery continued to dominate the competition and with so much coal being mined the company became one of the first to build its own railway lines to connect its collieries to the main lines in 1866. The railways moved the coal traffic from the mine to the main railway lines and canals to be transported to customers across the country. These railways would also be a source of income for the Smith family in the future.

Cannock Chase Colliery sank its eighth pit at Heath Hayes as the golden age of coal mining continued. In the next fifteen years mines were set up at a pace. In 1869 the West Cannock Colliery Company opened four plants at Hednesford in the Pye Green Valley. During the 1870s there was an extra boom in the coal industry because of the coal needed by the French to fight the Franco-Prussian War. Coal and coke were of major importance in the Franco-German puzzle during the first half of the twentieth century, coal being the main energy resource in Europe and coke being a rarer coal by-product necessary for the steel industry. Both of these commodities were concentrated near the Franco-German border.[13]

These were the reasons behind the continued hegemony of the British coal industry and increased job prospects for the working classes of Staffordshire including the Smiths. In 1871, East Cannock Colliery, Leighswood Colliery and Leacroft Colliery came into existence. Wimblebury Colliery started in 1872, and in 1873, sinking started at Mid Cannock Colliery. In 1874, Pool Pits mine was opened by the Cannock and Rugeley Colliery Company and the company sunk a second pit at Cannock Wood. And so it was in 1876, during these times of industrial advancement and urban build-up around the three towns of Rugeley, Hednesford and Cannock, that Stephen senior and his wife and Stephen and the rest of his siblings left Abbots Bromley for good and headed for the coal fields of Cannock Chase.

Chapter 2

Hazel Slade

In 1876, the Smiths, Stephen senior, and his heavily pregnant wife, Elizabeth, and their children John, 11 years old, Mary Ann, 7, Charles, 4 and Stephen junior, 2 packed up all their belongings onto the carriage of the family pony and trap and set out for the Cannock Chase Coalfields, their destination, the mining village of Hazel Slade just to the north of Hednesford on the eastern edge of the Chase. Stephen senior drove the horse from the front of the carriage with Elizabeth at his side. The four children sat in the carriage back to back on top of their belongings which were tied down with rope.

The journey away from the Smiths' and England's agricultural past and into theirs and their country's industrial future took five hours. They travelled along the Colton Road and through the village of that name. A small humpback bridge brought their pony and trap into the village and past the Anglo-Saxon church that was modified when the Normans conquered England. They added a bell tower to the Saxon settlement's church.[1] There the Smith's rested for a while. Stephen senior watched the farm labourers in the fields coming into the local pub 'Ye Olde Dun Cow' to slake their thirst at lunchtime.[2] It was a symbolic example of the lifestyle he and the majority of England's workers were now leaving behind as they headed from the fields of England to its towns.

Stephen and Elizabeth had first met in the fields of Colton and their eldest son John was born there in 1865 before they moved in with Elizabeth's family in Abbots Bromley soon afterwards due to financial hardship. Stephen hoped the coalfields and industrial life would push away financial insecurities for evermore. They moved onto the Rugeley road and to the town itself perched on the western edge of the Chase. The town stood on the River Trent, on the Grand Trunk canal, and on the Trent Valley railway at the junction of the railway to Cannock and Walsall.[3] It was the perfect place for coal to be transported across the country and it was bustling as the Smiths travelled through it. Comprised of several long busy streets, it had a large general post office, a railway station with telegraph communications, two banks, a hotel, a town hall, a church built in 1822, part of an old church, chapels for Independents, Wesleyans, and Roman Catholics, a mechanics institute, an endowed grammar-school, and an endowed national school for all children between the ages of 5 and 10. Abbots Bromley and the countryside already seemed a long way away.

The Rugeley road becomes the Hednesford road and vice versa depending on whether you are travelling east or west. The Smith family travelled on through Cannock Chase following the road as it wound south westerly towards Hazel Slade village. On the approach to the village the Smiths passed through a glade or dell in an area known as 'Hednesford Hills' which is within the southern sections of the Cannock Chase coalfield; the Smiths had not lost all their access to the countryside. They passed over the trickling Bentley Brook which eventually winds its way to the river Trent and as the trees that abound the area and beautiful vistas fell away the focal point of of the village appeared, the 'Slade Pub' which still stands on the corner of Cannock Wood Street and Rugeley Road leading into Hednesford Hills. The Smiths had arrived in Hazel Slade.[4]

Stephen Smith senior had not only secured a job with the Cannock and Rugeley Colliery Company but also a house. One of the main attractions for workers when applying for the multitude of mining jobs that had sprung up on Cannock Chase in the mid to late 1800s was if they were given a 'company cottage'. The nineteenth century equivalent of the company car was built en-masse as the Cannock Chase coalfield expanded. As the coalfield expanded so did Hazel Slade, and gradually a close knit community of terraced houses was built in the 1870s by the bosses of the Cannock and Rugeley Colliery Company.

The village was really starting to form by the time the Smiths arrived. All of the two bedroomed barrack type terraced houses and associated shops, schools and churches opened straight on to the streets. They had no private gardens; instead some miners started allotments, some alongside the Bentley Brook, others in Cannock Wood Street and behind Albert Street. As newcomers in 1876 it would be a while before the Smiths would be invited to start an allotment. The miners took great pride in their allotments, many with the odd racing pigeon pen, and these allotments, together with the Slade Pub, Brotherhood, and churches were a form of escape from the pit dust and their cramped and dingy shift work.

Hazel Slade

The year 1876 then was a fresh start for all concerned in the Smith household. Stephen senior was ready to start his new job in the mines of the Cannock and Rugeley Colliery at the age of 35. It was to be a shock to the system compared to his life as an agricultural labourer. Stephen's eldest son John was now eleven and had transferred to the village school in Hazel Slade having been taught in Abbots Bromley at the Clarke Free School. He would soon be expected to find a job to help support the family. Finances were still tight and the Smith family, as was the norm in this period, large and would get larger. Contraception had not reached the working classes of the industrial West Midlands.

Already in the family was eight-year-old Mary Ann, another scholar who eventually would marry and any income she made would support her husband and her new family. Charles at four years old and Stephen junior aged two were of course just toddlers. By the middle of 1876 the Smiths were just one month away from the arrival of Elizabeth Smith's fifth child, and to put it in brutal economic terms, the fifth dependent on Stephen senior.

Stephen's eldest son John was now eleven and had transferred to the village school in Hazel Slade having been taught in Abbots Bromley at the Clarke Free School before working in the fields from the age of six. He and his father would doubtless have wanted him to leave school but educational reforms and how the government now wanted to protect children delayed the Smiths' quest for economic salvation even if it had the best intentions. It was a different world to the one we live in now where we see education as a right not a privilege. The Smiths knew they needed to read and write but beyond that their expectation of education and what it could do for them was limited.

Parliament passed an act in 1842 which prohibited women and male children under the age of 10 from working below the surface at the collieries.[5] Then the Coal Mines Regulation Act of 1860 improved safety rules and raised the age limit for boys from 10 to 12.[6] While this new legislation was obviously the start of the government intervening in a more positive manner on behalf of the huddled masses, it delayed John Smith from earning money for the Smith family for another year. In 1876 in Hazel Slade, the Smith family six strong, and soon to be seven were totally reliant on Stephen Smith senior's ability to earn money in the Cannock and Rugeley Colliery and thus keep a roof over all their heads and food in their bellies. Stephen Smith senior was the key to seven people's survival. It was all on him and his single weekly wage.

There had been well thought out reasoning by Stephen senior behind moving from the agricultural world to the industrial one. Although mining was hard work and dangerous compared with other manual jobs, working underground was relatively well paid.[7] In the 1870s farm labourers were earning between 9 and 15 shillings.[8] Miners were earning around 20 shillings by the 1840s.[9] This had not gone unnoticed by many including Stephen senior. Even so, he was anxious for John to come of age as it would be a while before Charles and Stephen could contribute. Like most other households, the more children you had meant the more money you could earn, however, conversely there were more mouths to feed – a historical Catch-22 situation.

In the summer of 1876, William Smith was born in the Smiths' new house in Hazel Slade. In 1877, eldest son John was able to follow his father down the mine and a second wage entered the household. This was just as well as Ellen was born to Elizabeth in 1879, Henry would arrive in 1882 and Walter in 1885. This was a little portion of Cannock Chase where the family had lived, worked and grown up together most consistently in their lifetime. It seems like the place the Smiths most felt at home and Stephen would revisit time and time again and be based there at even at the peak of his powers and the height of his fame.

The home comforts of Hazel Slade and Hednesford would never be forgotten. The 1881 census tells us currently Stephen Smith senior and eldest son John were working at the colliery. Mary, Charles and Stephen junior were at school. William was five but not yet at school, Ellen was two and Henry and Walter had not arrived.[10] William would soon be going to school as the Elementary Education Act of 1880 made it compulsory for children to attend school between the ages of five and ten years of age. Stephen junior in fact stayed on at school until he was 12 as the law prevented him working at the colliery until then. In 1886 Stephen joined his father and brother John down the pit. A whole new underground world of hard labour and brutality was opened to him.

Maybe the shared hardships he endured here with the other male members of his family is why he was always drawn back here. A feeling of belonging, family bonds and perhaps wanting to look after the family who did not have the same abilities that allowed him to earn much more money than he could have ever thought possible for a fraction of the hardship and none of the danger that his siblings went through all their lives.

The coal face at the Cannock and Rugeley Colliery was a brutal place. Safety has always been an issue for mining from its early days to more recent mining accidents and catastrophes.[11] Explosions happened because of the presence of methane gas in the pits. Mining technology had improved safety by the time Stephen became a coal miner but it was still a dangerous job.

As the years went by and the Smiths involved themselves more and more in the Hazel Slade mining community, they too were able to get an allotment. Stephen senior raced pigeons and as the sons got older and drew a wage from the colliery, they followed their dad into The Slade Pub. Working in such perilous conditions gave miners a work hard, play hard attitude and many were hardened drinkers by the time they were in their teens. As well as frequenting the local hostelry with his father and brothers, Stephen played football for the mining company's football team. Big brother John had been fascinated with the cricketers and rugby players of Abbots Bromley. He'd played football in the streets of that village.

John took his brothers Charles, Stephen and William to play football and they would enjoy playing and improving their footballing skills on the moors adjoining the Cannock Chase Forest.[12] Despite being shorter and slighter than his brothers (we are not sure whether he was 5ft 4in or 5ft 6in as he was given these two different heights in the *Lichfield Mercury* in 1895, he weighed just 11st 6lbs in the two accounts that differed on his height) they could see he had great skill with a football. John recommended Stephen for the colliery team and even though he was still only a teenager, he soon became quite a star of local football where his speed and exquisite skill put him head and shoulders above his contemporaries.[13] Stephen senior was even bought pints in The Slade by fellow drinkers and getting a pat on the back from the Colliery Company owners such was the improvement in the Cannock and Rugeley Colliery football team's results since Stephen had joined. William, his younger brother by two years, was no slouch either and was also in the team by the age of 15.

Stephen, however, was the star of the show and John basked in the afterglow of being the man who introduced this phenomenon to the people of the Cannock Chase Coalfield. Steve 'Tich' Smith, as he came to be known, was just too good to only be playing for the colliery.[14] Steve was particularly noted for the accuracy of his passing.[15] Contemporaries noted that: 'Smith was a particularly close dribbler, with a fine turn of speed, he was only robbed of the ball with difficulty, and with anything approaching a chance would centre most accurately. Being on the small side, he often suffered from the lungeous opponent, and received more than his share of hard knocks. Quiet and unassuming, he proved a most unselfish partner, and could always be relied upon to do his utmost. A modest winner and a good loser.'[16]

And that's what people loved about Stephen Smith. He was small, with a slight frame, he didn't look like a footballer and yet he was strong, precise with his manipulations of the ball, took the hits but got up and carried on and got the upper hand with his opponent often. His quiet way meant he did not brag or walk too tall after each successful match. Smith also took rare setbacks with good grace. He would just go to The Slade and drink with his own kind, he had the common touch despite his gifts. Perhaps he didn't realise his own potential.

Smith was a man of supreme footballing talents, a man with a terrific shot in his boots.[17] And opposition keepers had to hold on to their shots because, if they let the ball run loose, there would be the moustachioed winger waiting to pounce. His performances for the Colliery team made him something of a local celebrity – if that word even existed in the nineteenth century and could be applied to coal miners who played football on an amateur basis and yet at the same time he was a man of the people. The working man loved Stephen Smith because he was one of them – an underdog. But every dog has its day. But in the 1890s he was still an underdog. His sporting activities at the weekend always had to take a back seat to his day job at Cannock and Rugeley Colliery, for it was still his day job that meant survival for him and his ten-person family all in their tiny terraced house in the mining village of Hazel Slade.[18]

Chapter 3

Hednesford

The 1891 census has the Smith family living at 25 Cross Street Rugeley.[1] This is misleading as the Smiths never left Hazel Slade. Why would they? Rugeley is on the eastern edge of the Chase, Hednesford on the western edge. Both places are about a mile from the colliery. It wouldn't make sense to move in terms of getting closer to their place of work as the Colliery was equidistant in terms of distance. Until 1934 Hazel Slade lay within the boundaries of Lichfield Rural District Council (Brereton Ward).[2] This included Rugeley which then enveloped Brereton so all Census information was recorded at Rugeley and Hazel Slade was in the Rugeley district thus considered part of Rugeley, much like now where it is considered another part of Hednesford.

The 1881 census backs up the view that the Smiths never left Hazel Slade. The census has the Smiths at Rugeley in 1881 even though William Smith was born in Hazel Slade in 1876, Ellen was born there in 1879, they didn't move to Rugeley in 1881. Henry was born in Hazel Slade in 1882 and Walter in 1885. It could be argued they moved to Rugeley by 1891, but the census says 25 Cross Street, Rugeley. There is no Cross Street in Rugeley but there is one in Hazel Slade.

The Cannock and Rugeley Colliery Company was very proud of its football team and very proud of Stephen Smith. Football kept people's morale high, so grumbles and requests for pay rises stayed low. The company didn't plan on losing Stephen any time soon; he made them look good. In the local area, however, Stephen's reputation as a top player was being taken seriously by now. Bigger local football clubs were now giving him more than a second glance.

In 1888 football had become officially professional at the highest level. The secretary of the top club in the West Midlands area, Aston Villa had set up the Football League for the 12 most prominent football clubs of the day. William McGregor had realised that the decision to pay players increased club's wage bills. It was therefore necessary to arrange more matches that could be played in front of large crowds. On 2 March, 1888, William McGregor circulated a letter to Aston Villa, Blackburn Rovers, Bolton Wanderers, Preston North End, and West Bromwich Albion suggesting that ten or twelve of the most prominent clubs in England combine to arrange home and away fixtures each season.[3]

This led to the following events in April 1888:

> The following month the Football League was formed. It consisted of six clubs from Lancashire (Preston North End, Accrington, Blackburn Rovers, Burnley, Bolton Wanderers and Everton) and six from the Midlands (Aston Villa, Derby County, Notts County, Stoke, West Bromwich Albion and Wolverhampton Wanderers). The main reason Sunderland was excluded was because the other clubs in the league objected to the costs of travelling to the North-East.[4]

In September 1888 the Football League's first season got underway. Football matches were now played regularly and not just in friendlies and cup competitions where if you lost one game your competitive season was all but over. Hednesford Town Football Club did not have the support through the turnstiles or the financial clout to turn professional. Despite this they had made a name for themselves in the regional cup competitions such as the Staffordshire County Cup and the Birmingham Senior Cup which saw Hednesford Town pit their wits against professional clubs from the region such as Aston Villa, Stoke, West Bromwich Albion and Wolverhampton Wanderers. On a local level, like Stephen, 'The Pitmen' had a strong reputation and could pick strong players who worked in all the local pits during the week and used their athletic physiques honed underground on the football field at the weekend. Stephen fitted the archetypal mould for a Hednesford Town 'Pit Man'.

While Stephen was just starting out for the Company team, Hednesford Town had already made a name for themselves in and around Birmingham and the Black Country. In fact, in the 1890s Hednesford had two top teams, Hednesford Swifts and Hednesford Town.[5] Mike Bradbury in his book, *Lost Teams of the Midlands*, explains how during the Victorian period mining helped the town of Hednesford grow and could support two different teams (initially even more teams than that) for a time before Town forged on and the Swifts fell by the wayside:

Different sources disagree on football history in Hednesford; it is generally believed that two local sides, Hill Top FC, joined forces with Red and Whites FC from West Hill and formed Hednesford Anglesey. This happened in 1880, the date of establishment which appears on the current Hednesford Town shirt. The team were either called Hednesford Town or Anglesey depending on preference. The Swifts side played at the Cross Keys ground behind the public house of the same name in the Old Hednesford district. Rivals The Town played at the Anglesey Ground in 'high town'.

The Anglesey was a large Regency mansion house, later a hotel to the nearby railway station, with a football ground right behind it, just as did the Cross Keys, which was sixteenth-century coaching inn on the Lichfield to Stafford route. The Anglesey had been built by one Edmund Peel of Fazeley near Tamworth. A wealthy landowner, he built it to house his many racehorses in the 1830s, since the Hednesford Hills were said to be the finest place on which to train racehorses in the Midlands. It became a hotel in 1864. The football ground was merely a patch of land fenced in with corrugated iron fencing, and thus, the ground and the team took on the early nickname of 'The Tins'. The home crowd used to 'drum' the sheets with both hands and feet, creating a noisy wall of sound, or as the local residents put it: a racket!

Eventually it seems Hednesford Swifts disappeared, and Bradbury believes it probably became absorbed into the Town Football Club. The club were founder members of the Birmingham & District League in 1889 and finished sixth in their first season. Despite finishing third in 1890–91, they left the league at the end of the season and played only friendly matches.[6] The Birmingham District League started in 1889, only a year after the Football League, with six Midlands clubs in the senior competition. It is not at all surprising that the new competition was among the first combination for non-league sides in the country. It also shows what a hotbed of footballing talent there was in the West Midlands and how good some of the amateur teams were at this time that the professional teams still deigned to play them in regional cup competitions and of course in the FA Cup.

Regional cup competitions were many in number during the 1890s as league football was still in its infancy. Cup matches also meant there was always something at stake to play for. Hednesford Town were a reasonably successful cup team at this time and reached the 1890 Dudley Charity Cup semi-final going down 4-1 to Wednesbury Old Athletic at Walsall despite bringing around 1,000 supporters of the 1,500 in attendance that day.[7] On 15 May that year they got to the Walsall Challenge Cup final, unfortunately they were thumped 7-1 by Walsall Town Swifts.[8]

Amateur clubs of the age had trouble in fulfilling all their fixtures in a league context. The cost of hosting lots of matches against opponents who would not necessarily capture the public's imagination and draw a crowd drained the coffers. People's imagination was more inclined towards knockout cup competitions where the context of the outcome of the result was immediate, unlike in a league format.

A big club like the Albion, Villa or Wolves turning up would produce a healthy gate and help a club survive. Amateur Victorian football clubs, like the people who followed them, existed almost hand to mouth. They felt like they were being left behind by the capitalism engulfing football and refused to accept it. When you look at the Industrial Revolution that had just happened and was still happening in Victorian England, football matches organised on an industrial scale for profit and growth went hand in hand with the development of liberal capitalism that the United Kingdom is famous for.

Professional football continued apace with the construction of the Football Alliance league which would eventually be absorbed into the Football League as its second professional division. Hednesford Town was high enough up the footballing food chain of the day to be invited to play in the 1890/91 FA Cup against Alliance side Small Heath of Birmingham.[9] They didn't make the next round but it showed that 'The Pit Men' were rubbing shoulders with some of the leading clubs in England from time to time.

As previously stated, it was in the regional cup competitions where Hednesford Town tended to excel. In March 1891 Hednesford marched on in the Wednesbury Charity Cup beating Great Bridge Unity 3-2 to reach the latter stages.[10] In March 1891, Hednesford Town had reached the semi-final of the Walsall Cup against great rivals Walsall Town Swifts. The Swifts often got the better of Hednesford on the pitch, and in the desperation of wanting to get to a cup final at the expense of superior local rivals the club sent scouts to all manner of local matches in the weeks building up to the game. Hednesford Town Football Club then had quite a pedigree regionally before it came calling for Stephen Smith's signature and a need for players of superior quality to what they already had.

The Cannock and Rugeley Colliery Company had its headquarters at 'The Grange' a large, fine, white property standing in its own grounds and home to the managing director.[11] Stephen Smith was a Company employee, so it was to this house that officials of Hednesford Town headed with entreaties. Smith could play for who he liked during his free time but felt his job would be at risk if his employers had not had caps doffed to them by way of permission. In truth it was great publicity for the Company and again helped keep morale high in the pits. One of their own now playing for one of the great amateur cup fighting teams of the area. Many workers already followed Hednesford Town and so the club had known about Stephen for some time. It was only a matter of time before another miner-come-footballer would sign for 'The Pitmen'.

And so it was that at the age of 17 on Tuesday, 31 March 1891, Stephen Smith, making his first-team debut, lined up as a left sided back in the semi-final of the Walsall Cup for Hednesford Town against Walsall Town Swifts.[12] Stephen must have been nervous making his debut, especially as a teenager in a semi-final of a cup competition against fierce local rivals. Local pride was very much on the line in a much more intense way than today's local derbies, as high profile as they are with television and social media commenting on everything. This is because every Hednesford Town player would also work with their teammate, know many members of the opposition team and on top of that a huge amount of the team's supporters were friends and work colleagues too. What people thought of your performance could not be avoided in the goldfish bowl of local amateur football that was at the same time just a few rungs down from the top professional football league in the world.

The two sides met at the Wednesbury Oval, home to another fierce local rival Wednesbury Old Athletic. The Oval was used for both football and cricket and as such the pitch was always immaculate due to the care and attention needed to maintain both pitch and wickets. The ground was located to the north-west of Wednesbury town centre, and featured a pavilion located close to St Paul's Road, which ran along the northern boundary. On a stunning spring day with the sun blazing in the sky the pavilion was full and the pitch surrounded by between 4,000 and 5,000 spectators, including a sizeable contingent from the Cannock Chase coalfield. It was a huge crowd for the time and status of the game. The size of the attendance would not be beaten until Walsall played Small Heath on the same ground during a Second Division game two years later. Walsall would be founder members of Football League Division Two when they went professional in 1892. This shows the pedigree of opponents Hednesford were competing with in the last decade of the nineteenth century.

The action flowed from one end of the pitch to the other. Walsall started to get the upper hand and forced three corners. Webster, the Hednesford keeper, was forced to punch clear a free-kick that was lumped into the box. Another Walsall shot went just past the post. The semi-final of the Walsall Cup was turning out to be a baptism of fire for Stephen.

Hednesford Town managed to steady themselves and rally. An effort went just over the Walsall bar. The Pitmen won a free-kick inside the Walsall half and the ball was sent into the Swift's area and bobbled around in the box before falling to Talbot the Hednesford half-back who smashed home to give his side the lead. The *Birmingham Daily Post* reported the goal as follows, 'Talbot gained the first point for the colliery district.' Hednesford were ahead, heading to a cup final and bragging rights over arch-rivals. Stephen could hardly believe his luck – all this on his debut.

It all seemed to go to the Hednesford player's heads. Walsall equalised immediately. Webster had to save Hednesford again soon after. Holmes of Walsall put his side 2-1 up and despite claims of offside from players and supporters the goal stood. In a matter of minutes the game had been turned on its head. A Walsall free-kick whipped in by Tonks was converted by Homes just before half-time and at the interval and Smith and his team-mates were shell-shocked.

Hednesford fought on in the second half and fired another shot over the bar. The end-to-end action and Webster saved his side once more. Edge, the Walsall keeper and former Pitman was then twice called into action. He was heckled by his former supporters all the game, such was the rivalry between both clubs. Hednesford were still in the game with ten minutes to go when all hell broke loose.

Shelley, the Walsall outside left, made it 4-1 to Swifts and that seemed to be the *coup de grace*. But Hednesford were not done yet. Hednesford centre forward, Rollins beat Edge with a shot to bring The Whites within two goals of their opponents. The *Post* described it as a 'brilliant shot'.

With three minutes to go Hednesford left winger, Oswald pulled the score back to 4-3 and chaos ensued. Could the comeback be completed? The crowd was raucous and intense.

The *Birmingham Daily Post* explained: 'In the last few minutes that remained Hednesford tried their utmost to equalise, but the defence was too strong for them. Result of a fast and rough game: Walsall 4 Hednesford 3.'

Walsall had held on. Just. The bragging rights were theirs. The crowd applauded both sides' efforts. Hednesford had put in a tremendous effort to go toe-to toe with a soon to be professional side in a cup semi-final. The club and its supporters were disappointed but rightly proud. Stephen was gutted. He didn't like to lose and whilst he accepted the defeat with grace, it was not a feeling he was anxious to experience on a regular basis. Stephen Smith wanted to win.

Amateur clubs like Hednesford struggled to compete due to the spread of professionalism. A mixture of bitterness over defeat in the Walsall Cup, where one Walsall goal was seen as offside by the Hednesford club and the lingering annoyance towards those who were, or were suspected of making a living out of the sport, led to a protest by The Pitmen to the Walsall FA about a Swifts player. 'Shamateurism' was a real bugbear amongst amateur purists at this time. Players were employed for factory or colliery teams and paid a higher wage if they were skilled footballers or amateurs with no job were paid 'expenses' fees to entice them to play. Clubs maintained these payments were merely to cover costs of a player's travel for example, though of course these payments could be sizeable.

On Tuesday, 21 April 1891 at a special meeting of the Walsall Football Association at the Dragon Hotel in Walsall, Hednesford Town submitted their complaint against Walsall Town Swifts for playing an ineligible player.[13] The meeting was a tense affair and led to the President of the Walsall FA storming out. Six other clubs backed Hednesford's claim. So the complaint had to be discussed, but the meeting wasn't pretty as the newspaper report details:

> (The meeting was) for the purpose of further hearing and deciding the protest of Hednesford Town against Walsall Town Swifts for having played an ineligible player in the semi-final ... who was alleged to have played in the close

> season and taken payment. The President declined to allow the question to be reopened and left the room. (The secretary) considered it his duty to protest against the question being reopened unless upon a vote of the meeting. Ultimately after some heated discussion ... that the question should be reopened. The amendment was carried by 8 to 6.
>
> (The) treasurer (of the FA) resigned his position and retired. (The) Secretary to the Walsall Town Swifts (retired) after stating that he should decline to give any evidence on the subject.

What the *Lichfield Mercury* doesn't make clear is that Walsall Town Swifts counter-claimed against Hednesford that the player concerned, Withington, had been paid in the summer during a match involving Hednesford, and also by Hednesford. Mr Freeman, the Hednesford representative at the meeting, explained that any money exchanged was for all players and shared between them by way of expenses and that Withington was a professional at Darlington so it was Walsall who had made the error by playing an ineligible player and anything to do with payments was an erroneous matter.

The *Birmingham Daily Post* explains this:[14]

> Mr Freeman said the sum of £5, was paid over simply to pay the expenses of the two clubs, and further that the former decision of the association was based on an erroneous impression of the circumstances. The proceeds of the match at Cannock (Hednesford), were not for charitable purposes and Withington was at the time a professional for Darlington and had not as alleged joined the Cannock club (Hednesford).

It is clear then that Walsall's controversial semi-final victory against local rivals had caused serious resentment and bitterness. It had also caused consternation and upheaval in the corridors of power at the Walsall FA and showed just how important competitive football had become to the people of England. That it was reported in many different newspapers of the day also supports this view. That the motion of complaint was only thrown out because no evidence could be gained from Walsall

Town Swift's secretary due to him walking out of the meeting shows the strength of feeling amongst clubs who thought rules had been broken and where professionalism or 'shamateurism' was suspected. Such were the growing pains of English football.

Hednesford Town and Stephen Smith's quest for glory in 1891 had not yet finished. On 9 May, Hednesford made the final of the Wednesbury Charity Cup against old foes Wednesbury Old Athletic.[15] Hednesford returned to the Wednesbury Oval once more where 2,000 fans turned out for the final which was part of a whole day of sport known as the Wednesbury Festival. Wednesbury were huge favourites having reached the final of the 1891 Birmingham Cup final. Their success was another example of the elite company Hednesford were keeping in those heady days.

Wednesbury played towards the entrance gates against a strong wind, Alderman R. Williams, President of the club kicking off on their behalf.[16] Hednesford, with Smith once again a defensive back, raced into a three goal lead by half time and could have scored more but for Llowarch in goal. It seemed certain Hednesford would finally be rewarded with silverware in this eventful season. But then Wednesbury clicked into gear. They pulled a goal back early in the second half and then laid siege to the Hednesford goal. A second Wednesbury goal followed as they mounted attack after attack as The Pitmen wilted. Just before the call of time they rushed the ball through and thus drew level with their opponents. The Hednesford players were devastated, exhausted and dejected. They had blown it again, just as against Walsall. As the *Birmingham Daily Post* explained:

> But for the magnificent goalkeeping of the visitors goalkeeper (Wednesbury) must have won easily. The home team wished to play an extra half an hour, but the Hednesford men refused. The result was a draw, 3 goals each.

Hednesford had no desire to lose again in controversial circumstances. They had once again played away from home and matched more illustrious opponents blow for blow. The question now was, though, who would get the cup?

In July, the Wednesbury Charity Football Association presented Hednesford Town and Wednesbury Old Athletic with gold medals of equal value for their efforts but the committee awarded the cup to

Hednesford Town. It is not clear in any press reports as to why this decision was made. Maybe because Hednesford were playing away from home and thus were seen to have the odds against them as the away team. Away goals have since become a decider of European ties in the latter part of the twentieth century so maybe a similar thought process followed here. Whatever the reason, Hednesford Town were the Wednesbury Charity Cup Holders for 1891, and Stephen Smith had the first cup winners medal and footballing honour of his senior career.

The competitive aspect of the 1891/92 season began in October for Hednesford Town. The club had only friendlies and cup fixtures to contend with having withdrawn from the Birmingham League. They were drawn away to Oldbury Town on 10 October.[17] It was hardly the glamour tie the club needed to increase revenue, especially with all the big Midland clubs in the professional Football League. Even if the big teams rested players in cup competitions which reduced crowds, this type of thing was not a modern phenomenon. The only other fixture on the horizon was a friendly against Stafford Rangers on 21 November, again, hardly a money spinner.[18]

As the season wore on Hednesford's pedigree continued to be seen, sometimes they performed to devastating effect, especially against teams from middle class areas whose predisposition towards Rugby Union and cricket meant the football teams were generally weaker. Tough, athletic miners facing doctors, teachers and solicitors whose jobs did not improve them physically and who saw the game merely as a sporting diversion as opposed to intense competition, led to many a one-sided encounter. For the men of Lichfield Leomansley F.C. Saturday was another pleasant day after a pleasant week in the office or classroom. For Hednesford's miners it was their only escape of the week from underneath the ground in the pitch black and a rare time during which to breath fresh air.

Hednesford were quickly ahead, and by half time were 4-0 up.[19] By the end of the massacre the men from Cannock Chase had claimed seven goals and a 7-0 win. Stephen Smith hadn't even made the team, at nearly 18 years old, his birthday was on 14 January and he was still finding his way in a man's world and a miner's one to boot. The season petered out with no league campaign and the Wednesbury Charity Cup was lost to Singers FC who would become Coventry City in another life.

The loss of the cup hurt the most, it was much prized and shown off by the Coventry club in shops across the city.[20] Hednesford Town and Stephen Smith hoped for better times when the next season came around.

In August of 1892, Hednesford Town's next season of football began in earnest. In the close season there had been much discussion amongst both professional and amateur clubs about having separate cup competitions rather than amateur clubs being at a disadvantage against clubs who could pay for the 'better' players. The offer of a trophy for the new competition by Sheffield FC was declined and for the moment all amateur teams continued to enter the FA Cup at the qualifying stage.[21] Amateur clubs to this day enter the FA Cup but also an amateur / non-league version known as the FA Trophy. Teams like Hednesford still believed they could mix it well enough with the professionals. Hednesford drew Hereford away from home. Unfortunately teams needed to win four matches to get to the first-round proper – the last 32 of the competition – and Hednesford did not make it past Hereford.

As 1892 turned into 1893, Stephen Smith's performances in the white and black of Hednesford Town would send his reputation soaring into a different footballing stratosphere as more and more people learned about the footballing prowess of the miner from Hazel Slade with magic in his left boot. He was now seen as a regular in the team, not played where there was a spare spot anymore, the mining men knew he was superior in skill and speed to them, he may have been small and suffered from injuries through opposition rough housing but he was the talisman of the team. He hadn't even turned but burly mining men in their thirties looked to him to dazzle the opponents from this outside left position, making goals aplenty or arriving at the far post to strike or gobble up rebounds.

On Saturday 7 January, Hednesford Town beat Leek Town 5-0 in the Staffordshire Cup first round. From the kick-off at the start of the second half with The Pitmen already two up, Smith picked up the ball and ran through the entire Leek Town defence and made it three.[22] Anyone in the Hednesford team who did not realise they were in the presence of greatness before this game realised it now. Hednesford and Stephen Smith marched on.

The biggest game of the season in any competition for Hednesford was against very near rivals Cannock Town. Many things about the town of Cannock grated on the people of Hednesford and Hazel Slade. First of all, the miners worked for a company called the Cannock and Rugeley Colliery Company. No mention of the other two places often assumed by outsiders to be parts of Cannock town. As seen above when Hednesford complained to the Walsall FA about Walsall Swift's alleged irregularities the press frequently referred to them as 'the Cannock club' in despatches. As well as that the coalfield Stephen and his team-mates/colleagues worked under was known as Cannock Chase Coalfield. The people of Hednesford and Hazel Slade felt a tad unrepresented and under-appreciated by the overbearing town of Cannock. People of Hazel Slade also pointed out that they were part of the boundaries of Lichfield Rural District Council (Brereton Ward).[23]

Football in 1893, as it has been for so many people, in so many places all over the world, before and since, was an expression of individuality and identity for the players and supporters of Hednesford Town Football Club. The two clubs met in the Wednesbury Charity Cup competition at Cannock Town's home ground on 14 January. All roads in the town led to Simm Lane Athletics Ground which is now Cannock Park.[24] The fields were also used for Galas, Agricultural Shows and Sporting activities and thus a community hub of great popularity. Crowds averaged between 400–2,000 and with Hednesford in town bringing a sizeable contingent of supporters, from just over a mile down the road, the attendance would have likely been considerably more than 2,000.[25]

Going into this game Hednesford were massive underdogs. This cup match was only their third competitive match of the season. Cannock Town by comparison had played five games in the Walsall District League, winning three and scoring 37 goals. They had recently beaten Walsall Rangers, 20-3 in the Walsall Cup.[26]

It must be remembered of course that two years previously Hednesford had won this particular trophy. So the outcome was not quite the foregone conclusion it might at first have seemed. Cannock Town had the first attack but Hednesford managed to clear their lines thanks to Brough.[27] Hadlington then cleared the ball from another Cannock attack as the home side continued to press.

Cannock nearly scored from a corner, and then went close through half-back Reynolds. Reynolds then blocked an attack at the other end as Hednesford tried to get a foothold in the game. Hollingshead went through on goal for Cannock but a foul in the build-up brought him back. Cannock then went close from a free-kick. Hednesford keeper Edge saved twice as the Pitmen managed to hold on until half-time, but only just. Hednesford regrouped and had the better of the first twenty minutes of the second half. The *Lichfield Mercury* explained that, 'for the first twenty minutes they had the better of the play. The home side however withstood the strain'.

Cannock rallied and both sides exchanged chances and the game was heading for a draw and a replay. But with five minutes to go, Stephen Smith who had been a peripheral figure all afternoon picked up the ball on the left of the pitch and waltzed past the Cannock defence before burying the ball past a helpless keeper. The journalist watching wrote that, 'Steve Smith defeated Powell who had no chance of saving.' Smith hadn't just defeated Powell but the entire town of Cannock.

Hednesford Town, often described as a team from Cannock by those who didn't know or care about the nuances of the region, had done it. After a couple of late efforts blocked by Edge the Hednesford keeper, the victory went to The Pitmen. The local press were so surprised by the result they looked for excuses for Cannock's defeat, such as key players being out and being at an unfamiliar new ground after the recent move from the Oak ground on Wolverhampton Road.

This victory was more than just progression into the next round of a cup competition. It was a victory for the underdog against supposed superior and overbearing neighbours. The bragging rights would be articulated throughout the Cannock and Rugeley Colliery until the next meeting. For the people of Hednesford and Hazel Slade it was proof of their existence separate from the town of Cannock and their footballing reputation was doubtless enhanced throughout the region. One man whose reputation was enhanced was Stephen Smith, the match winner, the deliverer of local pride. And as any football supporter from Birmingham to Barcelona will tell you, score a winner in a local derby, and your name lives in that club's particular folklore forevermore. Smith had secured mythic status among Hednesford Town followers and the local population in general. He bought not one single drink or cigarette out of his own pocket in The Slade Pub that night as the game was toasted and the women fluttered their eyelids. In fact, he wouldn't need to buy himself a drink again in Hazel Slade for a very long while.

Smith's star was rising, and it was not just the followers of football on the Cannock Chase Coalfield that were noticing it now. He probably didn't realise it then, but looking back on his life it is likely that Stephen Smith would agree that January 1893 was the pivotal month in the defining year of his life. Hednesford Town headed for Birmingham and the Perry Barr football ground for the final of the Birmingham Junior Cup and a chance of another piece of silverware as well as access to the senior competition. Although strictly still part of Staffordshire, Perry Barr was just a few miles from Birmingham City Centre and referred to as part of the city. The club which played at the Wellington Road Ground, Aston Villa Football Club, creators and founder members of the Football League and professionalism in general, were members of the Birmingham Association and considered a Birmingham club.

By 1893 Aston Villa had become the first Midlands club to win the FA Cup in 1887, had beaten Scottish Cup winners Hibernian 3-0 in an unofficial World Championship match that same year and had reached the FA Cup final in 1892 as well. To get to the final of a cup competition was a big deal even a junior one, to play at Wellington Road the home of Aston Villa FC even more so. It was a ground that had capacity for over 25,000 spectators, no Hednesford player had played in front of more than 5,000 people. On 21 January 1893 the footballers of Hednesford were about to play the biggest game of their lives at the most prestigious football ground in the English Midlands. The *Lichfield Mercury* set the scene: 'Hednesford Town played Redditch Town, at Perry Barr, in the final tie of the qualifying round for the Birmingham Cup, the Villa ground being placed at the disposal of the Birmingham Association. Redditch won the toss and elected to kick downhill.'[28]

The winning of the toss was the only success of the afternoon for the Redditch Town players. Hednesford attacked Redditch from the off. Redditch held firm until the twentieth minute when Rollins banged into the net but was ruled offside.' Then Hednesford broke through as the *Lichfield Mercury* explained using the flowery language of the day. 'Matters were made intolerably warm for the the Redditch custodian, who was twice called upon to clear, each time acquitting himself creditably, but finally found himself beaten by a capital low shot from Wootton who attacked from the right'. Spooner of Hednesford sent in a stinging shot that the Redditch keeper couldn't hold and the ball went into the net to give Hednesford a 2-0 half-time lead.

Steve Smith had been the source of many a Pitmen attack. Redditch simply couldn't cope with the slight and sprightly left winger. The barrage of Hednesford attacks continued and five minutes into the second half Spooner smashed in his second and Hednesford's third. Stephen Smith had terrorised Melen, the Redditch right back all through the match. In the end Melen, totally tormented by Smith, capitulated and lost possession to him in a dangerous position. Smith left him for dead and added the fourth Hednesford goal of the afternoon.

The crowd roared as Hednesford's teenage talisman dealt Redditch the decisive blow. The Birmingham Junior Cup was Hednesford's. Smith had been the architect and the crowd could see his superiority over his opponents and value to his colleagues. The Aston Villa committee members knew a top player when they saw one. Redditch pulled a goal back. Hednesford added a fifth. Wootton and Spooner fed by Smith continued to go close until the end. The victory, the glory, the trophy and the medals were the property of Hednesford Town.

There were celebrations back in Hednesford as the news came over the telegraph wire. Stephen Smith senior, now a platelayer for the colliery railway, basked in his son's glory once more at The Slade as the information filtered through to the village. William, Stephen's younger brother, had recently started playing for the Colliery and inspired by his sibling hoped to replicate similar footballing feats. But today was Steve's day, affectionately known in the village as 'Tich' due to his slight stature, he had once again brought vicarious fame to the village of Hazel Slade.

This morale boosting victory came at a time when the majority of the miners in the village were striking over a lowering of wages. Sickness and starvation was rife in the village and in 1893, the men went on strike for more pay.[29] Football now as then gave people an escape from their hardships if only for a few hours at a time. If nothing else the Smith family of Hazel Slade had pride and and reflective glory in Stephen's achievements. Glory doesn't put money in your pocket or food on the table. But what could anyone do? Mining was the only life Smith and his people knew.

Aston Villa held a dinner in the pavilion at their ground after the match for the players of both teams. No medals were given out as they needed to be engraved and the cup was lifted by Wootton the captain in the stands before being given back to the Birmingham Association, also for engraving. After the dinner the players were invited to join the Villa committee members and Birmingham dignitaries in the adjoining Crown and Cushion pub.

The players punished the ale and the woodbines in the tap room of the pub. Smith sat and smoked with Spooner and Wootton. The talk was of the satisfaction of victory, the delight at the knowledge that the Birmingham Association had provided both finalists with overnight accommodation at the nearby Aston Lower Grounds and their guilt at enjoying themselves despite all the troubles back home. But they agreed they had earned their day in the sun, or in this case a night in Birmingham with food and alcohol aplenty.

The hubbub in the Crown and Cushion carried on until the early hours. At one point Smith and his compatriots were approached by a thin bespectacled man of average height with a moustache and a brown homburg style hat. He was wearing a blazer, a waistcoat with a gold pocket watch and a heavily starched white shirt with the collar pointing upwards and then bent back down with a black tie wrapped around said collar. He looked to be in his mid thirties and he addressed them in a Liverpudlian accent.

He complimented the Hednesford men on their fine display. He'd heard about Smith's goal against Cannock and asked Steve to talk him through his wonder strike against Leek. Smith, modest as ever, did so briefly. The man praised Wootton and Spooner on their goal scoring exploits that season and they were more effusive in talking about their success. The man said he was a member of Aston Villa and a committee member to boot. The Villa committee member bought the players a round of beers and topped them up with whiskies whilst he smoked cigars himself. He continued to speak even though the players could not see him for the fog of cigar smoke. The man explained he was disappointed with Villa's FA Cup final loss the previous season and that his team were way off the pace to challenge for the Championship title, the only trophy still to elude them. Only two years previously Villa had finished low enough in the league to have to apply for re-election, something that to a man who had been a member since 1881 was a source of deep embarrassment and shame to him and his colleagues.

Stephen opined to the Villa member that as long as finances were good, which at Villa it was obvious that they were, wasn't that the main thing? All employees were getting paid he said referencing his home village's financial tribulations. The member said they didn't need to tell him that twice. He explained it was his idea to install turnstiles at the Perry Barr ground the previous year. The member said that sporting achievement was more important than money. 'Finance is important, but we should never forget that we are not talking about a mere business. This is the Aston Villa football club, and it deserves nothing short of the best.'[30] The member made to depart but just as he did so he turned back and explained that he was looking to improve Villa on the field as well as off. That his club needed to improve its current players off the field behaviour and training discipline and also improve the playing staff with new additions. He said he would keep an eye on the Hednesford men's progress and would be interested to talk again if they could keep up their consistency of performance. He then bade them a good night.

The players joked that the Villa man had had too much to drink and was exaggerating his importance for effect. They joked that they were going to sign for Villa now. They laughed heartily at the absurdity of such a suggestion. The Hednesford treasurer then came over and grilled the trio for the gossip. The treasurer was astonished with what they told him. The footballers were confused and then agog when the treasurer explained who the man was. It was Aston Villa Football Club's financial secretary, Frederick Rinder. The man would soon be Villa's chairman, he would sweep away the old order in Perry Barr and stay in his position until 1925.

Having won the Birmingham Junior Cup, Hednesford marched on in the senior version as well. March saw victory over Burton Wanderers by five goals to two.[31] Steve Smith was in the thick of it. He is mentioned throughout the match report as Hednesford caused Burton immense problems. The opposition resorted to rough treatment to stop him but they only ever managed it temporarily. Smith and co had won again.

At the end of March, old rivals Walsall Town Swifts returned to haunt Hednesford once more, beating them 4-2, in front of 1,000 fans, again in a semi-final, this time it was the Staffordshire Cup.[32] Walsall it must be remembered were now a professional club in the English Second Division.

Stephen Smith and his teammates were disappointed at another loss to Walsall and missing out on a cup final. Another disappointed man was Aston Villa finance secretary Fred Rinder. On the same day as Hednesford's defeat on Saturday, 25 March, Wolverhampton Wanderers lifted the FA Cup. Aston Villa's English Cup triumph back in 1887 seemed a long time ago.

As the *Birmingham Daily Post* explained through listing all past Cup winners, Albion and Wolves had now equalled Villa's solitary success.

In fact it could be argued Villa had been usurped as the top Midland's club. Wolves had reached the final twice, Albion three times. Villa were also ten points (five wins) behind First Division leaders Sunderland at this point. They would eventually finish 13 points behind Champions Sunderland, 7 wins back. As a historical aside it is interesting that the FA Cup final was held in late March. This fact explodes the myth that the cup final has always been held in May.

Hednesford Town were Birmingham Junior Cup winners, Staffordshire Cup semi-finalists and were discussing with another old rival, Wednesbury Old Athletic, where to play their latest Wednesbury Charity Cup semi-final match after the draw was made.[33] Hednesford already had a fine regional cup fighting pedigree but this year the whole footballing nation had sat up and now were on the brink of doing the unthinkable, the unprecedented, winning the Birmingham Junior and Senior Cups in the same season. Hednesford travelled to face recent FA Cup winners Wolverhampton Wanderers at the Molineux grounds, as it was known then, to contest the Birmingham Cup semi-final.[34] The leading men in the football region of the West Midlands looked on with interest.

The Molineux name originates from Benjamin Molineux, a successful local merchant who, in 1744, purchased land on which he built Molineux House and on which the stadium would eventually be built. The estate was purchased in 1860 by O.E. McGregor, who converted the land into a pleasure park open to the public. Molineux Grounds, as it was titled, included a wide range of facilities including an ice rink, a cycling track, a boating lake and, most crucially, an area for football. Games continued to be played in the grounds throughout the late nineteenth century, including football, cricket, croquet, and lacrosse, but they were never as popular as the cycle races.[35]

The Birmingham Cup semi-final of 1893 between FA Cup winners and Senior Cup holders Wolverhampton Wanderers and Junior cup winners Hednesford Town took place in front of over 2,000 spectators as the sun shone down brightly on Molineux. Many Hednesford supporters had made the trip to see if their team could do the unimaginable, support wise, 'both teams were fairly represented'.

The First Division professionals from Wolverhampton dominated from the off. It was noted that 'the inferiority of the visitors was noticeable from the kick off'. Harsh but truthful. Smith didn't get a kick.

A man described as a 'player who rose to the big occasion' was nowhere to be seen as Wolves bypassed him and his teammates in the forward positions.[36] Wolves had Hednesford penned in their own half for the entire game. Smith and The Pitmen's forward line could only watch as Wolves repeatedly waltzed through Town's defence. The ball kept careering into the Hednesford Town net. The reporter couldn't bear to watch and was discreet in his reporting of the carnage: 'A description of the play is scarcely necessary. At half-time the Wolves were leading by 8 goals to 0, and pressure being maintained to the end won by 12 goals to 1.[37]

Smith looked embarrassed when the crowd clapped his consolation goal. The man who had vanquished Cannock and steered his side to the Birmingham Junior Cup victory at Aston Villa's ground had been helpless on the left wing as his teammates had been dismembered by the Wolves. It was yet another semi-final defeat but instead of looking at the positives of his amateur side yet again having another great cup run Stephen was down. He was fed up as the players got the train home. He was grumpy when they had to get off at Stafford to get on another train to Hednesford rather than it being one journey. Back to the miner's strike of 1893 and poverty and hardship. Football glory helped soften the blow of humiliation at the hands of the mining company owners. When you get humiliated on the football field as well as constantly in daily life it all seemed too much to take.

Fred Rinder also felt humiliated as Wolves murdered Villa in the Birmingham Senior Cup final. Despite winning the Staffordshire Cup, beating Hednesford's conquerors in the final, Villa were no longer the top team in the Midlands. They may have finished above Wolves in the League but their FA Cup pedigree had been usurped by the men from the Molineux and West Bromwich Albion and the 3-1 Birmingham Cup final defeat had been comprehensive. Villa were going backwards. But unlike the maudlin Stephen Smith, Rinder was already making movements to change things for the better. In doing so he would change Stephen's world, and his entire family's world for that matter, out of all proportion to being something they could never have possibly expected in their wildest dreams.

Back in February 1893, at a now infamous Aston Villa Committee meeting at a hotel on Barwick Street in Birmingham City Centre, Rinder had shocked the club's members and supporters to the core with his oratory about Aston Villa's recent decline. He was the main instigator of the meeting at which he swept away the men who were running Villa into the ground, criticizing the board's tolerance of ill-discipline and players' drinking.[38]

The club was in turmoil, inside and out. Fans, players, members all at odds with one another. Performances were being criticised left right and centre. It just goes to show that criticism of well-paid footballers misbehaving off the field and underperforming on it is not a modern-day phenomenon. Young men earning good money and with time on their hands in a big city need to be closely monitored or things could get out of hand. At Aston Villa they already had and Frederick Rinder had had enough.

The local press called for William McGregor to return. The Villa director and President was the current Chairman of the Football League which he had founded. The famous Barwick Street Special Meeting took place on 24 February 1893. This meeting – though it was not realised at the time – proved to bring about the final 'clearing of the decks'; the final weeding out of weak individuals and wrong practices, to enable the club to make progress. This meeting also brought the footballing world to know about Mr Fred Rinder, 'who arrived in Barwick Street more in the form of a stormy petrel rather than as a peace descending dove'.

A new Committee was elected and pledged to make Aston Villa the greatest club in the world. It had been a brutal evening where former FA Cup winning captain and legendary star player Archie Hunter had been heckled for defending the current playing staff.[39] In fact it may well have been that when 'the hero of the club for many a year was jeered and heckled' it totally broke Archie Hunter's health. Already unwell, he soon became worse, and by the end of 1894, he had died. A journalist described the incident that fateful night, 'as the most painful I have experienced'.

George Ramsay, the club secretary who was also in charge of finding, coaching and selecting players, was one of the few men not asked to resign. The man who masterminded Villa's first and only FA Cup win in 1887 plus six Birmingham Senior Cups by 1892 was the definite beneficiary of that infamous meeting on Barwick Street. He remained as Secretary on the revamped Committee, this time with fellow visionaries and without the hindrance of the less far-sighted.[40]

Fred Rinder looked after the finances required to lure the best players to Aston Villa, and George Ramsay was able to capture virtually any footballer he wanted. By June of 1893 George Ramsay had decided he wanted to sign Stephen Smith from Hednesford Town. Rinder who had also seen and heard much of Smith agreed and set about capturing his signature.

After the Wolverhampton debacle in the Birmingham Cup, Smith had been desolate and distraught and unusually sullen after that defeat. He picked himself up and continued to bolster his burgeoning reputation. It was a reputation so strong that Aston Villa Football Club, reformed and reorganised and looking to end their winless run in the Football League Championship could not resist and saw him as an integral part of their brave new dawn.

Wednesday 17 May 1893 was a very busy evening in the life of Hednesford Town and Stephen Smith. He travelled to Birmingham that evening with his Town teammates to receive the medals they had won in the Birmingham Junior cup that meant qualification for the senior tournament, a tournament that they had nearly won as well.[41] They had won the final of the junior competition at Aston Villa's Wellington Road ground at Perry Barr. Villa's committee members were there. Fred Rinder arranged for Steve to meet them having had a positive reply from Smith about a discussion about signing for the Birmingham club. Out of courtesy, Rinder had also asked Hednesford Town for permission to speak to him that evening.

The Villa committee had come to congratulate the Hednesford players and sign Stephen Smith. They appeared out of the cigar smoke and directed waiters to bring over drinks to the Hednesford party's table. Rinder, Ramsay, the legendary William McGregor, the giant man with a giant beard, James Lees and the rest of the Committee joined the players and began to chat amiably and let their hair down.[42] George Ramsay, chief selector and owner of a jet black, pointy and waxed moustache of considerable size, explained to Steve how much Aston Villa wanted to sign him. Smith said how flattered he was and was interested in signing for the Villa. Rinder interjected that any player who signed for them would be fairly paid and bonuses earned would be put away as a sort of pension fund for when the player and club ended their association.[43] 'We'll look after you lad,' said McGregor, the Scottish behemoth.

It was all quite overwhelming for Steve. As his Hednesford colleagues caroused and enjoyed themselves through drink, he was discussing football and finances with four of the most important men in

English football. Rinder excused himself, saying he would be in contact again later in the week to talk terms, league forms and signatures and congratulated him on his exploits that season.

George Ramsay congratulated him and bought him another drink. Ramsay said he was putting a top squad together and he also had a top coach to train them all. Ramsay introduced a man on the table who had not yet spoken once, other than to say hello. The only other thing that Smith noticed the man do was to put his big flat cloth cap down on the table on arrival. The balding man with a floral cravat introduced himself as Joe Grierson, former coach of Middlesbrough Ironopolis. He explained his training methods and his tactics and Steve was impressed with his knowledge of the game and genuinely excited at the prospect of playing for this man. He answered every question Smith asked with detail and expertise.

It was the early hours of Thursday morning now and Steve Smith from the Black Country, who had only really heard the adenoidal accent of the West Midlands during his lifetime, had in a matter of minutes been spoken to in Scouse, Scottish and now the North East Yorkshire twang. It was about as exotic as it got for a man who had rarely been outside Staffordshire and Warwickshire in his entire lifetime. The Villa men decided to leave but Stephen assured them he would be in touch. They told him Fred Rinder was the money and details man. He would see him right.

Stephen Smith realised he was entering a whole other world; the only one where a member of the working class could find fame and fortune and at the same time respect, purely based on their actual skill not background. If you had ability in the footballing world, then as now, that was all that mattered, and Stephen Smith, the small and stocky, yet pacey footballer with a low centre of gravity, with two quick feet and a powerful shot and endless stamina to boot, had ability in abundance.

On Friday 7 June, 1893, the *Lichfield Mercury* reported the events of the previous Friday's annual meeting of Hednesford Town Football Club at the Anglesey Hotel behind The Tins Football Ground.[44] Club secretary Thomas Stokes presided over the meeting and reported on Hednesford's fine season. Despite not competing in a league competition the club played in 43 matches, winning 28 and losing just 9. The team entered into seven cup competitions, reaching five semi-finals and one final. They'd won the Birmingham Senior Cup qualifying competition winning medals for this and it had topped a season where they had achieved 'a very good record'.

The financial position of the club was also satisfactory as they had a small balance in hand. Despite this small profit the balance sheet showed that as an amateur club they could not afford to buy players or pay players if they wanted to go professional. The profit was a mere 3 shillings and 10 pence. The club was surviving but only just, it had to pay £94 in wages to employ non-playing administrators plus expenses to so players who you might argue were 'semi-professional' footballers to induce them to play.

Without going professional the club could not join the Football League and get in regular gate receipts. However, as in previous seasons when in a league the club had struggled to compete due to low attendances, Going professional would not necessarily help the club as the costs they would incur to host matches on a more regular basis could potentially kill the club as they would also struggle to pay regular wages to contracted players whose demands would legally have to be honoured. The amateur game was the immediate future for Hednesford Town.

But this was not the case for Stephen Smith who was about to enter football's professional ranks. He received his Birmingham and Dudley Cup medals at the annual meeting and it was also announced that he was departing to Aston Villa. He received warm congratulations and applause at this announcement. Wootton, Smith's partner in crime up front, who had joked disbelievingly with Smith that they would both join the Villa, won a contract with Burton Wanderers of the Midland League, which they would win in 1894 and be elected to the Football League.

The minutes of Hednesford's annual meeting read that, 'S. Smith, outside left forward, of Hednesford Town, has been transferred to Aston Villa'. It would be a signature that Fred Rinder would never forget acquiring. Famous author on all things Aston Villa, John Lerwill sent me an interview with Fred Rinder from the *Athletic News* in 1928. Here Rinder explained the unusual circumstances behind finally signing Steve Smith for Aston Villa:[45]

> One of the most amazing experiences was when I went to sign Steve Smith. He was working at Hednesford (Cannock and Rugeley) Colliery, and I was told that I should find him at home at five o'clock in the evening. But when I got there

> I found he was working on the night shift. He was in the engine house, winding the cage to get men out of the pit. When I got his signature it was between nine and ten at night: and then I had to find my way back to Hednesford. I got lost among the pit banks and wandered about in imminent danger of falling into the canal. It was a nasty experience. Finally, I determined to undergo no more thrills, so finding a canal boat I crept into the cabin and stayed there until morning!

The one and only Fred Rinder had gone underground armed with a league form for Smith to sign, having been told where to find him by Steve's mum and dad.[46] Steve was a coal-miner when he went to work that morning, when he next saw the light of day he was a professional footballer.

Thankfully Fred Rinder survived his ordeal and lodged the league form with the respective authorities informing the League that Smith would be on around £2 a week, plus a £5 bonus for winning key games; the bonus alone was five times what he earned in the pit, more than all his family's weekly wages added together.[47] Stephen Smith was now a footballer in the world's only fully professional league, playing for the club that founded the league and was one of its most famous, Aston Villa.

Chapter 4

Perry Barr

The spring of 1893 had been a momentous one for Stephen Smith. He was now a professional footballer with one of the world's best teams in the best league in the world. Only the Scottish league could come close to the English league, especially as they were the only two professional leagues anywhere in the world at the time. The Scottish league was not fully professional at this time, however, but of the two pre-eminent national teams of world football in this era Scotland had fared better in matches with England. The problem for Scotland was their best players headed down south, as professionalism took hold, for better wages and the English teams desire to utilise and learn the ways of the Scottish passing style.

Despite professionalism, players often had other jobs as they were not paid pre-season, some played professional cricket, others continued to do second jobs.[1] Stephen continued to work down the mine until August when he was expected for pre-season training. He was still registered as a mining engine driver in 1895 when he got married, showing that he was still involved in his old industry even as a professional footballer when he had the time.

Footballers' wages and working conditions have come a long way since then. It is highly unlikely that current Premier League footballers would be allowed a second job during the off season, never mind mining and they would certainly not need to supplement their wages with a second income.

In September 1893, Derby County proposed that the Football League should impose a maximum wage of £4 a week. At the time, most players were only part-time professionals and still had other jobs. These players did not receive as much as £4 a week and therefore the matter did not greatly concern them. It certainly did not concern Stephen when he signed on for Aston Villa. However, a minority of players were so good they were able to obtain as much as £10 a week.

This proposal posed a serious threat to their income. One such player was Stephen's soon to be captain and colleague John Devey. He and several other top players of the day at clubs such as Wolves, Liverpool, Everton and the two Manchester clubs, formed the AFU, Association Footballers Union and persuaded the FA to ignore proposals for a maximum wage. It was put off until 1901 when a £4 a week maximum wage was implemented which had dramatic consequences for both Aston Villa and Stephen, but there was a lot of water to flow under a lot of bridges before then.

Stephen's last summer in Hazel Slade before he started his new occupation ended when he was requested to report for pre-season training at Perry Barr on 1 August. He was now to be paid to play football, his hobby, his pastime that had helped him escape the coal mines. He could hardly believe his luck. He left his parents' house where he still lived on Cross Street, early in the morning to catch the train to Birmingham. He hugged his mum and shook his father's hand as he fairly burst with pride.

His siblings bade him farewell with a mixture of love and teasing and he hugged his brother William. They were close, bonded by a shared love of football, of kickabouts on the Chase. Stephen was William's idol and had started playing for the Colliery team having been inspired by his brother. He too was starting to be noticed, replacing Stephen himself on the left wing when he went to Hednesford. It was about 6.00 am but it was light and fresh, as cool as it would get before the summer heat would shine through as the day progressed. Stephen walked up the hill of the Hazel Slade valley, climbing up Cannock Wood Street. He turned left onto the Rugeley Road past the Slade Pub down the bank towards Hednesford. He walked parallel with the Hednesford Hills over the Rawnsley Road and into Hednesford. At the edge of Hednesford is Station Road and from there the platform where steam engines headed south to Birmingham.

Stephen walked towards the train station but was intercepted by a small brown-haired woman who asked him to stop. She must have been small because she was shorter than Stephen and he was between 5ft 4 inches and 5ft 6 inches. She was like Stephen in terms of her slightness as well as her height. She was a beautiful delicate creature that made Stephen's heart race, Susan Blastock, the daughter of his father's neighbours on Cross Street.

Susan, whose father ran the Slade Pub, had come to wish him good luck. She worked as a barmaid and had seen Stephen and the male members of his family most days of the week. The Slade was the focal point of the village. She had seen Stephen in the pub ever since she could remember, she was 20, he was 19. They had grown up together but also apart, knowing of each other but not knowing each other. He only really talked to her when he had drunk a few ales usually after a Hednesford Town or Colliery Company football victory. She knew he was quiet and shy and needed the Dutch Courage because of all the attention he got because of his exploits. She forgave him because of that.

Stephen awkwardly and nervously thanked her for coming to see him off. Susan had blue eyes and pale skin despite the summer sun. She had powdered her face a little as was the fashion, but she needn't have. She was the very embodiment of an English Rose. He had been bewildered by her for many years and saw her as some sort of goddess. Now it seemed as though there might be a chance to see more of her on a regular basis if he could get over his shyness in her presence.

Before that though, he must get on the next train to Birmingham to the 'city of a thousand trades', the 'workshop of the world', the second city of the British Empire in the heart of the industrial Midlands. He was about to meet his new teammates, the men who played for former unofficial world champions and English Cup winners, Aston Villa.

The train chugged down the Grand Junction railway towards Perry Barr station on the outskirts of north Birmingham. Stephen saw the famous suburb of Handsworth as the train travelled on to its destination through where the famous industrialists James Watt and William Murdoch had lived.[2] Perry Barr was certainly not the limit of Birmingham's sprawl northwards. The station encouraged further development to the north, and the opening of Handsworth and Smethwick stations on the Birmingham, Wolverhampton and Dudley Railways continued the northwards development.

Birmingham's northern suburban area had reached into Handsworth Wood, houses there being large and few to the acre. The northern limits of the country's second city seemed to go on forever as Stephen peered out of the carriage windows. South of the Holyhead/Soho Road, a much greater density of working-class housing was beginning to be developed. The whole place seemed massive compared to Abbots Bromley, Hazel Slade or even Hednesford.

Beyond Stephen Smith's final destination of Perry Barr, to the south of Aston Villa's headquarters was Birmingham city centre itself. The city the club represented and which now he would represent. The city of a thousand trades was the epicentre of the Industrial Revolution that had made Britain the wealthiest country in the world. And of course, it was the birthplace of the world's first professional football league. By the 1890s Birmingham was the home of metalworking, nail making, brass goods, jewellers and gunsmiths.[3] The carriages that were taking Stephen south to Perry Barr were built in Birmingham, as were bicycles, glass and cocoa and chocolate in Bournville. A huge Town Hall had been built to imitate the temple of Castor and Pollux in Rome. A huge Catholic Cathedral called St Chad's dominated the skyline, a vast array of public amenities were also built including hospitals, botanical gardens, public parks, a museum and art gallery and the huge council house building was the centrepiece of the city. Railways ran through Birmingham, north to Manchester and Liverpool and south to London, the city had its own electricity supply and electric trams.

Birmingham was truly a modern, vibrant city with all the technological advances that brought. This included a modern fire brigade, telephone exchange, library, school of art, technical college and Mason Science College which would become the University of Birmingham, one of the finest universities in the world. The West Midlands at this time had more banking offices per head than any other region in Britain, including London.[4] Stephen had never inhabited anywhere like this before. He would now be living and working in a city described in 1890, by a visiting American journalist as 'the best-governed city in the world'.[5] Stephen would now be part of Aston Villa's plans to give the city the best football team in the world.

Alighting from the train at Perry Barr station, Stephen walked southwards down a street called Birchfield Road. After about half a mile he could see a crossroads. Heading southward to the Aston area of Birmingham was a road called Aston Lane, at the corner of this crossroads was the Crown and Cushion public house. The northward road the other side of the Birchfield Road, was Wellington Road and on that corner was Aston Villa's Perry Barr football ground. Stephen had instructions to go first into the public house.

He opened the door of the Crown and Cushion and walked into the saloon area. Around twenty athletic male figures and a few considerably older turned around in unison to look at him. He suddenly felt very nervous. It was 9.00 am and yet some men were drinking ale and some were smoking.[6] As he stood there nonplussed he was welcomed by Villa's man with the hat. Joe Grierson the coach shook him by the hand and welcomed him to the Aston Villa Football Club. He saw George Ramsay and William McGregor at a table conversing intently. There was no sign of Fred Rinder.

'Mr Rinder told me to arrive at 9.00 am, have I missed him?' gabbled Stephen nervously. Grierson responded, 'You'll see Mr Ramsay, Mr Lees and Mr McGregor again later but Mr Rinder rarely mixes with the players. He just signs you and puts you in our custody. Don't worry you'll be fine with us, lad.'[7] Grierson proceeded to introduce Smith to his new teammates but unlike the Villa committee members he had met in the past these men required no introduction. Stephen couldn't quite believe these men were about to become his work colleagues.

'Come and meet Jack,' said Grierson and steered him to the middle of the bar room where a tall, well-built man was holding court surrounded by the other footballers, it was Villa captain, England football international and Warwickshire cricketer John Devey, who rather confusingly liked to be called Jack.[8] Devey stared at Smith through dark eyes and beamed a huge smile at him. 'Welcome young man, another fine recruit, I watched you play at Perry Barr earlier this year, I was impressed, lad.' Stephen blushed.

Stephen Smith was now introduced to more players by Devey, the club captain who had joined Villa two years previous at twenty-four. Devey had been criticised for being too old to be signed as he had been playing since he was fourteen and everyone assumed he was older.[9] He took over Archie Hunter's mantle and despite this pressure to emulate Villa's greatest hero he blasted in 26 league goals in 25 league appearances in his first season in 1891–92.[10] He was the only player who had ever scored more goals than appearances made in a single season in a Villa shirt. His goals helped Villa to the Cup final and a fourth place league finish. By the end of that season he was an England international.[11]

Devey hit another 20 goals the following season as well as a double century for Warwickshire and was desperate to bring silverware to Birmingham.[12] Devey then introduced Stephen to his idol. Smith couldn't speak as Charlie Athersmith shook his hand. Although Stephen was an outside left he was desperate to emulate Athersmith the Villa right winger. Athersmith seemed to loll and lean on something wherever he sat or stood. Not quite as tall or well built as Devey, he still had a piercing gaze and an aura about him.

Smith had seen Charlie play before and with his long flowing locks embarking on dazzling runs he was a sight to behold, Stephen wanted to be like Charlie.[13] Athersmith was only just 20 and already an England international, making his debut with Devey.[14] They had been part of England's British Championship winning side of 1892 that had confirmed the English as the best footballing nation on earth, despite Scotland still having won more editions of what was also known as the 'International Championship' than England at this time.

Athersmith had exploded onto the scene in March 1891 with a hat-trick in only his second Villa game.[15] He hit double figures from the wing as Devey's partner in crime in the 1891/92 season and again in 1892/93 but silverware still eluded him even if he had become an England regular. Charlie could see Stephen was nervous so he sat down next to him at a table and slouched down on a chair in the style you can see him do, in any 1890s Aston Villa team photograph and gave Smith a cigarette.

After a few pleasantries he was introduced to two of the club's all time legends who were sat at an adjoining table. Stephen thought his head would explode with starstruck awe. When Aston Villa last won the FA Cup it had been six years previous in 1887, the same year they beat Scottish Cup holders Hibernian to claim world domination as well as English hegemony. The only men still playing for the club that famous year were now staring back at him saying 'hello'. Albert Brown and Denny Hodgetts shook him by the hand and greeted him warmly. Albert had reigned at right wing until Athersmith came along. At 31 years of age his best years were behind him but Albert was revered by the club for all he had achieved, including an amazing 14 goals in 10 games on the way to FA Cup glory and he had hit nine goals the previous league season as well; he was still a top player and a man everyone admired.

The other man at the table was even more famous. It was Denny Hodgetts, a massive man, nearly six foot tall which was big for the times, stocky and with a big kind face, and despite being 30 years of age he had been and was still being picked for England.[16] He had won the British Championship twice, once with Devey and Athersmith, Villa really was a club packed full of internationals during these days and Smith just sat in awe as Denny welcomed him. Stephen didn't really know what he was doing in this place full of sporting behemoths. What could he say to the first Villa player to score in an FA Cup final?[17]

The main body of the squad was sent across Wellington Road to the Blacksmith's Yard to change. The grandstand at Perry Barr didn't have changing rooms even though teams often changed in the pub or by the side of the pitch as Stephen had done on his previous visit.[18] The yard provided very good facilities for the era, so much so that the Birchfield Harriers athletic club also utilised that area as their dressing rooms. Stephen and the other new signings were allowed to change in the pub as they were issued with new football boots, shin guards and the famous claret and blue jersey with white shorts and claret socks. Everyone would be wearing new shirts with a claret body and blue sleeves except Denny Hodgetts who kept his claret and blue quartered shirt which he preferred due to his sentimentality, the man who had scored Villa's first cup final goal pretty much did what he liked anyway.[19]

The new recruits were introduced to each other properly for the first time. Again, Stephen was in awe. The four men who joined with Smith were John Reynolds and Willie Groves from the Albion, James Welford and Bob Chatt.[20] Reynolds and Groves were the two half-backs that caused the Villa considerable problems in the 1892 Cup final that saw Albion win comfortably 3-0. Groves at this point though present for training couldn't yet play in competitive games for Villa as the League found that Villa had infringed the rule which debarred poaching, fined Villa £25 and declared that Groves was still an Albion player.[21] Fred Rinder had assured everyone at Villa including Groves that he would 'sort it'. No one expected anything different from Rinder.

A little over a year after 'Baldy' Reynolds had hit the third Albion goal against Villa in the cup final at The Oval, he had signed for Villa for just £40.[22] His prematurely receding hairline had and would again be the source of good-hearted banter with supporters throughout his career.[23] He had grown up in the North of Ireland and was one of a number of the new signings with an accent hard for Stephen to decipher. I wonder what they made of Stephen's Black Country twang?

The Scotsman, Welford, shook Stephen's hand heartily and made him wince as he towered over him and spoke in such a thick Glaswegian brogue that Smith struggled to understand all that he said. That just left Bob Chatt to introduce himself, he had come from Middlesbrough Ironopolis with the coach Grierson and could play at half-back or forward.[24] He was a strapping bloke and tall, though most were taller than Smith and he came with a decent reputation, his North East Riding of Yorkshire accent was also hard for the ear to decode and sometimes as with Welford, Stephen pretended to understand when perhaps he didn't. He was very friendly and talkative and in good form having hit over 50 goals in his past four seasons under Grierson's tutelage.[25]

Training began on the Perry Barr pitch and as the players trotted past the Committee members, Stephen remarked on how much he had loved playing here for Hednesford Town. William McGregor joked that he wouldn't have thought that when they first acquired the playing enclosure. He explained that, 'when the Villa first took it there was a hayrick not far from the centre of the ground, a number of trees along the touchlines, a pool not far away, and a nasty hill near the left-hand corner of the top goal'. Stephen Smith as an outside left would come to know that nasty hill very well throughout his Villa career at Perry Barr.

Stephen asked Charlie Athersmith why there were so many men in suits writing things down at the side of the pitch. 'They are press men, Steve, this is Aston Villa, they even write about how we train!' he laughed. Smith gulped. What a day, what a world. The Aston Villa squad of 1893/94 gathered around Ramsay and Grierson and listened to the North Easterner's words intently as he detailed what they would be doing that day. Dunning, Elliott, Baird, Reynolds, Cowan, Chatt, Athersmith, Logan, John Devey and his brother Will, Hodgetts, Woolley, Welford, Gillan, Groves, Hare, Smith, Randle, Benwell, Burton, Brown, Russell and Coulton were then put through their paces by Grierson as Ramsay and McGregor pondered the state of the squad and the newspaper men watched on and scribbled.

Grierson explained to the new signings that Villa had a certain way of playing and that he would turn them from footballers into 'Villa footballers'. Grierson told them that he planned to train the team so well that they would know exactly what to do when attacking and defending. Examples of this training later in the season during games highlighted the benefits of the hours they would spend doing as Grierson told them as explained by Simon Page in his book *Pinnacle of the Perry Barr Pets*:

> Cowan times a tackle to perfection and is left with the ball at his feet. Just behind and to the side would be his two wing halves who would have been covering Cowan as he made the

challenge. They would push out towards the wings should a side-ways pass be Cowan's best option. The two fullbacks would push up in order to catch forwards offside should the opposition win the ball back and try a quick break. The wingers start to move down the flanks where they would either find room for themselves or stretch the enemy defence leaving space for the inside-forwards to exploit. Whatever situation arose in a match, every Villa player knew what he had to do and what his comrades would be doing.

The quality of the players and the level of organisation that Grierson showed Stephen and his new teammates that day was proof that Smith had entered the top level of English sport and he needed to be always at his best in order to break into this side on a regular basis. This was not just professional football but elite professional football, something he had no prior experience of. He was terrified. He also couldn't get over the fact reporters turned up for training, trial matches between Villa's first and second team and friendly matches. The pressure was on.

The Birmingham and Midland papers reported all about the Villa build up to the new season which would begin on 2 September 1893.[26] The *Birmingham Daily Post* of 28 August detailed the 'coming football season' from the Villa point of view.[27] The article gives us an insight into Stephen's contractual situation with Villa, his place in the squad pecking order and also the further improvements to the Perry Barr grounds facilities and why it was linked to football supporter behaviour. Things seemed so different to modern football back in 1893 but also so inherently the same.

As well as being a Villa director, William McGregor was also the Football League President, known as 'the father of the great Football League'. McGregor's league had just ruled that a professional footballer's 'registration is now only binding for one season'. Players like Stephen who had just signed this type of contract might be affected, basically Smith had to hit the ground running or he would be out on his ear.

Despite the shortness of these new contracts all existing contracts would be honoured and if Stephen had a great season he would not be tied to Villa should he get a better deal elsewhere. The machinations regarding player contracts are not a modern scenario nor would it seem was freedom of contract, every year you could move, just as now if a player wants a move, despite the length of contract he can pretty much always force a move or wait until the last year of his contract when his club will be forced to sell him to get some money before his deal expires. Player power began in Victorian England.

The journalists of Birmingham obviously thought Smith was about to make a huge impact in his first year at the club. 'The Aston Villa trial matches have been watched with much interest ... as far as can be gathered, (the line-up for the opening game at home to West Brom) will be constituted as follows:- Benwell in goal, Baird and Elliot as backs, Reynolds, Cowan and Chatt as half backs, Hodgetts and Smith on the left wing, Devey in the centre, Athersmith and Logan on the right wing.'

Then as now pundits tried to analyse form and predict line-ups. Focus on footballers has always been intense since the professional era began, if not before.

The press also reported that Villa had placed an 'unclimbable iron fence' around the pitch to prevent 'spectators encroaching' or 'interfering' with players. Again, fan misbehaviour is not a modern problem. To guard against this 'interference' the club planned a 'new entrance onto the field from the dressing room' presumably from across the road at the Blacksmith's yard or perhaps from the public house. This is unclear.

Aston Villa's first game of the 1893/94 season would be against their most ancient and bitter rivals having signed two of their better players with the Albion trying desperately to get one of those deals annulled. It is a bitter rivalry that has waxed and waned in intensity but has always endured to this very day. Any game between the two is an occasion full of tension. With the likelihood of Reynolds making his debut against his former team and Groves being forbidden from playing, the press reported that there was fear there would be crowd disturbances over the matter of the transfers.

Stephen Smith's first season in the big league was about to start with a Brummie-Black Country bang.

Chapter 5

Culture Shock

Aston Villa versus West Bromwich Albion is in its third century of bitter rivalry. It is the oldest professional club football 'derby' match in existence, first played in 1885. Albion and Villa's grounds are separated by just 3 miles. Despite the town of West Bromwich never having been inside the city of Birmingham officially, a game between Albion and Villa is, to all intents and purposes a North Birmingham derby. Fans of both clubs live in the city of Birmingham, especially in the Handsworth area of Birmingham that divides the areas of Aston and West Bromwich. To the north of Birmingham, you will see many Albion and Villa strongholds of support offset occasionally by supporters of Wolverhampton Wanderers. To the south of the city, Villa continue to draw support but as with the city of Birmingham in general the competition for fans is fought against Birmingham City.

The rivalry between the two sides is intense and bitter not just because Villa Park is closer to The Hawthorns than Birmingham City's, St. Andrew's ground (by one mile), or because The Hawthorns is much closer to Villa Park than to Wolves' Molineux stadium, but because it is deeply rooted in a Victorian era battle for early English and regional cup supremacy. It was in the FA Cup where the intensity was at its greatest, the two clubs first meeting in the FA Cup in 1885 at Perry Barr drawing 0-0, Albion thumping Villa in the replay 3-0.[1] But the greatest battles were still to come, and again it was in the English Cup. In the 1887 final Hodgetts and Hunter scored the goals that claimed the cup for Villa at Albion's expense. Villa went on to beat Hibernian to claim to be the best team in the world that year, before Villa then won five and drew two of the first eight league encounters and were expected to sweep Albion away in the 1892 cup final. In the end Albion got their revenge thrashing Villa 3-0, with Reynolds and Groves starring, hence the bitterness over their transfers in 1893.

It would be Stephen Smith's first experience of this special rivalry that has continued into the twentieth and twenty-first centuries. The two clubs battled at the top of the league in the 1970s and 80s as they had in the Victorian period and then nearer the foot of the top-flight in the 2010s. The year 2015 saw a brutal cup quarter-final ending with a pitch invasion and serious crowd disorder at Villa Park before the teams then scrapped it out in the Championship play-offs of 2019 to get back to the promised land of the Premier League.

Unfortunately for Stephen, the Birmingham sports journalists who he had been so fascinated with had got their selection predictions incorrect. Smith would be behind the new iron fence with the supporters as Albert Woolley got the nod at outside left.[2] Smith accepted that it would be a struggle getting straight into the team and had it shown, not for the first time that when it came to predicting a team's tactics, journalists don't always get everything right. One thing journalists were right to point out at this time was that the popularity of the game of football was getting stronger and stronger. It was eclipsing all other sports as the nation's number one pastime.

On the opening day of the season Villa versus Albion was the most well attended match in the land. The Football League, on the opening day of the 1893/4 season was averaging attendances of over 10,000 per game at a time when most people still worked on a Saturday, had very little expendable income for pastimes, and it was very difficult and expensive to travel anywhere except on foot.[3] In the next hundred years, as people got more and more leisure time, huge numbers of them spent it watching association football.

By the day of the first game of the season, the Villa's number one 'fixer' Fred Rinder had finally sorted the transfer of Willie Groves from the Albion, but FA rules would not allow him to play that day.[4] The atmosphere was raucous and intense inside the Perry Barr ground. In the build up to the game the press reported there was fear there would be crowd disturbances over the matter of the transfer. *The Athletic News* explained why those fears were unfounded. The paper explained 'the Aston Villa Club are to be congratulated on the precautions they took to prevent a disturbance in their opening match with West Bromwich Albion'.[5] The paper continued, 'all round the ground high iron hurdles were placed inside the ordinary rails and this would effectually prevent any crowd getting over; but on Saturday the crowd never attempted anything of the sort behaving in an admirable manner and witnessed an exciting match in an exceedingly sportsmanlike manner'.

What a match it was. Stephen Smith was disappointed not to be playing but exhilarated by the setting, the amount of spectators, the tension and the footballing rivalry. The 'large amount of friction' due to 'the notorious Groves case' was evident but did not boil over.[6] The afternoon was 'warm, unpleasantly warm for football' and the sunshine 'was streaming over the great crowd'. A 'rousing and welcoming cheer greeted both teams' as they entered the fray. The crowd were less appreciative of the late arrival of the referee, a 'soupçon of annoyance' is how it was reported.

Charlie Athersmith started well for Villa in an even opening to the game, 'conspicuous for some fine runs'.[7] The *Birmingham Daily Post* reported that Athersmith and Hodgetts had shots blocked by the keeper around the thirty five-minute mark before an Albion player handled in the ensuing melee. A penalty kick was awarded to Villa. John Reynolds, just signed from Albion, the man who had put Villa to the sword in the 1892 Cup final, and 'has never failed yet to score under such circumstances, gave Villa the lead'.

The Villa crowd went wild, the noise was deafening in the stands, Stephen had never heard or seen anything like it. This derby match was a long way from Cannock versus Hednesford. Albion fans remonstrated with the referee and their ex-player in bitterness at what had just happened but their anger didn't last long. The match report explained that after going a goal behind, 'Albion played better, and before half-time Geddes scored from a Norman centre'. Perry Barr was stunned into silence. It was 1-1 at the break with both sets of supporters having plenty to say to each other.

Stephen was nervous, his teammates were a team of new players that as yet 'did not gel fluently'.[8] Worse was to follow as the *Birmingham Post* continued to explain. Villa swarmed over Albion's defence but could not make a breakthrough. Then disaster struck Stephen's teammates. The Albion forward Perry whipped in a corner kick and somehow, 'Cowan had the misfortune to head through his own goal'. The Albion fans erupted in delight as the rest of the ground looked around in silent disbelief. Villa were headed for defeat, Grierson a debut defeat as coach, Rinder's new line-up seemed as disjointed as the old one. The old enemy, the local nemesis was spoiling the opening day of Villa's brave new world. The old mistakes were still happening. Villa were still losing.

Denny Hodgetts, the darling of the Perry Barr crowd, the legendary cup winner and goalscorer, the man who wore claret and blue quarters whilst everyone else wore the shirt with blue sleeves, the Victorian man mountain had had enough. He did not like losing to the Albion one bit. It had been a long time since he had vanquished them in the English Cup. He wanted to do it again. Villa continued to press, Albion fouled out of desperation. Hodgetts stood over a number of free-kicks given away by the opposition. Soon after Albion equalised he whipped in a free-kick that beat everyone on the pitch except for John Devey and this other prolific Astonian legend headed Villa level. The crowd roared, Smith relaxed.

Hodgetts was causing Albion all sorts of problems but was penalised for fouling the keeper when Devey scored. The game was heading for a draw, unsatisfactory for Villa when you consider they had pilfered Albion's best players in the summer. Embarrassing, when you consider all the recruitment Ramsay and Rinder had invested in. Then two minutes from time the man who had pipped Smith to the left-wing berth in the starting line-up picked up the ball. Albert Woolley got away on the left, dodged about a bit, sent the ball to the centre and it was in the net, the centre had gone straight in.[9] In the grandstand it was bedlam, Smith was on his feet with Groves clapping his team-mates' endeavours, Rinder and Ramsay threw their hats in the air in relief, the Albion supporters were baited mercilessly. Crowd behaviour however did not get too out of hand, they were 'reasonably behaved under the circumstances'.

The roar when Villa's third went in had taken Stephen aback, the roar as the final whistle went and Villa had hung on to a slightly fortuitous victory was even more stunning to his ears. Was it luck, was it skill, Woolley's winner? Whether it was or not the press concluded that in the end it had been the 'superiority' of Villa's forward line, the likes of Hodgetts and Devey that had seen Villa home.[10] The old enemy had been bested and despite the fact the winner had been scored by the man who had taken Smith's place in the side, Stephen was exhilarated with what he had witnessed, he had been part of something special and knew it was always going to be difficult to get into this Aston Villa side full of Cup winners and England internationals.

Stephen went to congratulate his colleagues in the changing rooms at the blacksmith's yard. The *Athletic News* explained Villa's new security measures meant the players were unmolested as they left the pitch and spoke only to the press in enclosed parts of the ground.[11] Stephen marvelled at the Villa players being asked their opinions on the game within minutes of the match being over, again this was not a modern phenomenon:

> The players were completely isolated from the spectators, and immediately they left the ground they were placed under lock and key in the paddock. The only people who can get at them are members of the press and they are harmless enough.

By the end of Saturday 2 September, the new Football League season was underway, Aston Villa were up and running, the press men had their first stories of the new footballing term, all that was left was for Stephen Smith to launch his new footballing career but this would be easier said than done.

Villa's side was unchanged for the first four matches of the season, they drew away 1-1 at League Champions Sunderland in their second game, which was no mean feat as they had smashed in 100 goals the previous season and beaten Villa 6-1 and 6-0 into the bargain.[12] Villa thumped Stoke 5-1 at home before losing for the first time that season away at Everton, the man standing in Smith's way of a place in the team, Albert Woolley, had banged home four times from outside left and the legendary Hodgetts already had three goals as well.

Defeat to Everton had been by 4 goals to 2 in a game where Villa were 3 down within 15 minutes; Smith's rival Woolley scored his fifth goal in as many games.[13] Changes were made for the return fixture at home which Villa won 3-1 with two more goals from Woolley.[14] Smith had still not played a minute of football for Aston Villa in the Football League; it would be a long time before substitutes would be used in English football so Stephen was once again sitting in the grandstand as Villa finished September 1893 with a 1-1 draw at Perry Barr against Derby. Even Willie Groves had started for Villa by now making his debut against Derby due to an injury to Athersmith.[15]

It was hard for Stephen to make a case to play with the way Woolley was performing on the left and after the day's play against Derby, Villa were in second place in the league table. Stephen had little to report at The Slade Pub to Susan and his pals. He was getting frustrated but as the league table showed Aston Villa were doing just fine without him at that moment, only the old enemy West Bromwich Albion were ahead of them.

Stephen Smith, not yet in the first team and on the sidelines, could observe the type of pressure his new colleagues were under – pressure that he would also eventually be under. He worried that if he did not get a break soon his one year deal would not be renewed. Villa dropped to third after a 3-0 defeat at Sheffield United in a top three clash in their next match at the start of October. The press reported that Villa had been 'soundly thrashed'. That Villa were still third did not hold any water with the club's committee, they had only lost twice, failed to win for just two games in a row, but they had only won one of the first seven matches. They were not top of the league despite the investment in the squad by Rinder and they were not performing to a level that Ramsay and Grierson found acceptable. On top of that West Bromwich Albion were still above them in the league table.

Stephen was astonished further when the players were addressed by Committee members at a club meeting. Grierson wanted a team playing in his image following his rules. They were still a collection of individuals. Smith squirmed as the message was delivered loud and clear by the club big wigs. The *Athletic News* reported that the Villa committee issued a caution to the team that matters have to improve or they would lose their places. Senior players rolled their eyes, newcomers looked startled and everyone in the room was agitated. The team had just not gelled yet. Some players like Stephen Smith hadn't even played yet. Smith was the type of player who always gave everything for the cause and was too shy and quiet not to be a team player. The Committee's next words gave Smith hope he might get a chance soon, the press reported them as the men at the top wanted 'a good tryer, plucky and true', rather than players 'animated by personal pique and child-like jealousy'. The Aston Villa side of 1893 was not yet a team but Smith was ready to be a team player.

Villa's next three games saw some improvement, and for the latter two of those games Charlie Athersmith had returned for which everyone was grateful. The England international had been sorely missed on the right hand side. Nottingham Forest were beaten 2-1 and there were away draws at Stoke and Darwen.[16] John Devey scored in all three games, Groves was off the mark in claret and blue and Athersmith signified his return with a goal at Stoke. These results weren't fantastic by any means but they steadied the Villa ship somewhat and placated the Committee a while longer. This, however, delayed Smith's debut further and he was beginning to feel embarrassed that he was the only new signing yet to play for his new club.

Villa were back in second place but Sheffield United were the clear leaders and many teams below Villa had games in hand.[17] Villa were still not firing on all cylinders but expectations were still high amongst the committee and fans alike. The Villa now had three matches against the other sides in the top four in the table. Next up – West Bromwich Albion away. The match at Albion's Stoney Lane ground drew a huge attendance by the Black Country club's usual standards the coffers were swelled by a large contingent of away supporters that outnumbered the home fans. This game fired the supporters' imaginations like no other, and once again there would be a serious edge to the game as Groves made his return to his old stomping ground after the controversies of the summer. Smith again, watching from the side-lines was amazed how many fans Villa took away from home, never mind the large attendances at Perry Barr.

Villa's expensively assembled side finally clicked and the opponents who had made things so difficult on the opening day were blown away inside the first half. Stephen wondered if he would get a single kick in a Villa shirt after what he saw in the first half. Albert Woolley continued his imperious form on the left and Smith realised he had become quite jealous of his teammate despite another fantastic result for his own team. Villa were winning but Stephen had still not been able to take a single win bonus back to Staffordshire.

With Albion's best two players now in tandem in Villa's midfield, The Baggies were 'manifestly outclassed' and 'Groves, Cowan and Reynolds could not have played better', no doubt anxious not to lose face against their old employers, teammates, and fans.[18] That afternoon, 'the Villa forward line were simply perfection' and before long they were leading 5-0 before Albion pulled one back to make the score 5-1 at half-time.[19] According to the press, 'five goals to one fairly represented the play in the first half'.[20] Albion pulled two more goals back before Devey ended any hopes of a comeback with his second of the game and Villa's sixth. Before Albion's comeback and Devey's sixth, Villa had run amok. Goals from Devey, Cowan, Hare, Athersmith and Woolley with his seventh of the season from the left wing had left the pressmen purring.[21]

Stephen read the papers himself every day and was fed up of how much praise Albert Woolley was getting, with that and the adoration for the rest of the club's forward line Smith resigned himself to more second team games in the Birmingham and district league. He could have played in that league with Hednesford or Cannock Town, he thought to himself sourly.

The Committee's hard words from a few weeks ago seemed to have worked. Villa were now a point off the top and a point clear of Burnley in third while Albion had dropped to fifth.[22] Villa were no longer struggling in the league, but Stephen was still struggling to get a game. But how could he complain when Woolley had hit seven goals in the first eleven games?

On Saturday 28 October around midday, Stephen Smith got off at Perry Barr train station at the end of his usual commute from Hednesford and trudged rather disconsolately to his place of work. He was nearly blown over twice as the Autumn weather was windy and inclement to say the least. There were also intermittent smatterings of rain to contend with as he headed down Birchfield Road. He would be getting his usual £2 weekly wage which was over double his wage as a miner. It was enough to support him and his extended family, but without the £5 win bonuses you got if you made the first team line-up (of which there had been five already for Villa that season), you couldn't make the big money that could really improve his and his family's quality of life. Without getting into the team, under the new rules, which meant players only signed for a year at a time, he had no job security should Villa deem him surplus to requirements. As it stood he was definitely that. Villa had played eleven games, were over a third of the way through the season, four games away from the half-way point in the league and Stephen still had not played.

He cursed the abilities of his direct competitor on the left wing, Albert Woolley. The Hockley-born winger was undisputed number one performer in the Villa side at that moment. There was talk of an England cap for the man with 7 goals already that season and a man who had scored 4 in his first four games for the club when he joined at the back end of the previous season.[23] Woolley was the man of the hour. Smith and Woolley were both similar players, obviously in a positional sense but in a physical sense as well. Woolley was slight like Smith but unlike Smith who was small but well-built nonetheless, Woolley was sometimes described as having a 'weak physique' and sometimes 'unable to withstand the ravages' an 'athlete had to put up with in the winter'.[24] There was an intimation that in the colder parts of the year

Woolley could be rather sickly or disinclined to perform. Eleven goals in his previous fifteen games would suggest otherwise and yet all those goals were scored between April and October.

Inside the Crown and Cushion most Villa players had arrived. They were assembling for the crunch match with Burnley, third to Villa's second as both sides tried to hang on to the coat tails of early leaders Sheffield United. Charlie Athersmith, Stephen's idol and now good pal grinned at him. Hodgetts and Devey too. Albert Brown who had become a partner in crime on the sidelines soothing Smith's jealous anguish, 'the main man is here everyone!' he jested kindly. Grierson approached Stephen, 'kit all clean Stephen, is it?' he asked. 'Boots polished "Tich"?' asked George Ramsay. 'Er, yes', replied 'Tich' Smith as Steve was sometimes called on account of his small stature.[25]

'Can I ask why all the questions Mr Grierson?' inquired Smith, and almost immediately as his coach replied he realised Albert Woolley was not present. 'You're playing, outside left, next to Denny. Woolley is sick, he has a cold apparently,' explained Grierson without much sympathy, Stephen noted.

Stephen felt excited, then sick, then excited and downed a small whiskey handed to him by Charlie Athersmith. He took a smoke of one of his friend's Woodbines as well to calm himself and then made his way down to the Butcher's Yard on Wellington Road for the team talk. Only this time he would listen properly. Denny Hodgetts put a bear-like arm around him and said, 'stay wide of me and we will put some crosses on Jack Devey's head, make him even more famous, we might even manage to lay a goal on for Charlie if he's lucky'. Both men laughed. Smith was nervous but felt exhilarated. The great man Hodgetts had made him feel ten feet tall. His dream was coming true. In the Summer of 1893, he was an amateur footballer working down a mine. Now in the Autumn he was about to make his debut as a professional footballer in the only fully professional league in the world. A win against rivals Burnley and he would also be playing for a team atop the best league in the world.

Stephen and his Villa team mates walked out onto the Perry Barr pitch and the wind 'howled, growled and whistled around the arena and made the stands creak and groan under the pressure'. The 'fierce gale of wind, spoilt' the game and made conditions difficult for both teams.[26] The wind was responsible for the lack of 'pretty passing' both teams were unusually noted for, the wind 'hampered the players whether facing it or playing with it in their favour'. The *Birmingham Daily Post* reported the weather that day 'blew what nautical men call half a gale all through the game'. [27]

Maybe this was not a game for Woolley, suffering from a 'severe cold, it was a difficult enough game to play at 100 per cent fitness, never mind if you were struggling with extreme lethargy'. Woolley was 'indisposed', but Stephen 'Tich' Smith was in fine fettle and 'caused quite an eye opener by the manner in which he executed his work'.[28] Smith was in the thick of the action from the start, determined to seize his first chance in a Villa shirt and make his mark. He hadn't been scared on his first day down a mine in his early teens, he might still be only 19 years old but while 10,000 people watching him in a howling gale gave him some nervousness, he certainly did not fear his new surroundings. This was an opportunity for him and his family and to make his family and community proud. Smith picked up the ball on the left, navigated the Perry Barr slope in the northwest corner of the ground and smashed a fierce shot goalward, Hillman the Burnley keeper managed to fist the ball away as Smith and Villa started sprightly.

Villa were dominating possession, dealing with the conditions far better than Burnley. Were Burnley just poor that day or Villa still in fine form? Smith didn't care. But barely five minutes had gone and Smith had gone close again. The spectators were marvelling at this little wingman who they had never seen before despite him signing for Villa in the summer. Smith was making up for lost time and people were sitting up and taking notice. It took Stephen Smith ten minutes of his debut to announce himself properly to the Aston Villa supporters crammed into Perry Barr. They clapped Stephen as he marched up to take his first corner kick for Aston Villa. He whipped the ball, 'a beautiful centre' into the path of inside forward Charlie Hare, who 'banged it through' to give Villa the lead. The ferocity of Smith's shots, the accuracy of his crosses were already evident after just ten minutes. Fred Rinder looked at George Ramsay and said, 'I knew that boy was worth a night stuck in the Cannock Chase cut'. Ramsay, Grierson and McGregor chortled in unison in the main pavilion as the Villa onslaught on the Burnley goal continued.

Charlie Athersmith thumped the cross bar and Denny Hodgetts 'skimmed the post' with a shot as he and Smith dovetailed superbly. Then just before half-time Stephen Smith felt the agony and ecstasy of his newfound profession all in a matter of seconds. Hodgetts played

Smith through on goal and he smashed a hard and low shot into the bottom corner of the net and burst with pride as Perry Barr erupted to acclaim him in unison. A debut goal after just twenty minutes of professional football. He wheeled away in triumph and turned around to accept the congratulations of his team mates. But Denny Hodgetts and John Devey were having discussions with the referee. Charlie Hare said apologetically, 'look, the lino has given you off side, unlucky mate, you'll get one soon though, you're playing capital today'. Smith was more embarrassed that he thought he'd scored even though he was 'palpably offside' according to the newspapers more than disappointed he hadn't scored. But he had felt elated nonetheless and he wanted more of that.

* * *

As an aside, it seems that many journalists after the event marked Smith as scoring, the Aston Villa record books included. This is incorrect as the primary evidence of the newspapers of the day only state him scoring an offside goal. It would have been a better story had he scored but unfortunately, that is not the case. It amazes me how many things that are written down in history are taken as gospel and regurgitated. Smith himself, though the National Census has him born in Abbots Bromley, he is also reported as being born in Abbots Langley, Halesowen and Hazel Slade. All understandable because they either sound the same or are near to places he lived in but all incorrect. History can never be taken at face value, especially in an era where mass literacy was not a given and mass media, was based on a written press that had to record events quickly from memory before telegraphing back to headquarters to be printed that very same evening. This meant mistakes often happened particularly in the sporting papers where players were not as recognisable as they are now. One mistake would be reproduced repeatedly as facts were often not checked or questioned before publication.

* * *

Aided by the wind Villa pressed the Burnley defence severely and aimed pot shots at their keeper Hillman.[29] Just before halftime Smith dribbled in field from the left hand touchline and fed Devey who finished methodically. Devey, the great Villa captain, went straight to Smith to congratulate him for the fine ball. Stephen Smith walked off the pitch at half-time at Perry Barr on his debut with his side 2-0 up having made both goals, wowing the crowd and steering his new team towards the summit of the football league. Or as they said in those days, to the 'top of the list'.

The second half continued in the same vein as the first. The *Athletic News* described the match as 'a boisterous game at Birmingham'.[30] Both sides were very physical in their approach and the game often 'degenerated into an exhibition of bad temper'. In the second half the wind was more boisterous than ever. Burnley came back into the game and had a goal disallowed. Villa seemed to be rocking a little as nerves set in as they tried to hang onto the victory which would send them clear at the top. Dunning, the Villa keeper, had to tip a couple of shots round the post and Burnley won a succession of corners.

Stephen Smith was having the game of his life on his Villa debut and was desperate for victory and his first win bonus to take back to his family. He had made the Villa Committee and his teammates sit up with his first half performance. With Woolley suffering with illness he wanted to cement his place in the team. Hodgetts and he had joked about teeing up Charlie Athersmith and that's exactly what Smith did next. Smith took the ball from Hodgetts and centred for Athersmith who couldn't miss, 3-0 Villa, Stephen Smith had made all three goals with his precision passing and crossing. Burnley's brief fightback was over and the Perry Barr crowd knew it. They were jubilant and knew their club was heading top of the pile and maybe, just maybe they could stay there and be League Champions for the first time ever. Charlie Athersmith ran over and patted Smith on the back, and Hodgetts just chuckled and said, 'told you we'd set you up Charlie!'. Then he turned to Smith and said, 'you been the best player on this pitch today kid'. The legend had spoken. And that was all that mattered. Stephen Smith had arrived.

But there was still more to come from the new dream combination of Hodgetts and Smith down the left. The crowd was going wild at the pair's wing play. Their enthusiasm increased with a magnificent run in which he cleverly eluded all opposition before transferring the ball to Smith who waltzed round Crabtree, the Burnley defender, before laying the ball on a plate for Devey to tap in his second goal of the game, 4-0 Villa. Stephen Smith, in his first match as a professional footballer had made all four goals that his team had scored and sent them top of the league. Talk about timing. All the anxieties based on his early struggles to get in the team melted away from Stephen. He was meant to be on this pitch, in this team.

As the game wore on, Crabtree, the Burnley player dominated by Smith all game, had enough. He mercilessly, desperately clattered Smith as he went past him in full flight. The crowd booed and demanded action from the referee. Devey and Athersmith argued with members of the Burnley team. Stephen lay on the side of the pitch and had to be rolled off for the game to continue without him, his legs hacked to pieces all game. Smith had to quit the game for some time. It mattered not, Smith had engineered Villa into a four goal lead.

Despite Smith's punishment he was able to return to the field before the final whistle. He had to get back on to calm Charlie Athersmith who had resorted to hacking and tripping every opponent he encountered after Smith had gone off in retribution and solidarity with his new friend Stephen. Athersmith was even criticised for his actions by the press. The final whistle went. The players all shook hands but shared a few critical words about each other's conduct during the game. As Smith limped back to the paddock the crowd cheered and clapped him and Hodgetts put his arm around him and helped him to the safety of the butcher's yard. In that moment Stephen realised he was playing in a team top of the best league in the world. In one game he had proved he deserved to be among the best in the world, even if a few months ago he had been working under the ground of Cannock Chase.

No one knew who Stephen Smith was on Saturday, 28 October 1893 but by Monday 30 October many in the footballing world now did. Smith was now being praised alongside Devey and Hodgetts. The *Athletic News* explained, 'The Villa forwards all played well, Devey, Hodgetts and Smith especially so'. The *Birmingham Daily Post* was even more complimentary:[31]

> One of the great surprises was the defeat of the United at Sheffield, and thanks to the Albion, the Villa now head the list, and should increase their lead by knocking two points out of the Sheffielders. Smith, playing in place of Woolley, ... did yeoman service, and two fine centres, ... resulted in Athersmith and Devey scoring. Smith made a promising debut in a first League match. He is plucky, cool, unselfish and centres with remarkable accuracy, being a

most worthy substitute for Woolley. Indeed on Saturday's form he is a rival to that clever little player and the Villa Committee are most fortunate in possessing two such wing players who have the additional merit of being local men.

In the Crown and Cushion after the players had changed the ales flowed, the whiskeys were downed, cigarettes and cigars puffed on heartily. If it felt like a turning point for the club, it certainly was in every sense for Smith. He finally felt like he was part of the team.

A few days later and Villa were again in action at Perry Barr. Second placed Sheffield United arrived having been defeated by West Brom. But if they were able to win in Birmingham they would be clear of Villa at the top with games in hand. The same team that had beaten Burnley lined up for this match. In front of 10,000 fans Villa 'wiped out the disgrace of their defeat at Sheffield'.[32] Smith continued his glittering early form for Villa and the newspapers acknowledge his ability and how much the legendary Denny Hodgetts has already helped Stephen to flourish.

Villa were in superb form and were 'cheered' heartily by the crowd, and Villa 'gradually assumed the upper hand and Smith and Hodgetts were cheered for some clever and tricky passing'. Smith and Hodgetts were praised for 'the understanding between them' and Hodgetts fed Smith who made yet another goal, he whipped a ball across the face of the goal and Hare 'dashed in and scored'. 'Baldy' Reynolds and a second Hare goal put Villa 3-0 up before Smith claimed another assist as the Villans cruised to victory and Stephen basked in more acclaim.

Smith 'screwed the ball into goal from the corner flag' and Hare completed his hat-trick by bundling the ball home after Smith's cross was fumbled into his path. The journalist described Smith as 'a really fine wing player with a difficult shot' for goalkeepers to deal with. The press man also wrote that, 'Smith it should be mentioned, owes a great deal to Hodgetts, who plays most unselfishly to his little partner and gives him no end of chances to distinguish himself'. Smith was a good player but playing with some of the greatest players of the era was making him better and better. Villa were three points clear but if United won their two games in hand they would be back top of the League.

Chapter 6

The Team of All Talents

Stephen Smith's winning start in a Villa shirt came to an end with a 2-0 defeat at Blackburn Rovers. But as the *Birmingham Post* explained, 'Rovers are a hard lot to beat at home, and we venture to prophecy that very few clubs will come away from Ewood with a couple of points to their credit.'[1]

Despite Villa still being in pole position some of Smith's close friends in the team were criticised in the press for their performance in the team's first defeat in seven games. Stephen found it all a bit harsh but his experienced colleagues took it all with a pinch of salt. They were used to it. This was the pinnacle of professional football and then as now, a footballer's lot was to be built up and knocked down repeatedly in the media.

The Post said, 'Hodgetts was not as good as usual, Devey did not pass with certainty' and the whole team's display was 'disappointing'. Smith himself was commended for, 'several brilliant runs' which his teammates teased him about. Hodgetts started calling him 'Tich the golden boy' for a day of training until the great man got bored of it.

Serious days were ahead with a home match against Sunderland, the reigning champions. Villa had managed a draw in the North East, a vast improvement on the previous season's thrashings. Sunderland had warmed up for this match by beating Wolves 6-0 as Villa fell at Blackburn. Villa were still top with 18 points, two clear of West Brom but Albion had two games in hand. Sunderland were back in sixth place with eleven points but had four games in hand.[2] Sunderland were rightly seen as the best team in the land and arguably the best in the world. Wolves were cup holders and had been smashed to pieces. If they won their games in hand they would be clear of Villa at the top. And that is what people expected to happen. They had won the previous two league championships and Villa's own William McGregor declared them the 'Team of All Talents' after they beat Villa 6-0 and 6-1 in the season just gone.[3] Villa had won just one of seven league meetings with Sunderland, losing four of those matches by heavy scorelines.[4] Despite being top of the league, Villa were heavy underdogs and after defeat at Blackburn they were expected to be reeled in and overtaken by the red and whites.

The whole club was nervous about facing Sunderland, Steve's good friends and star players Charlie Athersmith and John Devey were due to be absent. Albert Woolley was still out with sickness as well and the *Birmingham Daily Post* documented Villa's apprehension about meeting their strong rivals explaining that: 'the match during the week had caused no end of anxiety to the committee. Athersmith was unfit to play on account of an injury to one of his feet and on Wednesday it was doubtful whether John Devey, who had undergone a great deal of domestic trouble, would be able to take the field. To meet Sunderland with a weak team meant defeat, for during the last few weeks the Wearsiders have been steadily regaining the form that made them last season's champions.'[5]

The 23-year-old reserve player Walter Randle replaced Athersmith. Despite being older than Smith by four years he seemed nervous having only previously played first team football for non-league Aston Unity.[6] Walter didn't have a great game in Athersmith's stead and was criticised in the press who reported, 'Randle ... was scarcely a success ... he lacked dash and centred badly on several occasions, when if he had put the ball in front of goal he would have caused the Sunderland defenders a lot of trouble.' Randle's debut was described as a 'big trial for a young player', the media was no less brutal in the Victorian period when it came to describing a footballer's performance. It also showed the high standards expected of a debutant professional footballer in the 1890s particularly at the top end of the top division. Thankfully Stephen's debut had been much kinder and more successful and, by comparison with Randle, underlined his ability and skill at the highest level.

The Victorian period was a time before antibiotics and catching a cold could be physically debilitating or even fatal. Woolley was suffering and John Devey's wife was seemingly at death's door suffering with a heavy cold. Devey was anxiously waiting for his wife's health to improve and had no thought of football in his mind.[7] This was how Aston Villa football club prepared for the biggest game of the season so far. Fifteen thousand fans packed into the Perry Barr ground expectantly waiting for their heroes to arrive.[8]

As the Villa players got changed for the match it wasn't clear what the line-up would be. Randle put his boots on with jittery anxiety, tying and retying his boots. Albert Brown, the veteran, the cup winning legend from days of yore, wouldn't get changed even though he was the replacement for John Devey. 'Jack will make it, he won't let the Villa down, he can't, he's not built that way,' Brown calmly explained. 'His wife was improving when I visited on Wednesday, and she told him to play.' Stephen wasn't convinced as the Deveys had been going through the mill all week.

In the end though, Smith had to bow to Albert Brown's experience as at ten minutes to three o'clock, John Devey, Villa's captain and talisman appeared, looking tired but beaming. 'Alright lads, are we ready to thrash the team of all talents?!' he bellowed. Albert Brown lit a woodbine and Smith felt exalted, relieved, and ready to make sure Aston Villa stayed, in the parlance of the day, 'at the top of the list'. The crowd could be heard roaring on the other side of Wellington Road.

The game was tense and tight throughout the ninety minutes. Much of it was essentially played out in the quagmire of midfield. Attacks would start with pretty combination play that was invariably broken up by the skilful tackling of the half backs. In the first half Stephen Smith was thwarted at every opportunity when going forward. He and his teammates were obstructed on several occasions by Doig the Sunderland keeper and there was no score at half-time. It had been a tense and tight affair and the result was on a knife edge. But as Devey, whose mere presence had spread calm throughout the dressing room explained, that even a draw would be a good result as it would check Sunderland's upward trajectory and keep the Villa at the top of the table. But that was easier said than done.

Stephen Smith was determined to make his mark on the game, cement his team's place at the top of the table and his own place in the team, which despite the good start to his career, would be under pressure as soon as Woolley was fit again. Stephen certainly tried his best, as the *Sunderland Daily Echo* noted, 'Smith and Hodgetts were getting dangerously near the goal,' and 'Smith ran cleverly along the line and gave Doig a sharp shot to deal with', Smith also 'hit the post as he attempted to centre the ball'.[9] Villa continued to attack and the crowd went wild, roaring on Villa's performance against a seemingly invincible opponent who always seemed to get the better of their team. On top of this Villa were showing their own title credentials by dominating the reigning champions.

Smith and his team-mates had been inspired by the appearance of their captain despite all his troubles and who was leading by example on the pitch. Smith would have done anything to make John Devey proud of him. And then the inevitable happened – Villa won a free-kick in a dangerous position.[10] Villa continued to be roared on by their supporters and the captain Devey responded to their fervent encouragement. From the free-kick, the ball was beautifully placed by Groves and amidst great cheering John Devey headed into the net. Stephen Smith had never admired a player more than his captain John Devey and his admiration grew further after that goal.

This could happen, he thought, Aston Villa could beat Sunderland. For the large parts of the rest of the game Villa were just hanging on, scarcely believing they were leading. Sunderland were even down to ten men during this assault on the Villa defence. As the *Birmingham Post* put it, 'Sunderland now played up with great determination and despite the fact they lost the services of Hannah for about ten minutes, they pressed severely and sorely tried the Villa defence.' Miller the Sunderland forward then picked up the ball and cut through the Villa defence to 'easily beat Dunning'. Villa were now teetering on the brink of defeat as Sunderland pummelled them. The goal was scored whilst Sunderland only had ten men, and when Hannah resumed a minute or two later the visitors seemed to have a 'capital' chance of winning.

Smith was struggling to have any impact whatsoever as the game was mainly compressed in midfield. The crowd was tense as the game hung in the balance, there was more nervous energy than noise at this stage as the adversaries went toe to toe. Wilson was denied on several occasions by Villa keeper, Dunning. Randle went close for Villa in reply. With ten minutes of this titanic struggle between champions and pretenders remaining, the decisive event in the match took place. Smith fed Hodgetts who got away from his marker and was about to shoot when he was tripped from behind for a penalty. This was the chance! If Villa could win this match they would have a huge lead over the one team that could stop them claiming their first league title.

The crowd and both sets of players held their collective breath as John 'Baldy' Reynolds sauntered up, as casual as you like and did just as he had in the exact same situation on the opening day against Albion:

'A penalty kick was awarded and entrusted to Reynolds who maintained his reputation and gave the Villa the winning goal.'

The crowd erupted and Reynolds was mobbed. Villa didn't seem to touch the ball for the final five minutes of the game. Smith himself was concentrating only on defending. When the final whistle went Steve Smith and many of his teammates sank to the ground in exhaustion. The crowd roared in exultation of its team and the *Birmingham Daily Post* reported that, Villa had, 'just managed to scrape through against Sunderland' and no game that weekend had been 'more exciting, for the result was always in doubt, and it was not until the referee's whistle was heard that the Villa supporters breathed freely'. The win was also described as 'lucky' but Villa and Stephen Smith didn't care.

Stephen was breathless and speechless, Villa were now four points clear at the top of the table, ahead of old rivals Albion and even more importantly, nine points clear of Sunderland having played half their fixtures. A league championship winners medal in his first season as a professional footballer was a real possibility for the teenager who had been a miner until six months previously. Smith was praised in the press as were the greats, Hodgetts and Devey, while Groves and Reynolds were described as the best half-back pairing in the country.

Stephen Smith realised he was making his mark and justifying his selection in one of the finest teams in the land. Villa beat Bolton 1-0, Dunning returned in goal and Athersmith returned from injury as Preston were beaten 2-0. Three further wins, making it six wins on the bounce kept Villa top of the list.[11] Stephen was often reminded of the precarious nature of a professional sportsman's health during the Victorian period. In a time before antibiotics, wintertime often caused footballers to fall ill with cold and flu symptoms. Smith had got his chance in the side because Albert Woolley had been struck down with illness for months and when Sheffield Wednesday visited Perry Barr, Albert Brown was called on to deputise for Charlie Hare who was 'indisposed' with illness.[12]

Hare, who'd hit five goals in five games as Villa climbed to first place in the winter, was out for several games and then, at the start of the New Year was announced as retired from the game because of ill-health. Although Hare made a comeback briefly the following season and tried to make another comeback with Arsenal after that, it was too much for Charlie and he was forced to retire, Stephen was very upset for his teammate and friend, he thought highly of him and was sorry to see him go. Woolley's illness, Devey's wife's sickness, Hare's ill-health all showed that the basic instincts needed in staying alive or being relatively healthy on a general day-to-day level could be far more difficult than maintaining fitness to play professional sport for the Victorians.

During the run of six wins Smith missed the last of those through illness himself, a 3-1 win at Newton Heath on 16 December, but was back for the next match against Wolves. Smith knew Albert Woolley was getting back to full health and also knew he needed to stay fit and in form to keep his shirt. But this was life at the top level, Villa were eight points clear of second place Blackburn in the standings, though Rovers had four games in hand and in theory could draw level at the top if they won them all.[13] Life at the top level also encompassed getting paid the best wages possible and the *Birmingham Post* reported that the proposal of a maximum wage was rejected out of hand much to the relief of those players that it affected and to the indifference of the vast majority who got nowhere near the proposed maximum.

Despite this the press at the time, as they often do now, criticised the amount some players were paid: 'As was generally foreseen, the pet scheme of the League Management Committee for the reduction and limiting of the wages paid professional football players received its rejection on Friday in Manchester. The resolution... met with much hostile criticism ... failing to obtain a two thirds majority... It could hardly be expected that the players materially affected would have tamely submitted to a reduction of their pay.'

(Again there was a worry then as now that there would be a lack of competition from more than a few clubs due to the finances of the bigger clubs, while others as in the 21st century struggled economically due to trying to buy success.)

'Now ... we do not deny that the wages paid to many players are extravagantly high, and as a result, the majority of clubs are in an unfavourable position ... clubs have no right to pay wages they could not afford to pay.'

(An obsession with buying expensive foreign imports did not help, though in those days the expensive foreigners were from Scotland.)

'Had clubs only borne this fact in mind and looked less to Scotland and more to England for their players their finances would be in a healthier state and their available strength equally as great.'

Stephen Smith would have his own wages issues in the years to come but for now he earned a wage that was nowhere near the maximum and was uninterested in these matters. He was more interested in the next game against Wolves. Villa were now in the final third of the season, the last ten games, the home straight. They had a buffer of points at the top of the table but could not afford too many slip ups. Unfortunately, they had one, a big one at Molineux losing 3-0, though Wolves then having hindered Villa's title hopes, helped them by beating second place Blackburn 5-1 on Boxing Day.[14]

Villa and Smith rectified their poor performance against Wolves by thumping strugglers Darwen 9-0 on Boxing Day.[15] For Smith, having made his first team debut in his first season, his next milestone was even more satisfying. The 'Villa were much too good for their visitors, 9-0 was the heaviest scoring that has taken place this season' wrote the *Birmingham Post'*.[16] The fifteen thousand in attendance roared with delight as Villa took their opponents apart. Steve and his great pal Charlie Athersmith were praised for their crossing ability, they 'centred in a manner that left nothing to be desired'. FA Cup legend Albert Brown put Athersmith clear to put one up, although no longer a regular he was still able when called upon. Hodgetts the other cup legend made it two, Reynolds made it three, Hodgetts four to 'loud applause and cheering'. John Devey hit number five, Brown added a goal to his previous assist for six as Darwen's goal was 'strongly besieged'. Hodgetts made it seven, and then it happened, Villa's eighth goal was Stephen Smith's first goal in professional football. It was probably the ugliest goal of his career. Smith forced a corner after a brilliant individual run, and taking the kick himself placed the ball well in front of goal. It was cleared, but 'Reynolds pulled it over his head and with the keeper reaching to stop it was charged through' by Smith forcing the keeper and ball over the line. It was not a foul in 1893, and so 26 December of that year saw Smith open his Aston Villa account. As he was retrieved from the net by Reynolds he was mobbed by Hodgetts, Devey and Athersmith. Stephen was bursting with pride and happiness and couldn't help think back to his disallowed goal on his debut and how he'd celebrated prematurely. This time, before he knew what to do his teammates had accosted him with playful glee.

John Devey made it 9-0 and Villa were six points clear of nearest challengers Burnley who only had two games in hand. Smith was now a permanent fixture in the side of Champions elect and had scored his first goal to add to the many goals he had made for others. The *Burnley Express* believed their local side were the only 'real disputants with Aston Villa for Championship honours'.[17] The paper went on to demand that, 'Burnley be determined to win their next ten league games'. The paper was indeed correct that Villa were not home and dry just yet. They pointed out that, 'Aston Villa can get 48 points if they win their remaining eight matches, Burnley, Blackburn and Wolves can be on 46 if they win all theirs. As Aston Villa have to appear at Turf Moor the Burnley team may possibly equal, if not surpass them, in points'. The team that Smith made his league debut against could yet scupper his footballing dreams.

Chapter 7

On the Sidelines

The first league match of 1894 saw Stephen Smith out of the side. Despite his first goal for Villa, Albert Woolley was now fully over his illness and Ramsay and Grierson wanted to give the man who had scored seven goals in the first eleven matches of the season a chance to get back up and running. One thing that Stephen couldn't argue with was that he needed to score more goals. The Villa Committee were desperate to win the title and thought Woolley, who was first choice left winger at the start of the season, could add an extra dimension to the attack. Smith wasn't happy at being back in the stands at Wellington Road and the brutal realisation that the committee were worried about his goal output and that they had a point that Woolley was perhaps a better bet was brought home in the next game away to Sheffield Wednesday.

In a 2-2 draw that strengthened Villa's position at the top due to Burnley's defeat to Blackburn, Albert Woolley scored a second half equaliser on his return. It was a vital goal for the team but Smith's heart sank. Woolley, seemed to have everything, pace, skill and goals. The press described Woolley as a 'clever wing'.[1] Smith wished he was more like his teammate.

January and February seemed to pass Stephen by as he watched Villa march on from the side-lines. Villa thumped Preston 5-2, Wolves were then dismantled 4-2 in the FA Cup, Newton Heath were thrashed 5-1 with the great John Devey netting a hat-trick.[2] Smith had to watch frustratedly as Villa overcame Sunderland in two more epic clashes to get to the third round of the cup winning 3-1 at Wellington Road after a 2-2 draw in the North East. Villa had proved their league win over Sunderland was no fluke, but Stephen had missed out again.

He took solace in his friends and family in Hazel Slade. Susan Blastock was a sympathetic listener in the Slade Pub and as far as his community was concerned all they cared about was that he was part of a side who would surely become English Champions. 'Got your medal yet Tich?' was a common shout to Smith on the streets of his village. One of their own was one of the best in the world, even if Stephen himself didn't feel like it at that time.

Having beaten Newton Heath 5-1 on 3 February Villa were seven points clear with five league games left to play and an FA Cup third round tie with Sheffield Wednesday in the offing.[3] Villa had a big lead and the most points that Blackburn and Burnley could now get was 44 points. Eight points from the last five matches would clinch the title. There was also still a chance of emulating the Preston team of 1888/89 by doing the league and cup double. Unfortunately for Stephen he was a spectator as they travelled to Sheffield for the cup match on 24 February.

February 1894 had seen Villa embroiled in the FA Cup with the league match against Newton Heath sandwiched in between the Wolves cup victory and the two cup epics against Sunderland. After three strength sapping Cup matches, Villa played Sheffield Wednesday three days after the last Sunderland cup match, another big gate was present.[4] There were 20,000 fans in attendance compared to the 3,000 for the league match.[5] When Villa had played at home to Sunderland in the cup there had been 25,000 in attendance compared to 15,000 for the league game, proof positive of the cup being seen as just as important, if not more so, than league success. This is a big difference compared to modern day football where Premier League positions are seen as the be all and end all.

Bob Chatt, another player now starting ahead of Smith, scored twice to give Villa a 2-1 lead with three minutes to go. The pressmen felt confident to go and wire the result but Wednesday equalised and then scored a winner in extra time.[6] Reporters had to be quick on the draw to get their copy filed for the late editions of the day, but they were premature, those days are long gone now with the instant technology and live feeds from games that are part and parcel of modern life. It was an unexpected defeat and one where Villa were criticised for not capitalising on their chances.

The partisan *Birmingham Post* was much more sympathetic describing Wednesday as 'lucky' twice and played large parts of the game without Woolley and Chatt who were described as 'seriously injured' during the game.[7] Woolley also had an equaliser ruled out late on. Stephen just wished he could be out on the field helping his team. He'd not played a first class match for two months and in an era before substitutes if you weren't in the starting line-up you had no chance of playing, and of course in Stephen's mind, as a former miner, always worrying about when the next set of wages would be paid, it meant no chance of a win bonus either.

Chapter 8

English Champion

Albert Woolley had played seven straight games in place of Stephen Smith but had been nowhere near as prolific as he had been at the start of the season. Woolley hadn't been as effective as he was in September but only Devey, Hodgetts and Athersmith had scored more. But Stephen would get a chance to play against Bolton Wanderers with the title in touching distance. This was because of injuries Woolley sustained in the cup match with Wednesday. The *Athletic News* reported that 'young Woolley was so bashed about at Sheffield –oh! These English Cup ties – that he only had one leg of any use'.[1]

This was Stephen's second chance to usurp Woolley in the team due to his fitness issues and it was a chance Smith was determined to take. Stephen also started to think that maybe Woolley wasn't as lucky as he thought and certainly wasn't jealous of his repeated fitness predicaments. Smith himself had just recovered from a 'machinery incident' as he kept his hand in at Cannock and Rugeley Colliery when not playing to keep his wages topped up. The club would not have been happy with him and it may have contributed to his enforced absence from the starting line-up, although there is no evidence to suggest this was the case. Woolley was the first choice left wing and had been in fine form before his illness in the winter.

This type of part-time activity would certainly not be allowed by a football club in the modern day but of course a player nowadays would not need to supplement his income. Despite talk of maximum wages for footballers, in those days most players, unless established stars, had wages only slightly better than the average working man and if you weren't playing you couldn't get a bonus. In the summer months footballers were not usually paid by their clubs either but while multi-talented sportsmen like John Devey played first classic cricket for Warwickshire, Stephen Smith went back down the mines as a haulage engineer. In the 1901 census Smith's main employment is stated to be a haulage engineer.[2]

It would also be unthinkable in the modern era for international football fixtures to be played on the same day as topflight club fixtures, let alone for a club attempting to be league champions to be forced by the Football Association to play without their best players, players they pay big wages to, because they were expected to report for England team duty. But that was the way of it in 1894. With so many players missing the *Athletic News* explained that, 'there was not very much hope among the Villa supporters of the home men keeping up their unbeaten record' (at Perry Barr).

It was a bad weekend all round for the footballers of Aston Villa. John Devey scored for England against the Irish but the presence of Villa's captain as well as star Villa men Reynolds and Hodgetts, couldn't prevent a 2-2 draw against a team England had defeated on each of the previous twelve occasions.[3] It would be Scotland who would win the British Championship that year and claim the title of world champions in the only professional international football tournament in existence. It was their sixth title compared to England's five since the competition's inception. Scottish football was pre-eminent in the world at this time.

For the rest of the team playing Bolton at Perry Barr, Villa's unbeaten home record was lost. Villa were 2-1 up just as against Sheffield Wednesday but lost the lead and then conceded the winning goal to the Wanderers with a few minutes remaining.[4] Villa were still top of the league but faltering badly and then lost 2-1 to non-league Loughborough in the Birmingham Cup again conceding late on in the match.

Stephen felt pressured, it had been a whirlwind season, not playing, playing, losing his place and worrying about feeding his family so much that he even took up part-time work back at the colliery. Now, even though he was back in the team, Villa were threatening to blow their chance of a first ever league championship in the club's history. Sheffield Wednesday had been horrible to watch, Bolton was unfortunate but Loughborough was embarrassing. Rinder, Ramsay, McGregor, Grierson and The Committee were getting edgy. The spectators at Perry Barr were hoping for glory but after years of disappointment, expecting the worst.

Three wins from the last five games would do it, no matter what any of Villa's opponents did. The chance to be the best team in England and arguably the best in the world was still in Villa's grasp. It was still in Stephen Smith's grasp, the miner, son of a farm labourer born in the country village of Abbots Bromley, brought up in industrial squalor on the edge of Cannock Chase. No one in Hazel Slade had ever even got close to anything like what Stephen was potentially about to achieve. The world Smith had come from was about making ends meet, not about national fame and adulation.

No one really knew anything about Hazel Slade in Birmingham, never mind the rest of England. Stephen was about to put all the places that had been part of his development as a human being and a footballer – Abbots Bromley, Hazel Slade, Cannock and Rugeley Colliery and Hednesford Town Football Club, squarely and firmly on the map.

Twenty thousand supporters greeted the players as they entered the Perry Barr arena.[5] This was it, thought Stephen, Villa had been stuttering in both league and cup. They couldn't afford anymore slip-ups. The embarrassment of the loss to Loughborough weighed heavily on Smith and his teammates. How could a team that lost to a non-league club be considered as having a chance of being named English champions?

The sun beat down on players and fans alike as the game commenced. The *Birmingham Post* set the meteorological scene, 'the weather is, in fact, cricketing weather ... summerlike'.[6] Blackburn were riding high in the league though with no realistic chance of winning the title and into the semi-finals of the cup. It would be a tough challenge for a Villa team short on confidence and under plenty of pressure to claim what could be a vital and season defining victory. Blackburn's fans were in extremely good spirits compared to the anxious home spectators. There were, 'several hundred excursionists who were greatly in evidence by reason of their playing concertinas and tin whistles whilst several of them possessed umbrellas of blue and white alpaca probably made with a view to the final for the English Cup'.

Stephen and all the players struggled in the heat. Blackburn started the better and dominated the first twenty five minutes as Villa played up hill with the sun in their eyes. Things didn't go well at all early on with the 'visitors the decidedly better players' in the first twenty-five minutes.[7] Then disaster happened, Rover's incessant pressure told and the concertinas were in full cry in a near silent Perry Barr ground as Blackburn scored. Were Villa really going to blow it again?

There were thirty minutes on the clock before Villa went close to scoring, Smith surged down the wing with a 'beautiful run' ending in John Devey being tripped before getting a shot away and nothing created from the resultant free-kick. Villa needed improvement and quickly. Smith and Devey seemed the most likely as Villa floundered in the nervous atmosphere. Villa needed something before the break and Reynold's ball into the box was flicked on by Devey for Chatt to head home. With the scores level the Villa made desperate efforts ahead before the interval but found the defence too strong.

The second half went to and fro as both sides went for a winning goal. Chatt's shot went wide by just 'a few inches'. Villa's defence then completely lost Blackburn forward Haydock who found himself unmarked 'from a distance of two yards' but he hit the post leading to howls of 'derision' from the crowd. Heckling the opposition's attempts to score goes back to the earliest days of professional football. Nevertheless Villa players and fans alike knew they had been lucky to survive.

Villa attacked relentlessly, they were desperate for the victory that would put them on the brink of the ultimate prize that had eluded them for so long. Smith tried everything he could to get his side ahead and make his mark on history. In doing so he invited ridicule from his opponents supporters and the watching press. Another Villa attack saw the ball fall to Stephen with the goal at his mercy, 'but with an open goal he lifted the ball over the top of the bar'. He couldn't believe it. He wondered how many people would blame him if they failed to win the game. Hodgetts and Devey told him to keep going, Athersmith too. He did as he was told.

With fifteen minutes to go, 'Villa supporters were beginning to get anxious', but Stephen Smith wanted to write his name down in football history and had the bravery and resilience to forget about his horrendous miss and steer the match in Aston Villa's favour. The *Birmingham Post* reported Smith's crucial piece of play: 'Smith received a long pass, made a brilliant run and centred when the ball was about a foot from the goal-line. The ball flashed across goal to Chatt, and he headed through gracefully and as easily as though he were merely bowing to a lady. A great roar went up from the crowd, and they felt that the game was won and so it proved.'

Smith had made the goal that had won the game and put Villa on the brink of the title just a few minutes after seemingly missing a glorious chance that was destined to cost them the victory. His resilience and determination after apparent humiliation and despair summed up Smith's never say die attitude and star quality to serve his turn to the end and win the day. Smith and Chatt, two of the new signings from Rinder and Grierson's brave new dawn had got Villa over the line in a game described as 'a great game' and Villa 'had not had such hard work to win since they defeated Sunderland' at Perry Barr in that epic encounter earlier in the league season.

For Stephen Smith the plaudits were plentiful and he was given much credit for the way he 'atoned for the mistake by the beautiful run and fine centre which gave Villa the victory'. Smith was described as having 'performed brilliantly'. The praise for Smith was in stark contrast to the assessment of his great pals. Hodgetts 'did not start well', Devey was 'not at his best' and Athersmith's 'centering was very inaccurate'. The *Birmingham Post* was in no doubt as to who the man of the hour was. It was 20-year-old part-time miner and professional football player, Stephen Smith.

It was a victory that after the trying recent weeks led the Birmingham press to declare after Sunderland lost unexpectedly to Stoke that 'The Championship of the League is now practically assured to Aston Villa'. The importance of Villa's near achievement was also trumpeted:

> They have therefore to only win one of their three remaining fixtures to gain the highest honours of English Association football for there is no doubt that the League Cup carries with it greater prestige than the older trophy. To win the one a team must be the best for the whole of a season. The team that wins the cup are entitled to all the credit for their performances and many would like to see them pitted against the winners of the league ... although the majority of persons would no doubt favour the chances of the Birmingham club.

The *Birmingham Post* explained that not only were Villa vying to be champions of England in the ensuing days following the Blackburn victory, but international glory as well against the best Scottish clubs of the day. If Aston Villa could top the English League and beat the best teams in Scotland, no one could dispute Aston Villa and Stephen Smith's designs on being the best in the world. The *Post* wrote, 'Saturday's victory (over Blackburn) has restored confidence in the Villa, and if they defeat the Wolverhampton Wanderers ... and the Glasgow Rangers ... they will fully recover any prestige they may have lost through the Loughborough disaster.'

They would be playing two games in two days, the second game may only have been a friendly but these games were crucial for the club to gain extra revenue and also there was the chance to pit their wits against the best teams from Scotland, then considered the best in the world. First up, though, would be Wolverhampton Wanderers at Perry Barr and a chance for Stephen to carve his name in football history as part of his club's first ever title winning team. A victory would lead to Championship glory and Smith remained in the team once more ahead of his rival Albert Woolley.

Again, the weather was beautiful and another large crowd was present, they were there to watch history in the making, to see the Aston Villa Football Club finally become Champions of England.[8] The players were nervous, they had come so far in this season, had started slowly, found brilliant form and then wobbled a little before composing themselves for one final push to glory. The game was fast paced despite the heat and Villa attacked the Wolves defence throughout. Chatt was criticised for several misses in the first half and Smith went close when put clear by Hodgetts but couldn't beat the last man to get a shot at goal. Charlie Athersmith then hit the crossbar and Chatt was denied again. It seemed a Villa goal would never come and neither would the league title.

As so often for Villa, Denny Hodgetts was a calming presence, the Astonian legend constantly encouraging his team mates especially young Stephen. With one waft of his mighty left boot he sent the ball into the box and Athersmith bundled keeper and ball into the net much to the Villa players' relief. They headed in at half-time just forty-five minutes away from greatness. Stephen Smith was fast out of the blocks in the second half as he looked to claim his championship medal barely a year into his professional career. He dribbled the ball down the left flank as was his trademark and his 'centre came right across the front (of goal) but Chatt failed to get the ball'. Wolves were now there for the taking and Wanderers' attacks were 'rendered useless' by Bair and Reynolds in midfield, Hassall their keeper regularly 'saved brilliantly amidst loud cheering', the title was in sight.

The press report is a litany of Villa attacks as they went for glory:

> Some beautiful passing by Hodgetts and Smith gave the Villa a strong attack but Chatt unfortunately got offside. A further Villa attack was finished by Reynolds shooting out

(wide?). Cowan just headed over the bar. An exciting tussle in the Wolverhampton goal mouth was next witnessed but the Villa could not get the ball through.

It seemed a matter of time before Villa got a second and took their crown. Something that has not changed however long football has gone on is Aston Villa's ability to court disaster in the dying embers of matches. In 1894, Sheffield and Loughborough had benefited from this weakness and when Elliot tripped Wolves forward Wykes 'badly', Kinsey stepped up and 'put the ball into the net', it was the turn of Wolverhampton to gain an Astonian gift. In the few minutes that remained the Villa made desperate efforts to score but failed.

The champagne and ales were kept on ice in The Crown and Cushion and Stephen's family who had come to the game went home without being able to say their son was a champion just yet. His brother William was now in talks with Willenhall Town about playing for them on a semi-professional level. Stephen was proud of him and his little brother was proud of Stephen and that day's game would seem more and more ironic as William's own footballing career progressed. But that story, like the one about the English League title being lifted, was for another day.

The *Birmingham Post* was not happy with Aston Villa stating that, 'but for bad shooting would have made the League Championship their own' however the paper did concede that 'Villa cannot now be passed by any other club in the competition'. Before the title could be secured, the Villa money men had to be satisfied and the very next day the famous Glasgow Rangers club, who had just beaten Scottish League Champions Celtic in the Scottish Cup final, were now in town for an exhibition match with the international reputations of two of the leading clubs in England and Scotland at stake.

In the modern era teams compete in the Champions League and World Club Cup to decide international hegemony. Back in 1894 the only two professional leagues in the world battled it out amongst themselves for prestige and the title of unofficial 'World Champions'. Rangers had beaten the Scottish champions, and now had the English champions elect in their sights. Over 5,000 people took time off work on a Tuesday afternoon at a time when free time was at a premium in society, such was the draw of these two elite clubs of the Victorian age.

Aston Villa on Tuesday 27 March, not quite English league champions, made their first steps in their bid for world domination against Rangers. On the day of the game with Athersmith injured, the old warhorse and cup veteran but now very much a squad player, Albert Brown came in on the right wing.[9] It was a sign of how far Albert Woolley had fallen since the early days of the season and also January and February when Smith felt he would never fully dislodge him from the team. Smith was now one of the first names on the team sheet after his meteoric rise and had played in fifteen of the final nineteen games of the league season having not played in any of the first eleven.[10]

The sun was 'scorching' as Villa took on a team with no fewer than eight internationals in it. Villa took out their frustrations from the previous day on Rangers. Compared to the Wolves match the reporter stated that, 'there was a marked improvement in the shooting all round'. Stephen Smith was by now a fans' favourite at Perry Barr and 'Smith was cheered for a brilliant run'. The amount of times that Smith was highlighted as having embarked on a brilliant run had been numerous and this would continue throughout his career. And of course many of his slaloming runs led to Villa goals. Smith, 'dodging two of his opponents ... dropped the ball in front of goal and Brown ... sent in a terrific shot ... and it rolled across the line for the first goal'.

Smith and Villa were too good for Rangers, they had been too good for all the teams in England too, they were surely the best team in Britain and in 1894 that also meant the world. Chatt and Devey made it 3-0 before half-time as Villa ran riot, maybe Celtic would have been seen as a bigger challenge, but Rangers had beaten them in the Scottish cup final with ease. Villa were so dominant that near the end of the match with Villa leading 3-1, Reynolds could afford to deliberately miss a penalty that Rangers were very upset had been awarded. It is highly unlikely that would happen in a modern-day Champions League match but it did at Perry Barr. Villa were so superior though that they felt they could afford to do it, win and yet not humiliate their illustrious opponents.

The Scottish national side might have been number one in 1894 but in club football it was the English clubs that were top notch, none more so than Aston Villa. And so to Lancashire and the match with Burnley, Villa needing one point for the title faced a side 'fighting Derby for third place'.[11] Jack Reynolds and Bob Chatt were away on England duty and despite the press already referring to Villa 'as the League Champions on view', Stephen and his team-mates were anxious to get the game started, they had dragged out proceedings for so long after seemingly being certainties to win the title for the first time. The pressure had almost got the better of them and now the players were desperate to wrap things up.

The *Birmingham Post* reported it as only being a matter of time and that the supporters were confident the title would come.[12] The supporters hadn't seemed so confident when Villa were being held at home to Blackburn. Burnley fans believed that Villa would be too good for their team, with only 7,000 fans turning up for such a decisive game.[13] Villa started nervously and Burnley, according to the *Birmingham Daily Post*, 'had rather the best of matters and their goal had been threatened on more than one occasion'. As the nerves heightened Cowan headed a Smith cross into the net, the Burnley fans didn't seem to believe they were behind such had been their dominance, 'the spectators were too surprised to appreciate the point', wrote the *Athletic News*.

In a tight game with so much riding on it, both sides seemed handicapped by nerves except one man, Stephen Smith. He was described as 'noticeable' for his 'smartness on the Villa outside left'. Smith would often be seen as a player for the big occasion as his football career wore on. But despite Smith's verve on the left Dunning spilled a shot into his goal just before the break and it was 1-1 at the interval. Villa were determined to make it hard for themselves, or so it seemed.

Groves put Villa 2-1 up before they were pegged back again quickly. A draw would suffice but a goal for Burnley could still ruin the season. Stephen Smith had other ideas and from his throw in on the left hand side Devey flicked the ball on and it fortuitously, 'passed through a bundle of legs before reaching the net'. Thank God for the skipper, thought Smith as Villa went ahead. In the next moment of the match a thing of beauty happened that made Stephen almost cry with relief. His great friend Charlie Athersmith, who'd welcomed him to the club and looked after him through the bad times when he couldn't get in the team, put in a wicked right-wing cross and the legend, the man Steve loved and admired above all others, his playing partner on the left hand side, Denny Hodgetts bulleted a header into the net and the game and the League Championship of England was won.

The rest of the game was played out in a blur of euphoria and ended 6-3 to the Birmingham club. How had this happened? How had the son of a farm worker, who still worked in the mines when ends needed to be met, become a League Champion professional footballer? The answer was that through determination, skill and the resilience to come back despite every knock back experienced in the brutal world of professional football, Stephen Smith had, from the humblest of beginnings forced his way into a team that was the best in the land, maybe the world, and as this game had once again shown he was an integral part of a team that would go down in history as the first ever Aston Villa side, the first ever team from the Midlands to be League Champions.

As a born and bred Midlander Stephen Smith was a true local hero, the epitome of what the working man could now achieve and earn, unrestrained, on the sports field, previously the preserve of privileged and monied landed amateurs. The world of football and sport in general was changing rapidly. This revolutionary period was seeing a Victorian upper class pastime become the game of the people and Stephen Smith was slap bang in the middle of it. The people of Abbots Bromley, Cannock Chase, Hednesford, Birmingham and across the English Midlands knew his name and cheered his appearance on a football field, even more so because as the popular modern phrase goes, and has always been important to footballer supporters then and now, he was 'one of their own'.

Most professional footballers play their entire career without winning the League Title. Stephen Smith managed it just ten months into his footballing life, ten months after working full time underground in the mines of Cannock Chase. That he managed to perform at the highest level while still sporadically doing shift work in the Cannock and Rugeley Colliery makes his achievement even more remarkable. But then Stephen Smith was a remarkable man. He was not just a local hero, but a man of the people and one of the original working-class footballing heroes.

The *Birmingham Daily Post* was lavish in their praise for Stephen and his club's achievements. The paper reported:

> The Aston Villa are now Champions of the League (sic) ... For months past the Villa have headed the table... and though their position has been challenged...they have always had such an excellent lead...their supporters had little doubt to their ultimate success...The Villa have recovered their temporary loss of form that followed their

Sheffield disappointment and are again performing with that excellence and consistency which has won them the League Cup and the right to assume the title of Champions of England.[14]

But there was one more challenge to meet, as detailed on the same page of the newspaper:

> Birmingham people will be afforded an opportunity of welcoming their champions at Perry Barr today for a match has been arranged with the great Scottish club the Celtic. They are the champions of the Scotch League and occupy in their own country a position similar to which the Villa hold in this. Both clubs will be fully represented and the contest should be a great one.

The two best teams from the only two professional leagues anywhere in the world, and thus by implication the best leagues in the world, would now face off for the title of unofficial 'world champions'. Having thrashed Glasgow Rangers who had in turn thumped Celtic with Smith in fine form, Villa were expected to confirm their status as the best team on the planet having also of course ended their Sunderland curse earlier in the season. And they did just that but Smith and teammate Bob Chatt had to sit in the stands of the Perry Barr ground.

Leg injuries and muscle fatigue after game after game in league, cup and now challenge matches to generate gate money, on top of Smith's continued moon-lighting as a miner had taken its toll. Of course had he been fit Smith would have played, he was now a key player in the team and had taken Rangers, an arguably better team than Celtic, apart virtually single handed.

Despite this he hated missing games, especially the big matches where he so often shone. Injury would be part and parcel of his time at Aston Villa due to wear and tear and being targeted by less skilful opponents. He was a true flair player whom the fans adored but when Villa beat Celtic to be crowned unofficial 'World Champions' on that day unfortunately he missed out. But without Smith who had destroyed Rangers earlier that Spring, Villa would not have been able to claim the title in the first place.

Four thousand fans were in attendance despite it being a workday. The fans wanted to celebrate with the players and show their appreciation for winning the league. Smith and Chatt's hands were sore from all the handshaking they did in the grandstand. Athersmith went close before Celtic went ahead with McMahon firing past Dunning.[15] Athersmith then whipped in a centre that Devey headed goalwards and the crowd thought had gone in the net, but the Celtic keeper turned the ball wide. Villa equalised fortuitously when the ball bounced into the net after the 'Villa rushed the ball, the goal keeper and one of the backs as well into the net', Villa were level but no individual player was credited with the goal. It was thus 1-1 at the break.

Early in the second half, Athersmith, in fine form, put a corner onto Devey's head and the ball flew in to give Villa the lead. Celtic then pressed and pressed for an equaliser and the locals gave Celtic's McMahon a round of applause as he equalised from twenty-five yards out. Hodgetts, the legend, the man who had sealed the title had seen enough and fed Devey 'and he scored with a beautiful shot which the goalkeeper tired in vain to reach'. Smith watched in awe as the three men he admired most took the victory and the plaudits at the final whistle as the ground erupted. Smith was happy to watch his friends take the glory, the 20-year-old had contributed much but had a long way to go to match his friend's legendary status. Bob Chatt and Stephen Smith stood and applauded their teammates and realised they were part of a team that was the best in England, the best in Britain and in 1894 that also meant the best in the world.

Chapter 9

Apotheosis

The final game of the season saw Villa beat Nottingham Forest 3-1 with Athersmith scoring 'after Smith made a brilliant run down the left', his trademark action which once again led to that overused description in the *Birmingham Post*.[1] Smith's consistency was now a given and an expectation of the spectators down at Perry Barr. The *Athletic News* reported that 'it was the intention of the club to entertain their players to a dinner, at which the League Cup will be handed over'.[2] Nowadays the players lift the trophy from a podium in front of their fans beamed around the world to television audiences. In 1894 the celebrations were more understated.

Part of the celebrations later in the month saw newly promoted local rivals Small Heath, the forerunner of Birmingham City, put on a dinner for Aston Villa at the Old Royal Hotel on Temple Row in the city centre.[3] The dinner was just a few streets away from Barwick Street and the infamous meeting that changed the direction of the club. Back then the two clubs had a healthy and friendly rivalry, a dinner like this would be unheard of in the modern era where the Second City derby has become one of the most bitterly contested rivalries fraught with crowd misbehaviour from both club's supporters.

Villa's players posed for a photograph to commemorate the title win in front of the pavilion at the Aston Lower Grounds.[4] Players and Committee members stood together unlike the team photos of today which are just manager, backroom staff and the playing squad. In the 1890s football clubs were managed by Committee even if trainer Grierson had a large degree of autonomy. Stephen Smith sat on the front row next to the trophy and Albert Woolley, his great rival for the left-wing berth. Woolley had signed on for another season and Smith still feared the competition.

Stephen need not have been worried, Smith's form the following season kept Woolley out of the side and he was transferred to Derby

County. Albert Woolley never shook off his susceptibility to illness and Derby refused to pay him when he became ill again. At the age of 24, still in dispute with Derby over his contract, he died on 3 February, 1896 of 'rapid consumption'; possibly out of guilt, unmarried Woolley's parents were paid the lump sum of £45 in compensation.[5]

Summer had arrived and Smith went back to Hazel Slade and the Cannock coalfields having signed on for another season with Villa. He never forgot Albert Woolley, a player he at first so envied, and he never forgot how lucky he was in comparison. Health in the Victorian period was a fickle mistress.

Back in the mining village of Hazel Slade Stephen tried to focus on his job as an engine haulier in the colliery. In the Slade Pub he once again didn't have to buy a round of ales. Susan Blastock was serving most of those drinks so it was an ideal opportunity for Stephen and her to get reacquainted. She was very glad he was back on a less infrequent basis. So were Stephen's family, particularly his proud father Stephen senior and Willenhall Town's newest recruit, his brother, William Smith.

Stephen was treated as a hero at work and in the street, the quiet Smith found it all quite overwhelming at times but knew he was lucky. He had health, fame and two incomes at a time when most people barely had one regular weekly wage. Susan wanted to know what Stephen wanted out of life. Smith just wanted to spend time with her when he could, away from the pressures of First Division football and the grind and grime of the colliery. 'I won't wait forever Stephen,' said Susan one day. Stephen, like most men, knew exactly what that meant. As well as working at the Slade she now had a part-time live-in job working as a domestic servant in Birmingham and had life plans of her own.

The 1894/95 football season was Stephen Smith's finest as a footballing individual. This was despite Sunderland regaining their crown in devastating fashion winning twenty-one matches and finishing eight points clear of Villa in third. Smith scored eighteen goals and missed just four league and cup games, his tally of strikes only being beaten by the incomparable John Devey.[6] He would finish the season as an England international to boot.

The burgeoning consistency of the previous season was fully evident in 1894/95. It must be remembered that he was still only 21 years old at the end of this season. In terms of more modern local heroes, only Gary Shaw the Brummie born striker who won the league with Villa in

1981 could be said to have had such a youthful impact in claret and blue. Gabriel Agbonlahor and Jack Grealish were older before they became the parochial folk heroes they are today.

Shaw, Agbonlahor and Grealish have all, in modern times, made their marks on the Second City Derby. Their winning goals in this bitter fixture, contested more fervently than ever in the twenty-first century probably due to having little other success to fixate upon, are the stuff of legend. But it all started with Stephen Smith when the opening day fixture of the season was against Small Heath – later to become Birmingham City – the first ever league meeting between the two clubs and as the previous pre-season 'celebration dinner' had shown, it was not a fixture then with any animosity. Small Heath were much more deferential back then to their illustrious neighbours.

The fixture between the two was of less importance to Villa until West Bromwich Albion fell down the leagues in the 1980s. Villa often won the day. After years in the wilderness themselves, the Blues returned to the topflight in 2002 and started to dominate Villa and were unbeaten in the fixture for six straight matches as well as beating Villa in the League Cup quarter-final in 2011 on the way to winning the trophy. Birmingham's two trophy wins, both in the League Cup, have seen Villa defeated. Crowd violence has never been far away from the contest in recent years, Villa keeper Enckelman was accosted in 2002 as fans invaded the pitch after he conceded an own goal. In the rematch in 2003, a headbutt by Villa player Dion Dublin on Blues midfielder Robbie Savage saw him sent off as mayhem ensued in the stands.

In the 2010 League Cup quarter final victory Blues fans invaded the pitch and only police intervention stopped them attacking the Villa fans in the away end. In 2019 as Villa extended their unbeaten run in the league fixture to fourteen years, Jack Grealish, having been assaulted on the pitch by a Blues supporter who was later imprisoned, snatched a late winner.

In front of twenty thousand fans at Perry Barr on 1 September in 1894, Stephen Smith scored the first ever Villa goal in this league fixture and set his side on their way to a 2-1 victory. Smith's goal was an equaliser after Small Heath took a shock lead, 'the goal rather took the Villa supporters by surprise'. Smith scored after, 'the Villa forwards began to attack very persistently, the ball came to Smith who dodged the back, secured an opening and equalised amidst great cheering'.[7]

Thirty seconds afterwards Gordon scored, 'receiving a superb centre from Smith and scoring easily'. Smith, the man of the match, had been the decisive factor in the first Second City league fixture. His genius had allowed a sub-par Villa to scrape home in a game they were expected to win comfortably. The *Birmingham Post* reported:

> In the Villa front rank Smith was certainly the best performer; indeed to our minds he was the best forward on the pitch. He kept going all the time and his dodging and centring alike were excellent. He was splendidly fed by Hodgetts, to whose unselfishness the little outside left winger owed a great deal of his prominence. The left wing was a capital wing on Saturday and the Villa Committee will doubtless hesitate before making changes in that direction.

Stephen Smith was the first local hero to put his indelible mark in this most contentious of fixtures and secure the bragging rights for the men from north Birmingham. He would be the first in a long line of men who would go down in history with legendary status on both sides of the divide. Smith scored in the next two league fixtures as well. Victory at Liverpool was achieved in part by Smith scoring with a shot that went in off the post.[8] Villa then faced their greatest rivals to the title of 'Unofficial World Champions' during the period of 1894 to 1900.[9] Sunderland had also won their first two games of the season and were desperate to retrieve the league title taken from them by Villa. There were 20,000 at Perry Barr that day, 18,000 at Everton and other matches reaching 8,000 as further signs of an increasing interest in football in those days became apparent.

The two best teams in the country, the champions against the previous year's winners, both with one hundred percent records, went toe to toe and Smith was in the thick of it. Hodgetts returned next to Smith on the left, much to everyone's relief, particularly Stephen who always felt more confident lining up next to his great mentor and friend.

Villa, backed by the huge crowd set about Sunderland with gusto. After five minutes Hodgetts found Smith 'who was lying up close to goal' and Villa were ahead. Three goals in three games for Stephen was nearly four when, 'Reynolds got the ball away, Smith at once took up the run, and going off at top speed, he beat his back and flew straight for goal and something very like a huge moan could be heard round the ring as he banged it against the side net.'[10]

Smith was single-handedly besting one of the top teams in the land but just before half-time the Sunderland forward Campbell wriggled past Welford and completely beat the Villa keeper Wilkes to equalise. Honours were even at the break. In the second half the Perry Barr crowd grew more and more edgy as Villa started to make mistakes. Villa conceded a late goal to Sunderland and even as far away as Scotland their second half performance drew criticism. The *Scottish Referee* newspaper reported that, 'Hannah scored the second and as it proved the winning goal for the visitors, who looked easy winners.'[11]

The Perry Barr spectators were 'incensed' at what they saw as time wasting by Sunderland players near the end. But Villa had lost at home for the first time in over a year. Defeat was an unsatisfactory end to a day that had begun with 'the League Championship flag which Villa had made to commemorate last season's triumph floating gaily in the breeze and was the object of much admiration'. To this day the Scottish League has a flag hoisting ceremony to celebrate their Champions. In England it is down to personal preference if a flag is flown, but no ceremony has ever caught on.

The *Athletic News* criticised the performances of Smith's great friends Hodgetts, Devey and Athersmith and in the Crown and Cushion after the match, Smith squirmed uncomfortably as Villa Committee members told Athersmith in no uncertain terms that if he were to be sent off in a match 'we will not pay you when you are suspended Charlie'.[12] He had been criticised in the press for 'resorting to bashing tactics' on opponents when frustrated. Stephen had played well but his team had lost, his pals, the heroes of last season were not performing well and were under the cosh from press and committee men alike. They drank their ale and smoked their Woodbines quietly that night.

Things looked back to normal a week later with an away win at Derby. Villa won 2-0 with Smith making the first goal for Devey.[13] But Steve's great friend Hodgetts had been dropped again and that caused tensions in the camp. Two more away games without Hodgetts followed and things did not go well. Villa were beaten 4-1 at Stoke and the criticism of the Birmingham press was vitriolic, 'It is inexplicable that the champions of last season should have to an ignominious thrashing at the hands of the team which previously stood at the very bottom of the First Division, and the effect cannot but be to create serious misgivings among supporters of the Villa colours.' The *Birmingham Post* was unimpressed with Villa's 'inconsistent form', and Villa's 'discomfiture was unexpected'.[14]

Alarm bells continued to ring a week later after another defeat, this time 2-1 at Nottingham Forest. Things were not going well for the League Champions and all the players including Stephen had seen their form desert them. The squad and supporters were disconcerted about the treatment of Denny Hodgetts who had been dropped from the last three games and Villa had floundered without him. Having managed to win – fortuitously – against the bottom club and then having lost to two lowly teams, questions were again being asked about the Villa.[15] The *Athletic News* commented that, 'it is quite evident that there will have to be an overhauling of the machinery and an adjustment of the working parts if the reputation of the Villa club is to be maintained'. Villa were already eight points behind leaders Everton who had won all of their seven games to date.

Next up was the old enemy. West Bromwich Albion. Hodgetts returned to the starting line-up and Stephen Smith found himself dropped from the team. Villa's committee had been criticised by supporters in the past over deselecting Hodgetts and now they were doing the same to a player seen as a reliable fan's favourite, a younger version of Hodgetts himself. Villa were victorious against their old rivals by three goals to one as Smith watched from the sidelines in the old grandstand. The press explained just how relieved the Villa Committee was after the match. The *Birmingham Post* wrote that, 'The action of the Aston Villa Committee in again rearranging their team will doubtless meet with the approbation of their supporters for the action was justified by success. But dread to think what would have been said had the experiment proved fruitless.'

Smith feared another prolonged spell on the side-lines like last season but Villa's form didn't improve. Against lowly local rivals Small Heath only a controversial Hodgetts penalty saved Villa from defeat. Villa lost for the fourth time in seven matches a week later meaning the title had been as good as lost just nine games into its defence. A 2-1 defeat at Sheffield United was the latest catastrophe for the team.

Stephen managed to get back into the side for the next game against Liverpool. With John Devey injured, Smith deputised at inside right against a team struggling worse than Villa and who would finish bottom of the table and relegated come the following Spring. Smith had started the season well but faded as badly as his teammates as the title was surrendered meekly. Against Liverpool Smith clicked back into gear before attaining previously unseen levels of ability, skill and above all goals, scoring that dragged Villa away from lower mid table mediocrity up to a respectable third place finish.

When Smith returned to the team and was eventually joined by fit-again captain John Devey, the team went on a mid-season charge that was almost unstoppable. Had Villa not been such slow starters they would have been champions again. Smith didn't want to lose his place again, didn't want to lose out on any more win bonuses that were crucial to sustaining his family's existence. He also wanted to carry on making history – and that's exactly what Stephen Smith did.

A Stephen Smith and John Devey inspired Villa won thirteen and drew four of the remaining twenty-one league games of the season. Smith's form was imperious. Liverpool were thumped 5-0 after even more selection changes which again didn't go unnoticed in the papers who wrote, 'it may be mentioned at once that the Villa had again undergone a change'. The *Birmingham Post*[16] was effusive in its praise of Smith detailing that 'Athersmith and Smith were the best right wing tried this season'. The *Post* continued, 'Athersmith... dodged very cleverly and some of his passes out to Smith were splendidly judged; and Smith for his part never failed to take them and on nearly every occasion made fine use of the opportunities that presented themselves'. Smith was tripped for the penalty that led to the third goal after a fine run with Baldy Reynolds converting.[17] Smith's run and centre that gave Dorrell the chance to score the fourth goals was described as 'the most brilliant bit of work in the match'. Smith and Villa were back up and running.

In consecutive games in November, Preston and Sheffield United were beaten 4-1 and 5-0 at Perry Barr.[18] The match report for the Preston game explained that, 'The absence of Dorrell, through an injury to his foot brought Chatt into the team ... Smith was ordered into his old position on the extreme left ... He acquitted himself admirably; indeed the play of the left wing was excellent throughout'.[19] Smith's crossing ability could not be bettered in the Villa team and 'a fine centre from Smith gave Hodgetts a chance and he scored with a shot worthy of his best days'. The apprentice was now helping the master regain his reputation.

Against Sheffield United there were only 300 people in the ground at kick off due to the torrential rain, though the attendance was 7,000 by the end.[20] Unlike modern football, facilities at football grounds rarely extended to roofs except in the main grandstand for the more affluent supporter. Inclement weather led to lower crowds and losses in profits as a cold caught by standing in the winter rain could, in the 1890s lead to death. Only the hardiest of footballing folk were in attendance for this match which the weather caused a 'tremendous loss financially to the home executive'.

Smith was denied twice by 'Fatty' Foulkes the famous goalkeeper of the day including on one occasion when he was described as 'absurdly offside'. Smith also shot, 'across the goal mouth but Devey was too slow'. As the rain teemed down, Villa's barrage on the United goal was also torrential, Chatt scored twice, Devey two more and then Reynolds made it five. Stephen couldn't quite believe that the game was being played and in the ensuing days after the game Sheffield tried to get the game replayed but to no avail, Smith could hear his own teeth chattering and some players walked off the pitch to the dressing room before the game had finished.[21]

The *Sheffield Telegraph* reporter stated that, 'the players seemed to be doing precisely as they liked' with no real thought for the rules of the game. Stephen stood amazed on the opposite side of the pitch as his good friend Charlie Athersmith motored down the wing with the ball and an umbrella over his head much to Smith's and the crowd's amusement. It is unlikely that this kind of thing would be tolerated today. It would likely be picked up by VAR! Amazingly the result of the match stood.

As frivolous as the scene sounds, Foulkes, the Sheffield keeper, went down with stomach cramp and players were dithering and 'shaking as if they had fits of the ague', showing how bad the conditions were.[22] It was the type of match and conditions that would lead to the premature death of Albert Woolley and curtailed the lives of many Victorian footballers in their 30s. Cold and sickness was a killer but players had to play no matter what, fixtures had to be completed just as in the present day. Stephen would remember this match with anger and sadness in his retirement when he lost good friends before their time.

Defeat against West Brom in the reverse league fixture, as the *Birmingham Post* described how Abion spectators were well pleased that their victory, 'destroys what little hope remained to the Villa of retaining the League Cup'. This was under the bold typeface 'THE ALBION VANQUISH THE VILLA'. Derby victories and local bragging rights being secured are something that has and always will make football so seductive to supporters and sell more newspapers. The tribal victory is more satisfying and the gloating more visceral when you can see the anguish of your neighbours first-hand in the streets and at work in the aftermath of your glory as they have it rubbed in their faces. Defeat to the Albion was the most unpalatable of all.

The only crumb of comfort in the 3-2 loss to their fiercest rivals was Smith's equaliser to make it 2-2. Athersmith had crossed the ball to the far post where Smith reached the ball before his marker and then cut inside his opponent, 'dodged that player and touched it into the net. It was a cool bit of play that was rewarded with loud cheers'. But Smith himself was not on top form, Denny Hodgetts was missing due to a family bereavement and Smith didn't play as well with his replacement Purslow. In the match Hodgetts was reported as being 'missed by Smith on many occasions'.

Stung by the criticism after their derby day humiliation, Villa won six in a row in the league, eight out of nine in an unbeaten surge towards the upper reaches of the league.[23] Forest were thrashed 4-1, Smith making the final goal for Devey before facing Blackburn.[24] In the build up to that game the great Archie Hunter, Denny Hodgetts' fellow goal scorer in Villa's only ever FA Cup final victory in 1887 against West Bromwich Albion, died of heart failure. He'd been ill since collapsing from a heart attack playing against Everton.[25] Years of playing in inclement weather at a time when medicine to deal with cold and flu was in its infancy, when electricity and central heating and fresh water in homes were not the norm had finally taken its toll. Hunter was just 35 years of age.

Denny was distraught that his great friend had died. Stephen had spoken to Hodgetts about the funeral in the butcher's yard as they got changed, in which Denny had been a pallbearer amongst other Villa legends from the cup winning side.[26] Smith had already known that Hodgetts had been very upset at the funeral having spoken to former Hednesford and Villa player Eli Davis, who had won the cup with Eli and Denny and still had a lot to do with Hednesford Town and thus knew Stephen. Smith and Hodgetts had become close due to their positions on the field and Hodgetts' natural ability to lead through deeds on the pitch and kindness off it. He'd done what only two Villa men had ever done, score in an English Cup final, and now the other man was dead.

'We need to win the cup, win it for Archie, win it so that we aren't the only ones who ever do,' said Hodgetts to Stephen. 'Archie was desperate for the Villa to win the cup again'. Hodgetts continued. 'They heckled him at Barwick Street, Steve, when things were going badly in 1892, at the meeting. He was their hero and the Committee and supporters jeered him. He scored in every round of the cup, no one has ever done that, and won Villa the cup on his own.' Steve stayed quiet. Everyone did when the great man spoke.

Against Blackburn at Ewood Park, Smith and his colleagues were determined to do Archie Hunter proud. The *Birmingham Post* described the depth of the outpouring of emotion for the only man to lift the FA Cup:[27]

> The Villa players on Saturday wore crepe armlets in memory of the late Archie Hunter and never was such a mark of respect more truly deserved. Throughout his last illness he has been most anxious to hear about the club's performance and so keen has been his interest that he has been propped up in bed whenever his condition permitted it, in order that he might see the crowd on its way to Perry Barr, the scene of so many of his triumphs.

Archie Hunter was a Victorian sporting celebrity and was Villa's first great footballer and an idol to the Perry Barr supporters for more than a decade.[28] The question was now, who was going to take his place in the Perry Barr Pantheon? Denny Hodgetts was already in it, Stephen Smith would do his very best to join his great friend there.

Blackburn Rovers away was a good start. The game against Blackburn started fifteen minutes late as the referee missed his railway connection. After the 'burly form of Mr Fox' the referee, 'came into view' it was Blackburn who took the lead. Just before half-time after concerted pressure from a corner, the ball fell to Devey who found Smith, he put the ball through the keeper's legs into the net.[29] Hodgetts beamed at his left wing partner. Villa headed for the dressing room as the whistle went but due to the game running behind schedule, a shorter half-time was conducted on the pitch, 'in full view of the spectators'. I'm not sure if modern Premier League players would take too kindly to half-time on the pitch with the potential 'banter' opportunities it would give to supporters.

Villa continued to press after the break and after just a few minutes Smith picked up the ball on the left and screwed a shot past the Blackburn keeper to give his side the lead. The *Athletic News* described Smith's finish as 'magnificent' and he was hungry for more glory. Hodgetts and Smith continued to terrorise the home defence. The *Birmingham Post* described Hodgetts' play as 'extremely good generalship' as he 'gave Smith many good openings which that player took full advantage of ... his scoring shots would have beaten any goal-keeper'.

Smith beat the keeper again with another of his shots to claim his hat-trick with fifteen minutes to go and seal the victory. He even put the ball in the net again for a fourth time but was adjudged offside, although it did not take away from a performance that honoured Archie Hunter's memory. Smith and Hodgetts had seen to that on a day of real emotion for the players and the club. The press gave them enthusiastic praise over the following days.

Smith was described as 'fleet-footed', and that 'his shooting was a treat to see', Smith and Hodgetts were called 'a dangerous wing'. Smith was happy with his performance and the praise he was getting, but even more content for his friend Hodgetts who had been through the mill not just in the previous week, but also throughout the season. He'd done it for Hunter and in doing so had done it for Hodgetts as well.

Inspired by the thoughts of emulating and honouring a lost great, Villa hit twenty-four goals in the next six games. Sheffield Wednesday were beaten 3-1, Blackburn 3-0 and Hodgetts scored twice in a 4-0 win at Molineux, the Wolves supporters were seen leaving long before the end, so comprehensively beaten were their team.[30] Villa then thrashed Stoke 6-0 with Charlie Athersmith scoring three; amazingly after such a poor start to the season Villa were now on top of the league, but Everton had the same number of points with four games in hand.

Sunderland were just one point behind with five games in hand and just one defeat, and were next up in the North East, if Villa were to have any chance of the title they would have had to have beaten their seemingly almost invincible opponents on their home ground. On their own patch, Sunderland had won nine out of nine, scoring 36 and conceding just 6, Villa had lost more than they had won on their travels. The table looked like this:

	Played	**Points**
Aston Villa	20	27
Everton	16	27
Sunderland	15	26

So, the two giants of the English game faced off yet again on 2 January 1895; the two clubs that were coming to dominate the English footballing landscape. Sunderland, the more established masters looking to retain their crown against the upstart pretenders full of talent and potential, if not the trophies to match. In an amazingly exciting match consistent with previous epic encounters ended in a 4-4 draw. Villa valiantly matched their much-lauded opponents and became the first side to come away with a point from Newcastle Road. But with so many games in hand Sunderland and Everton would now slug it out for the League title.

As Villa finished strongly in third place, Smith ended the league season with thirteen goals in twenty-six games, only the great John Devey, with sixteen scored more.[31] It was his best ever goal scoring return in a single season in a claret and blue shirt. The winter of 1895 was a very cold and wet one. Attendances were down as people avoided the elements and the potential for illness that came with it. Villa's epic draw at Sunderland had seen 12,000 fans at Newcastle Road, there had been 22,000 fans at the ground during the winter of 1894, a 10,000 drop in spectators was huge even allowing for the fact the game in 1894 was a glamourous FA Cup tie. Villa's average crowd was affected by the inclement weather during this season with attendance down by 2,000 fans.[32]

Back in Hazel Slade, Stephen was relieved to be able to give more of his wages to keep his family going due to all his recent win bonuses. The family was still struggling like many others due to regular bouts of sickness and hunger brought about by poor wages and working conditions, Stephen himself had been part of the most recent miner's strike in 1893.[33] His parents were delighted to see him, as were his brothers who wanted to talk football of course. William was doing great things at Willenhall Town and getting noticed by professional scouts.[34]

In the Slade Inn there was only one person he wanted to see. He ordered a round of ales for his father and brothers at the bar and waited for Susan Blastock to serve them up. 'Hello Tich', she said. 'How's the famous footballer?' He was well aware he had not seen her much since Christmas and it was now late January. He sensed her annoyance. She was so small and delicate and beautiful; he loved her but he was shy.

'Hello Tiny', he replied. It is what he called her as he very rarely encountered people shorter than him and it was a running joke between the two of them. They reacquainted themselves in between her serving all her other customers and people accosting him to fete the great local football player. Stephen knew he had to make a commitment to Susan soon, she was 22 years old, which was old to be unmarried in the 1890s in her social class.[35] She needed to be married soon. Smith was worried about the fact that as he was supporting his whole family that he wouldn't be able to support her as well. As a footballer and a mining engineer he knew he hardly got to see her as it was. Stephen's father gave him some further local intelligence – other local men were interested in squiring Susan around the village.

William found Stephen's predicament hilarious. 'Just ask her and get it done, Steve, bring her back another medal and an England cap to impress her,' he chimed mischievously, so Stephen finally plucked up the courage and asked the question. The next day, with Susan's excited acceptance you would think that he would have done all he needed to do by asking her to be his wife. But in Victorian Britain the fact two people loved each other and wanted to get married was a very small part of the marital process; and for a shy man like Stephen Smith, it was even more excruciating. Before the six-month engagement with his wife was formalised he needed to ask Susan's father which required him going to the Slade Pub and explaining his intentions and prospects. Susan's father was delighted of course to have his daughter betrothed to the great hero of Hazel Slade.

Within a few days, Stephen and Susan's family had organised the finer details including contacting the local vicar and announcing it in the local press and a summer wedding for Stephen Smith and Susan Blastock was on the cards, pending the end of the football season of course. Susan was impatient to wed, and see Stephen whenever she could, but at least now under the rules of Victorian engagement they could stroll out alone, hold hands and take unchaperoned walks – at least when Smith wasn't on a football pitch or down a mine. The footballer whose fame was growing would now also be in the paper publicising his nuptials. Not in *OK! Magazine* or with pictures in the national press, but the fans the clubs he had played for would certainly have been interested that he was getting married. He was becoming something of a local celebrity and was still only 21 years old.

In February the English Cup as it was called then, now universally known as the FA Cup, began in earnest. Aston Villa were drawn at home to Derby County who were struggling at the foot of the First Division and expected to win handsomely. In the first half, Athersmith hit the bar and Reynolds, Cowan, Devey and Smith were praised for some 'smart work'. Then the maestro that was John Devey, 'having a clear opening, rushed towards goal, and from a distance of nearly twenty yards scored with a straight fast shot'.[36]

Villa held the lead until just after half-time when their defence let a cross shot, 'aiming for the goal, skimming four or five yards in front' of the goalkeeper and England striker Steve Bloomer, 'with no one near to clear the danger' was allowed to score 'easily'. In the end Villa scraped home with a big slice of luck. Steve Smith picked up a pass from Hodgetts far out on the left and after a 'pretty run' his 'red hot shot' then 'glanced off Methven's (a Derby defender) calf through the goal, and the Villa once more had the lead'.[37]

Smith was the Villa hero once more, averting, with a large slice of luck, an embarrassing result and the prospect of a strength sapping replayed match. The relief to the Villa supporters was apparent with the applause that greeted the goal and the final whistle as Wilkes the Villa keeper was kept busy until the end. The *Birmingham Post* wrote that Smith 'put in work worthy of (his) reputation', a reputation that was growing with every star performance and vital goal.

February continued with the next round of the FA Cup. The second-round match was again at Perry Barr against Second Division Newcastle United.[38] The weather in contrast to a fortnight previously produced a 'beautifully fine day'. There was no repeat of the Derby performance as Villa smashed The Toon 7-1. Dorell scored twice, as did Athersmith and Devey while Russell added the seventh. Villa's forwards were described as having 'a field day', individually the forwards were described in the following ways; 'Hodgetts and Smith were a fine wing, Devey a capital centre, whilst Athersmith and Dorrell did very well together.'[39] Aston Villa marched on to the quarter-finals.

Stephen Smith's star climbed even higher after the next match, a 6-2 demolition of Nottingham Forest. The *Birmingham Post* explained that, 'Villa won easily on Saturday ... the four clubs left to contest the semi-finals are therefore Aston Villa, Sunderland, Sheffield Wednesday and West Bromwich Albion, and two splendid contests should result'.[40] The paper also wanted Villa to be drawn against Sunderland as they had the best chance of beating the red and whites leaving Albion the easier prospect of victory over Wednesday leading to the 'clubs meeting in the final as they did in 1892, when the Albion gained that memorable and unexpected victory at the Kennington Oval'.

Villa had got into this situation thanks to two more goals by Smith. When Forest got to within a goal of Villa making it 3-2, 'their hopes were speedily dashed, for Smith quickly scored from a free-kick and followed this up by 'shooting a fifth point'. The local reporter who had been critical of Hodgetts at the start of the year remarked that, 'Hodgetts, as usual was a splendid partner to Smith whom he fed most unselfishly and Smith was a constant source of trouble' to the Forest defence. The plaudits for Smith did not stop there with the *Post* also stating that, 'he dodged cleverly and his centres were always true, (and) Smith made the run of the afternoon' in one Villa attack.

It wasn't just the local press that Smith had wowed. The *Athletic News* reported Smith as 'the twinkling little left winger' such was his performance and also that 'Smith and Chatt were shining lights amongst the forwards'.[41] The reporter also exclaimed that the victory will 'probably make them favourites for the cup'. The pressure and expectation on Stephen and his colleagues never eased during these heady days. As well as more press coverage from the papers and more supporters in the stands than ever before, there was a different attitude to behaviour evident in the average spectator. They were more interactive with what was happening on the pitch. Polite applause was not the only way of expressing a reaction to what was happening on the pitch. After Villa's first two goals their fans 'danced with delight and raved with enthusiasm'.

When Forest scored their fans 'sang a loud if somewhat discordant song of jubilation' and when they got to within a goal of Villa, their supporters 'hollered in a way that crumbled the snowflake from off the curdled sky'. What was the reason for this boisterousness? Well, according to the *Athletic News* reporter it was the, 'whisky and other alcoholic compounds (sold to) to the multitude – at least as many who could get the liquid sin which shone invitingly in the crystal glasses, so near and yet so far'.

Football and alcohol have always gone hand in hand for its supporters. But back then, unlike now, thanks to restrictions imposed on drinking alcohol in full view of the pitch (due to football hooliganism mainly in the last quarter of the twentieth century), fans could drink as much as they liked, wherever they liked in the enclosure. They went to enjoy themselves no matter the score, whether people approved or not. A visit to a football match was not for the faint hearted in the 1890s and rarely would women and children be seen. A family day out it was not, a moniker which would only really be applied to football from the late 1990s onwards when it became less a working-class game. Very rarely did Smith invite his mother, sister or fiancée to 'go down the match'.

The draw for the semi-finals of the English Cup was made on the afternoon of 9 March and reported in the *Athletic News* on the 11th. The draw and the reaction to it were recorded in great detail. The paper also gave a huge sense of the importance of the competition to the nation at large. It stated in a section entitled 'Midland notes' written by a correspondent from Birmingham that:

> Birmingham and West Bromwich were in a state of feverish anxiety early on Saturday afternoon awaiting the result of the draw for the semi-finals of the English Cup. The announcement that The Villans and Throstles had steered clear of each other was received with a good deal of satisfaction by the supporters of both clubs, for there is now a chance – aye, a big chance too – that our two local league clubs will contest the final issue.

The day of the great match, the FA Cup semi-final between the best two sides in England, if not the world, was contested on 16 March 1895. The *Morning Post* of London set the scene accordingly. Its reporter wrote that, 'all general interest in the Association (football) community on Saturday was absorbed by the semi-finals of the English Cup, in which the two great league teams of Aston Villa and Sunderland were engaged at Blackburn', (for the) 'chief prize of the year'.[42] Despite the advent of regular professional football in the League format, for many football purists the English Cup, the much older trophy was still the tournament that beguiled them the most.

Despite the fact Sunderland were about to win the League title for a third time in the first seven seasons of the competition, they had never won the cup and Villa had only won it once themselves. Both sides had a mental block when it came to achieving success in this competition. Yet while the League Championship trophy had not been out of Birmingham or Wearside since 1891, both teams wanted to change their luckless history in this competition.

The Ewood Park ground of the Blackburn Rovers was chosen for this tie, and with everything favourable for the game a crowd of 20,000 gathered. The *Athletic News* reported that many believed that this game should have been the final tie instead. It wrote that, 'as Sunderland and Aston Villa came out of the hat together at the last draw for the English Cup not a few sagaciously shook their heads with a murmur that the final tie would be played at Blackburn the following Saturday'.

Not for the first time in the history of football, the authorities tried to cash in on the big occasion by raising ticket prices and the official attendance of the game was questioned. The *Birmingham Post* explained that, 'the attendance at Blackburn was not nearly so numerous as had been anticipated, only about 15,000 persons being present whereas as twice that number was expected'. It was the opinion of the paper that, 'the charge of a shilling for admission doubtless accounted for the absence of a great many people'.

The *Athletic News* of 18 March was more scathing in its criticism of the ticketing prices:

> The vast array of empty benches on the best stand was a silent protest against the exclusive prices of 4 shillings and 7 shillings and 6 pence ... the British working man considers he is being "had" if he is called upon to pay more than sixpence ... at sixpence the ground would have been ... full – in fact I don't think it would have held the people.

Further controversy came when Jack 'Baldy' Reynolds told reporters he was in the Villa team and then Villa stated he would not be playing, only for him to be the first Villa man out on the field. The club had not been happy he had been speaking to the press and the leaking of team news was covered up as much as possible. Every single psychological edge must be maintained in the build up to a big football match in any era, even if some of your players are a bit too friendly with the press. It was this intense back drop and build up to the semi-final that Smith and his colleagues now had to put behind them. They had to do their talking on the pitch against a seemingly invincible opposition they had failed to beat twice already that season – for themselves, for their club and for Archie Hunter.

The Ewood Park pitch was in 'splendid condition', Sunderland won the toss and allowed Villa to kick off while they lined up playing 'against a slight wind'. Villa dominated the early exchanges and had lots of possession; they were described as passing the ball 'about with almost bewildering smartness in front of the Sunderland goal'. The *Athletic News* reporter opined that he 'would not have been surprised if the Sunderland goal had fallen in the first five minutes'. Villa attacked at will but couldn't break through Sunderland's 'magnificent defence' and 'during the first six minutes (Sunderland keeper) Doig stopped at least four attempts by the Villa to score'.[43] Smith and his team-mates were scratching their heads as to how they were not ahead. Smith himself was worried that it was not going to be his side's day.

On a rare foray into the Villa half Sunderland won a throw that was loaded into the Villa box and was 'travelling insidiously towards the Villa goal'. After a scramble in the box the ball fell to Jimmy Hannah, the Scotland winger, who hit a shot that did not get a full connection on the ball as he fell over in the process. Nevertheless the ball managed to roll past Wilkes into the net. Massively against the run of play, Sunderland were ahead.

It was all too much for some Villa fans described as 'excited Birmingham gentry' who were having 'arguments' that were 'decidedly noisy' with Sunderland fans about the fact their team was behind. On top of this was the now usual grumbling at the referee's decisions against a supporter's chosen team which was also in the air.[44] These are examples of how intense the feeling had become for supporters in terms of the attachments to their local teams and the sometimes boisterous behaviour that was now becoming part and parcel of the antics of football fans in the Victorian Age.

The goal rocked Villa back on their heels and Sunderland had further efforts to extend their lead before half-time. Wilson, the Sunderland captain, worried the Villa defence and fans alike, 'and there was a palpable hush' every time he touched the ball. Villa were wilting under the pressure of the occasion and 'a misunderstanding by Russell and Welford' let the Sunderland forward shoot at goal but 'the ball passed a few inches over the top of the crossbar'.

Stephen Smith always seemed to do well against Sunderland and he was determined to get his side back on level terms. He picked up the ball on the left-hand side and went on a 'brilliant run' that was described as 'worthy of note' and Smith 'appeared likely to equalise'. He was just about to loose off a shot at goal when he was tripped by McNeill, the Sunderland full back that he was terrorising. For a split-second Smith thought he had won a penalty for his team and Hodgetts and Athersmith howled at the referee to give the decision in Villa's favour.

Fortunately for Sunderland the foul was given outside the area and the free-kick came to nothing. Sunderland survived further Villa attacks and Doig, the Sunderland keeper, was praised for his saves by the reporter. Villa had been thwarted by him on every occasion and the players trudged into the Ewood Park changing rooms disconsolately. As the players took a pew and half-time refreshments, the captain Jack Devey stood up, as did his chief lieutenant Denny Hodgetts.

Trainer Joe Grierson and main selector George Ramsay remained silent as William McGregor also sat in on proceedings. Devey wasn't happy. Villa had failed to breach Sunderland's deep lying defence and were heading out of the cup as the game stood. 'We've played well but we need to do better, this lot have taken our League title, let's make sure they don't take our shot at the English Cup,' exclaimed Villa's leader in chief. Listen to what Denny has noticed about them, follow the plan and we can win this,' added Devey. When Devey spoke all the players listened. When Hodgetts the cup legend was talking, the respect for what he had to say was equal if not more so than the captain's opinions.

Hodgetts cleared his throat and explained his tactical theory for the second half. 'First of all shut the door. Don't let any of them hear the plan. Now lads, we must change our tactics. You have seen how our wings are being held – well, Chatt, Devey and I will keep the ball to ourselves until we have drawn both halves and backs, and then the ball will go right or left, and Charlie and Steve must go for all they are worth.'[45] The players agreed on the plan and Smith nodded, he knew just what to do.

Players and management were working in concert to find a breakthrough, and it shows that tactical awareness wasn't just the preserve of the coaching staff in football. Football clubs were run by committee in this era and footballers were part of the tactical committee that led to decisions made on the field. One man or manager did not have the final say back then. In any case, players and Committee men alike strode out for the second half in confident fashion.

Within a couple of minutes of the re-start disaster struck and Villa's cup dream looked dead in the water. Hannah headed past Wilkes into the Villa net and at 2-0 the game seemed over. Campbell, the Sunderland forward, however, was penalised for a foul on the keeper. The Sunderland men had been 'overjoyed' but the goal was chalked off. Villa steadied themselves and as the second half wore on they mounted attack after attack hitting the wingers wherever possible 'in a capital exhibition of the passing game'.[46] Smith carried the fight to the opposition with skill and finesse and no little pace. His performance in the second half of this match would change his life forever, his reputation reaching its zenith at just 21 years of age.

The *Athletic News* reported what the Villa fans at Ewood Park were saying about Smith in a match that came to symbolise his apotheosis at Aston Villa. The paper reported that:

> Smith is a little wonder, and went for Wilson (the Sunderland captain and defender) as if he were a 14 stone gentleman instead of a 130 pounder and can't he run? 'Why blimey', the Birmingham sportsman behind me remarked, 'the little 'un ain't there for nothin' he ain't. He's running Wilson clean off his legs, he is'. Well, it wasn't as bad as that, but certainly he gave the Sunderland Captain a warm time of it and once on the wing he beat them all, chiefly owing to his own individual cleverness.

Villa plugged away with Hodgetts' suggested tactics, holding the ball in the middle, first with Reynolds, then with Devey and then 'the ball went out towards the left' into the path of Stephen Smith. William McGregor, who was of course, present that day, recalled how Smith 'had one trick which he could do better than any man I have watched, he used to walk past an opponent from practically a stationary position, and rarely did he fail to get right clear.'[47] Then as the *Athletic News* reported it, 'little Smith made a dash round McNeill planted the ball clean past Doig' for the equaliser.

Smith was elated and raised his arms in delight, he was mobbed by his teammates who marvelled at his ability to strike a football. The crowd also went wild and the neutrals started to back Villa in the match. The Villa's success was hailed with tremendous cheering and it was at once evident they were the favourites with the crowd. Smith now believed they could win, in only his second season as a professional footballer he was one goal away from the English Cup final, a league and cup in the first two years of his career, by the age of just 21 no less and ultimately, immortality in Villa folklore. Shy and reticent off the pitch, the ultimate footballing warrior on it, Smith had tasted glory and wanted more of it.

Apotheosis

The Hodgetts master plan continued to be followed by the team. Devey in the centre of attack sent the ball left for Hodgetts and he in turn played in Smith, the 'ball was touched from one to the other with beautiful precision and was passed to Smith'. Smith cut inside McNeill again and having terrorised his opponent once more bore down on Doig's goal.[48] Having sprinted past McNeill, Smith skilfully hit a left foot shot past the keeper with the outside of his foot into the corner of the net. The Sunderland defenders 'stood there dumbfounded' as Smith wheeled away 'amidst tremendous cheering' as the crowd roared with delight. Smith was embraced by his team-mates once again, the biggest hug for the tiny flying winger coming from Denny Hodgetts himself. Smith had scored twice in quick succession against the champions elect and had single handedly steered his team in the direction of the cup final.

In the last fifteen minutes having been relatively underworked, Wilkes the Villa keeper was called on to make several saves 'but he kept his head at a very important time and saved several good shots'. The final whistle blew and the Villa players flocked to Smith to congratulate him as the Sunderland players stood around distraught, the crowd cheered and clapped Smith as he walked off almost sheepishly, raising his hand only quickly to acknowledge the applause which was now also from his team-mates as he left the arena. The Villa's victory was extremely popular and they were loudly cheered as they left the field.

The plaudits for Hodgetts the tactical mastermind and Smith the matchwinner were many and numerous in the aftermath of the victory. The *Birmingham Post* wrote that, 'Smith and Hodgetts were the Villa's best wing, thanks in no small degree, to the judicious care of his partner, Smith was enabled to distinguish himself greatly, and was indeed the best forward on the field'. The *Athletic News* was even more effusive in its praise of Smith detailing how 'Smith was the executant' who ended Sunderland's hopes.

On Smith's winning strikes the paper stated that, 'He scored both goals and in each instance it was chiefly owing to his own individual cleverness. That second point was a beauty for such a youngster, nine players out of every ten would have either sent it over or straight at Doig, but Smith did neither – he placed the ball where Doig was not. It was so neatly done (the defence) stood there dumbfounded'.

Amid jubilant scenes in the dressing room John Devey and William McGregor made speeches of celebration as champagne and ale was quaffed whilst cigarettes, cheroots and cigars were puffed. Devey spoke first, 'that was the greatest footballing performance I have ever seen lads' and his teammates roared with approval'.[49]

McGregor came next congratulating the players and then addressing Stephen personally he said, 'no one but you could have scored those goals today lad, it was always going to be you, it's one of the best performances I have ever seen, you will play for England soon enough, Archie would be proud!' The players responded with 'hurrah for Tich!' and 'hear hear!' and Smith felt elation and pride as well as euphoria mixed with alcohol as the celebrations continued. A heady mix indeed for a young man.

William McGregor recorded his memory of this FA Cup semi-final in his column in the *Sports Argus* fourteen years later. His recollections of Smith's performance were still crystal clear:

> The display of Steve Smith was one of the best I have ever seen. None of Sunderland's defenders seemed to be able to cope with him. On each occasion he got quite near in, but his position was such that to score seemed virtually impossible. Nevertheless, although Doig, the wonderful, wary and vigilant goalkeeper, was on the alert, Smith each time planted the ball into the net with the most wonderful and skilful judgement, two of the finest goals ever scored by one player on the same afternoon ... He was cheered to the echo by the onlookers; he was feted by his fellow-players, and, what was better, he gained his international cap against Scotland.

The players caught the train back to Birmingham and the drink continued to flow liberally. The fans were there to meet the players when they arrived back at New Street Station that night, with the news that it would once again be old rivals West Bromwich Albion they would face in the final. The city centre was all of a frenzy with the news, and this was reported in the local press:

> Their reception at New Street Station, where they arrived at midnight, was of the most cordial character, the players being loudly cheered by a large number of enthusiastic supporters who had awaited their arrival.[50]

Chapter 10

World Champion

The players continued their celebrations in the bars and hotels on Temple Row and around the Gas Street Basin and were received jubilantly by the general public many of whom bought them drinks. Decidedly worse for wear, in their favourite pub the Tap and Spile on Gas Street, Smith and Hodgetts stopped to sit down and think about what they had achieved. They were so close to achieving their dream, they raised a toast with their tankards of frothy ale and clinked them together, saying in unison, 'for you Archie'.

The praise for Smith's performance continued throughout the week and he was particularly exalted by *Pearsons's Weekly*:

> To no one man was (Villa's) victory due more than to Steve Smith, their diminutive outside left. Smith is not exactly a lightweight considering his height, but he had the additional advantage, in his endeavours to elude the big Sunderland backs, of being assisted and judiciously "covered" by burly Dennis Hodgetts. Smith is not yet twenty-one years old (he was, he turned 21 in January) but has been playing for the Villa since 1893. He was born at Cannock (Abbots Bromley) near Rugeley, and after distinguishing himself in the local team went to Hednesford Town, where his ability was recognised by Aston Villa. He is very fleet of foot and one of the trickiest players; his swift cross shots are the terror of League goalkeepers.[1]

Smith's performances that season and in the cup semi-final had made him a household name, his diagonal shot across the keeper, his trademark. The nation was starting to pay his performance more attention. The Football Association certainly were and called him up to play for England against Scotland in the final match of the British Home Championship contested between England, Scotland, Wales and Ireland. The 'International Championship' as it was then known was the only international football tournament of its kind anywhere in the world at that time. The winners thus rightly claimed the title 'International Champions' and could claim to be the best side in the world.

As these were the only four internationally competing sides anywhere in the world the opportunity to play international football was incredibly rare, just three times per year, and there was no experimentation with friendly matches and international caps given out for mere warm-up games and friendlies as is now the case. You hit the ground running if you were picked as every game was a competitive test match in a first-class tournament. Stephen Smith had done in less than two years as a professional footballer, what the very vast majority of professional players just did not do (it was very rare for even the very greatest of Villa players to play more than ten times for their country in this era – John Devey gained two caps, Denny Hodgetts six caps, John Reynolds eight caps and Charlie Athersmith twelve caps), even once in their career at this time, play for England, never mind also win the League in his first season and get to a cup final in his second.

The reaction to Smith's inclusion was highly positive as reported in *The Scottish Referee*:

> Steve Smith's selection has proved extremely popular in Birmingham. Last season he was for the most part in the reserve team of Aston Villa (very harsh as he played in the majority of Villa's league matches and was a regular by the end of the season – but this shows how far he had come in a very short space of time) but he was not to be denied, and he has taken part in nearly all the Villa's League matches this season. He is not very tall, but there is plenty of him, and he takes a lot of bumping off the back. In the English Cup semi-final at Blackburn a fortnight ago Smith tricked Hugh Wilson repeatedly, much to the amazement of the Sunderland captain.[2]

There was immense pride at The Cannock and Rugeley Colliery where Smith still worked part-time and used to play for the colliery company's football team. It was reported in *The Cannock Chase Courier* that:

> The annual dinner of the Cannock and Rugeley Cricket Club was held at the Cannock and Rugeley Workmen's Club at Rawnsley on Tuesday. Captain, R.S. Williamson (said) he was pleased to find besides cricket, football flourished on the Colliery and it was something to be proud of to be able to send a man good enough to play for Aston Villa, and in the International matches. He referred to Steve Smith. He was very pleased they could boast of an International Footballer in the Colliery.

In the 1894–95 British Home Championship, England and Ireland played the first match of the competition, the Irish suffering a 9–0 defeat in Derby to give England the immediate advantage. Ireland and Wales then played a 2–2 draw in Belfast before England and Wales drew at the Queen's Club, the only international football match ever played there. Wales finished their competition as Scotland entered it, the teams drawing in Wrexham to give Wales three points in an unbeaten tournament. Scotland beat Ireland in their second game, ending Ireland's tournament with a single point before England and Scotland, level on points, were scheduled to play out the decider at Goodison Park on 6 April.

The build-up to the week before the match was intense and readers of the newspapers of the day would be able to digest, devour and pour over numerous articles analysing and comparing the respective line-ups and chances of success for both teams. *The Scottish Referee* on the Monday before the match produced a detailed preview which assessed the two sides:

> These are the two teams chosen to do battle for England and Scotland in the last and greatest of all the Internationals. The match will be the 24th that has taken place between the two countries. Scotland won 11 matches and (scored) 59 goals, England won 6 matches and (scored) 48 goals. In proceeding to critically examine these two teams, it is singular that the selections in both countries meet with the general approval of the public.

Historically Scotland had always been the stronger footballing nation, hence why teams like Sunderland paid big money to get their best players to come south. Scotland were the reigning champions in the tournament but had not beaten England since 1889. However, despite 'Baldy' Reynolds scoring a late goal for England in the last fixture, Scotland had held on for a draw and clinched the title. Scotland then were international champions but England had not lost to them for six years. This encounter then felt like a decisive one, to decide the argument once and for all as to who was the best international football team in the world.

To the Scots and the English, irrespective of who won the tournament, there was an assumption by both nations that you were only a true champion team if you beat your oldest and deadliest rival, a local derby that meant you were World Champions. The *Scottish Referee* was of the opinion that beating England was the be all and end all, the ultimate prize in football and vice versa for the English, 'going shoulder to shoulder, using all the powers, physical and mental, at their command, it is possible, our last victory in 1889 will be repealed and Scotland regains her position as International Champion'.

The English game was still coming to terms with its move away from amateurism to professionalism. Part of the build up to team selection was that the best amateurs were given the chance to play the professionals and from that a team was picked to play against Scotland. The professionals beat the amateurs 7-0 and thus professional players dominated the England line-up.

The old world of rich amateurs like Lord Kinnaird dominating the sport was on its way out as paid players who saw the game as a career, not just a pastime to help the rich idle away their day, players who, to protect their livelihood and attain a better quality of life, trained hard and pushed themselves to improved excellence, players like Steven Smith.

The professionals deserved to be representing England, to represent the working man who followed the sport, in those days players and fans were one in the same, making a living, trying to survive. Amateur players who bemoaned that sport was now all about money, could bemoan professionalism because in their mansions and on their manors, they could afford to. Stephen Smith and his family like many other footballers of the 1890s could not.

Stephen Smith and Jack Reynolds, the two Villa teammates, roomed together in Liverpool the night before the game with Scotland at Goodison Park. The Football League that same night named their line-up for the match against the Scottish League. The Football League did not pick amateurs like the Football Association. They could pick the best eleven professionals in their League. They decided to pick only English players even though they could pick foreign nationals including Scots. Playing for the League XIs was as much of an honour as playing for your FA at this time as no amateurs were involved.

A telegram to the hotel detailed what the rest of England would know the next morning, that Smith and Reynolds would both be picked for that team along with Athersmith, Devey and that great old survivor, Denny Hodgetts.[3] Stephen Smith was in 1895 again picked to play with the best players in the world for the best teams in the world. He was truly at the top of his game. Smith was just happy he would be playing with his best friends.

As well as detailing the above Football League selections, the *Manchester Courier* explained the fever pitch excitement in Scotland as the national team set off for Liverpool:

> England v Scotland – No alterations have been announced in either team for this match at Everton today. The Scotch team accompanied by many of the Association officials, left by the St. Enoch Street Station, Glasgow, at 1:30, a crowd of 4,000 spectators being present. These became so excited that they burst the barriers, and the police had to use their batons to keep them back.

Stephen Smith went to bed in the Alexandra Hotel in Liverpool on the eve of his England debut a household name in both England and Scotland.[4] He was exalted in England for his consistency that season and in particular his vanquishing of a Sunderland team in the FA Cup, who would soon be League Champions and then World Champions after beating Scottish Champions Hearts 5-3.[5] The press north of the border had done their due diligence on him as soon as he was selected against Scotland. They described Stephen as a player who would not combine with his team mate Gosling as he was an amateur he had never played with before, but was also 'very tricky on the ball' and needed to be watched by Simpson in the Scots defence.[6]

On the morning of the game Smith posed for photographs with his fellow teammates. He wore his dark blue velvet England cap for his individual photo as he leaned on a wooden plinth in his shirt, three-quarter length trousers, shin pads and boots. His cap was embroidered with the year of his debut, 1895 as well as the rose of England. England players still get a dark blue velvet cap for every season they play for England to this day, the only change being the three lions crest has replaced the rose. He then sat on the front row, on the far right of the picture taken for the team that took on Scotland that day. Jack Reynolds was on the back row to the left.

In these modern days of satellite television football fans often bemoan the myriad of different kick off times there can be to suit the viewers at home in their armchairs. But in the Victorian era games tended to start at 2pm on a Saturday afternoon in the autumn and wintertime instead of the perceived 'sacrosanct 3pm kick-off on a Saturday since the dawn of time' myth. With no floodlights at this time, a winter sport needed to get games finished before it went dark. In the spring games could start at 2.30pm, 3pm or even 4 or 5pm.

There were 20,000 fans inside Goodison Park over half an hour before the 4pm kick-off, such was the excitement and expectation surrounding the match. Nowadays supporters have designated seats in all seater stadiums at first class venues so early arrivals to football grounds are not uncommon. Back then where fans were crammed into tight paddocks and were expected to stand in uncovered stadiums whatever the weather, it was unusual for supporters to get into the ground more than a few minutes before they had to, especially as refreshments and toilets would on the whole only be found in the pubs outside the grounds. It was very difficult to get any refreshment whilst jammed onto a football terrace with thousands of other people.

The Scottish players were running late for the kick-off as they had left their team photograph to just before kick-off. The *Athletic News* was incredulous about this turn of events writing that, 'there was an unpardonable delay owing to the late arrival of the Scotch players who had been in the usual photographic pose and it was ten minutes after time when the game was started'. The crowd had swelled to 35,000 when the game kicked off.

Stephen Smith and his colleagues had marched out to great cheers even though England had been led out by the amateur R.C. Gosling who had got the nod ahead of Everton's Chadwick and had been named captain into the bargain. Smith was getting nervous as he stood around waiting for the Scots. What on earth was a miner doing playing for

England in the game to decide the International Championship anyway? He hoped he would do everyone back in Staffordshire proud.

As the English waited for their opponents to appear to play the Victorian equivalent of the World Cup Final, the Scottish supporters were in fine voice in stark contrast to the English fans. The Scottish Referee described the scene:

> The Scots were as numerous as they were loyal. They made their presence known, and their lusty lungs gave out in turn our traditional airs, and enthusiasm worthy of the occasion were wrought up. The English were not so demonstrative, and possibly the inclusion of Gosling instead of Chadwick cooled their interest.[7]

The Scots arrived at ten past four to contest the deciding game between 'the four countries where football is played' as the *Athletic News* put it. In 1895 in terms of international and professional football, outside of the United Kingdom, which included all of Ireland at this time, nowhere else mattered. The first Olympic football tournament was not until 1908, the next oldest international tournament was the South American Championship established in 1916.

The Scottish Captain Oswald, 'lost no time in shaking hands with Gosling' and the 'hurly-burly began as the teams lined up and at 4:13 Goodall (the England forward) set the ball in motion. Stephen Smith, the miner from the industrial midlands who had left school at 12 years old, lined up on the left with Gosling the Cambridge University educated, Old Etonian and Corinthian. The game of football was fast becoming a game of the working classes but it started in English Public schools like Eton played by men like Gosling. Nowadays men like that play Rugby, Cricket and Hockey but back then the aristocratic amateur was still a facet of the game. Smith chuckled at the thought of how different he and his partner were. Gosling was not only upper class to Smith's working class but also well over six feet in height in comparison to the diminutive Smith.[8] They only had one thing in common – football.

The Scots started the game well, roared on by their boisterous support. Gosling and Smith, whose portraits were sketched along with the other men of both line-ups on the front of the match-day edition of the *Scottish Referee*, struggled to make an impact during the early exchanges.

McPherson and Lambie, the Scotland forwards, were causing England problems and Lodge in defence blocked their shots on goal.

Gosling, whom many Evertonians and professionals believed didn't deserve to be in the team, never mind made captain after the pre-match trials, picked up the ball. It could have been that only Lord Kinnaird's intervention had maintained an amateur presence in the team. The President of the FA of course was a former amateur Old Etonian and part of the soon to be bygone era of the private school, Cambridge, old boy network and had potentially pulled some strings. Gosling was determined to prove people wrong in a sport where the world was changing quicker than other parts of England. Where ability not high birth was the more respected social currency. Gosling with his large imposing frame dribbled through 'a maze of players' and got into the 18-yard box but the Scottish defence blocked him off.

Gosling and debutant Smith had points to prove for different reasons as the game went back and forth. The game was reported as being 'fast and furious' as both Scotland and England's left flanks started to get the majority of possession. Gosling and Smith, the unlikely duo, began to combine for the English. The Victorian class divide was bridged as Gosling and Smith began 'doing most of the leading work'.

Smith's Villa compatriot 'Baldy' Reynolds was also starting to get into the game as England began to force the pace. Reynolds met a cross into the box a little too late and lifted his shot over the bar and then after good work from Smith and Gosling, who were indulging in 'aggressive movements' as they combined 'admirably together', Reynolds shot wide of the mark. The Scots were now struggling to deal with the pace of the English forwards and a goal seemed inevitable.

Smith was growing in confidence as England pressed. A 'brilliant run' by Smith and an exchange of passes with Gosling saw him send in a trademark 'screw-shot' across goal that the keeper fumbled and the ball rolled towards the goal. Stephen thought he'd scored on his debut for England, but a Scottish defender just about managed to shovel the ball away from the goal-line at the last moment. Smith's heart was racing, he'd dreamt about scoring the night before. He was so close.[9]

Half-way through the first period Scotland won a corner kick, the ball was put into the penalty area and Waddell the Scottish forward smashed it past Sutcliffe in the England net. Smith's heart sank, he was playing well, he desperately wanted to win the championship. Goodison Park was silent save a few rowdy Scots. Sutcliffe complained he'd been

Above: The Abbots Bromley horn dance – a rural tradition that affirmed villager's hunting rights. (Public Domain)

Right: Stephen Smith's athletics trophy won in 1891 for Hazelslade Athletics Sports Club. When he was 17 he had just won his first football honour with Hednesford Town a month earlier. (Used with permission from Cannock Chase Museum)

The Perry Barr Enclosure – Villa v Albion – first day of the 1893/94 season. (Public Domain)

Stephen Smith's wages during his first season's contract in 1893/94 – before bonuses was £2 a week. (Brian Halls)

Stephen Smith was an FA Cup winner in 1895 helping Aston Villa avenge the cup defeat against bitter rivals West Bromwich Albion of two years earlier. The victory was a fitting tribute to the memory of Archie Hunter Villa's legendary captain who had inspired the club's only other cup triumph back in 1887. Smith is sat on the front row, far right, to the left his great friend and team-mate on the left flank Denny Hodgetts sits next to him. Second from the left on the front row is Smith's other close team-mate Charlie Athersmith. (Public domain)

ENGLISH TEAM.

N. L. JACKSON.   L. V. LODGE.   J. REID (Referee.)   J. W. SUTCLIFFE.   R. E. LYTHGOE
J. REYNOLDS.   J. HOLT.   E. NEEDHAM.   J. CRABTREE.   C. J. HUGHES.
W. J. BASSETT.   S. BLOOMER.   J. GOODALL.   R. C. GOSLING.   S. SMITH.

Smith taking his place in the England team for the decisive match in the 1895 International Championship. (Alamy stock photo. Copyright purchased)

Above: Smith won trophy after trophy at Aston Villa, this was his collection at the end of 1898/99 season. (Public domain)

Left: Steve's brother, Billy Smith in Portsmouth kit. (Ray Stubbington/ Rod Cowan)

Above: Portsmouth – Southern League Champions in 1902. Stephen is pictured sitting down third from the right (of those sitting down). (Pompey Historical Society Archive)

Right: Billy Smith's Southern League medal. Stephen claimed one in 1902. (Ray Stubbington/ Rod Cowan)

Above: Stephen Smith (second from the left, middle row) with the Portsmouth squad in 1905. To the left next to Steve is Dan Cunliffe, his team-mate at both Pompey and New Brompton. Brother Billy is fourth from the right on the middle row. (Pompey Historical Society Archive)

Left: Billy Smith during his service in The Great War. (Ray Stubbington/ Rod Cowan)

Right: Smith as a 49 year old turning out in a veterans match with ex England international footballers from his era in 1923. (Public Domain)

Below: Stephen Smith's final resting place in Benson churchyard. His burial plot is underneath the tree running parallel with the headstone furthest to the left in the picture that is very close to being underneath the hedge. Smith's burial place has no remaining headstone or memorial. (Owen Arthur)

Benson Parish Churchyard. Nearly every plot has a head stone or memorial except Stephen's. (Owen Arthur)

impeded and thankfully for England the referee agreed and disallowed the goal. Smith was sweating through effort and now with relief.

Moments later England were up the other end attacking once more. Smith ran up on the left hand side to support England centre forward Steve Bloomer who ran through on goal. Stephen needn't have bothered, England's number one striker smashed a low shot past the Scotland keeper and it was 1-0. The crowd erupted with joy and Smith rushed to congratulate Bloomer with a firm handshake.

A few minutes later and Smith picked up the ball, as ever on the left flank. He'd been sent careering down the wing thanks to a pass from Gosling, before knocking it back to the Eton man who fed Goodall and his shot forced the Scottish keeper McArthur to parry the ball. Unfortunately for Scotland the ball rebounded off Scottish back Gibson and dropped over the goal line into the net; 2-0 to England and Stephen laughed with glee at his team's good fortune. He'd been a key part of the second goal and adrenalin was coursing through his veins. He was playing for England, beating the Scots in the International Championship. He didn't think the people in the Slade Pub would believe it. Things couldn't get any better.

The English were now passing the ball about at will and Gosling was the next to go close but his shot was too weak. Gosling though craved creating chances most of all, the press men opined that, 'his one idea was to give Smith every chance'. Just before half-time, Gosling put the ball into the Scotland penalty box but it was cleared to the left hand edge of the area, Stephen, seeing he could get there first, burst towards the ball that was falling perfectly toward him and in particular his fabled left foot.

As the ball hit the ground in front of him, Smith smashed a shot with such pace and accuracy that the ball rose violently into the top corner of the net, so brutal was the shot from Smith 'that the Scottish custodian had no chance of intercepting it'. Stephen Smith had just scored for England. The crowd roared its approval, the pride Smith felt after winning the League title and reaching the Cup Final and then getting picked to play for England, and then playing for England, all paled into insignificance compared to scoring for England. Smith, undemonstrative, quiet, humble Stephen Smith felt as though his heart would burst in the delirium and the fog of his euphoria. His goal had surely secured the International Championship for England. The only rivals to England's crown vanquished and it was not yet half-time. Ecstasy. Pure ecstasy. England and Steve 'Titch Tich' Smith. The best in the world.

Smith's goal was described as a 'beautiful lofty shot, which travelled at such pace and so accurately' that the goal-keeper didn't stand a chance of stopping it. Smith would make a career out of thunderous, precision strikes such as this. The second half of the game was the most satisfying of his life. The game was won, the championship secured, a goal on his debut, Smith played without pressure and with the freedom that happens very rarely for a professional footballer, when the opposition are beaten and it's just a matter of how many more goals will be scored. This was just one of those occasions.

Gosling and Smith dovetailed on the left to devastating effect and Smith's crosses into the box caused havoc in the Scottish defence. Smith went close with 'a brilliant screw shot', as the English were 'running round the Scotchmen'. The English just couldn't finish their chances. In the end, the Scots somehow survived without conceding another goal. The outcome of the game had long been decided, but the praise for Stephen Smith's England debut was long and loud after he had walked off to the cheers and applause of the Goodison Park crowd. The Scottish pipers, so loud at the start of the match, did not play at the finish.

The *Athletic News* reported that 'the Scotchmen were outclassed' in a game where Smith was described as, 'a very speedy, brilliant man, and the point which he scored was undoubtedly the goal of the match'.

The *Birmingham Post* was very proud of this local hero who was doing the Midlands proud:

> Unquestionably the shining light on the English side was young Smith of the Aston Villa. His brilliant runs and clever centres placed him head and shoulders above any other forward on the field. Smith's shooting, too, whenever he had an opportunity, was of the most deadly character and the third goal he scored was an absolute beauty.

North of the border they were also impressed with Stephen:

> Smith is a little dandy, very fast on the ball and a good shot and centre. His third goal was a beauty. The goal which Smith secured at the end of the first-half was the finest of the three. It meant England won the Championship again.[10]

Smith and his teammates shook hands heartily in the dressing rooms and celebrated their success. It was England's sixth title putting them one ahead of Scotland in that regard. Of course they smoked and also began to drink ale rather than to hydrate as would be the case in the modern era. 'Baldy' Reynolds got Smith in a playful head-lock as the horseplay continued. Reynolds promised Smith a great night of celebration in Liverpool now they were once more champions. This was something that Stephen did not doubt. Jack Reynolds' drinking and carousing were legendary and Smith had not been at Villa long before Reynolds had been fined and dropped 'for going on a spree' in Birmingham City centre. Smith was elated at his footballing success but also worried at what 'Baldy' had in store for him.[11]

The Scottish team was rooming at the Compton Hotel and the Englishmen at the Alexandra, but professional football was and still is a small world and there were plans afoot for both sets of players to meet up once official engagements in Liverpool had been fulfilled. The players of both teams had to behave the night before the game as the two association officials were all in the same hotels as the footballers, even 'Baldy' Reynolds had a reasonably early night.[12]

That Saturday night the English team dined at a banquet in the Alexandra Hotel presided over by Lord Kinnaird the F.A.'s President. He regaled the team with stories of his playing days for Scotland due to his parent's heritage and of course his FA Cup Final victories for the Old Etonians and the Wanderers. The players were respectful about the old man's reminiscences but of course most players like Smith, Reynolds and Bloomer were working class men who were doing a job that helped them feed their families. Men like Kinnaird were a dying breed, men who had so much money and land that they could afford to play football for free and for fun. For Smith and company it was a job first and foremost.

The world was changing, amateur players at the top level of English football had all but died out by 1895, and was non-existent within twenty years of the Football League being created. Players nowadays are still generally working class, and players come from academies and comprehensive state schools not private schools as they did in the very beginning. Association Football was made by the upper classes and the public school system, but it has been embraced and taken over by the working man and that has not really changed since the late 1880s.

Working class and some middle-class children now grow up wanting to play for their local team while private and grammar school kids play Rugby, Cricket and Hockey. It is, however, a legitimate career path and there is a system in place to scout the best young talent. Back in 1895 working class kids grew up hoping to live past eight or nine years of age and get a job in a mill or a pit to help their family survive. Those that ended up playing football ended up in that job more by luck than judgement and needed to work other jobs as well. They weren't doing the job for the love of their local club either, or to fulfil their childhood dreams, they were doing it to survive.

People talk about money ruining the game in the modern era. That players only play for money, not like in the good old days. But in reality, players who played football as we know it, in a league format, cup matches and international games always played for money. The only men who played purely for the sport and not the money were the tremendously rich landed gentry from the 1860s and 70s. This is because they could afford to do it (although many men took secret payments or well-paid factory jobs if they were good players and would play for the local team usually run by the factory owner – it was known as 'shamateurism'). Those good old days were long gone by the 1890s, if they ever truly existed at all.

There was a great gathering of international players, fans, officials and pressmen at the Compton Hotel.[13] The players drank together and agreed England were the better team. The English celebrated their Championship, the Scots drowned their sorrows. The Bee Hotel was also hit by the teams as well. Reynolds and Smith were taken around Liverpool by their England teammates. Smith was in a haze of drunken, satisfied blurriness as Reynolds, despite being married, chased the local ladies. Stephen took the congratulations of colleagues and opponents as well as supporters all night. They returned to the Alexandra the next morning, as it was getting light once more, in a marvellously drunken haze, their wits befuddled in the springtime morning light. Smith's head was spinning as it hit the pillow. When he woke at midday to get the train home with the rest of the Midlanders in the England team, he realised that despite his sore head, he'd survived his night out with 'Baldy' Reynolds and that he was still a World Champion.

Smith's performances that season had, of course, also led to him being picked for another prestige match. The English Football League

XI versus the Scottish Football League XI. For a long period, the annual fixture between the English and Scottish leagues was only second in importance to the matches between the two national teams.

In 1895 Stephen got the call to play, yet another proud moment in his flourishing career and another example of the enhancement of his reputation across the country. The players from the best two leagues in the world did battle at Celtic Park. Pricing had been a major discussion point in the British media all season and the Celtic club were praised for its prices for this game. The *Scottish Referee* reported that, 'the sixpenny gate proved to be highly popular with the public (over 30,000 fans attended), who are not adverse to parting with the humble tanner but decidedly object to give more. The calls, moreover, on the public purse this season have already been pretty numerous, and our football managers should not forget that fact.'

People were now starting to get a little expendable income to go with more leisure time but if the price was not right, they voted with their feet. The match was also seen as comparable with the international played at Goodison a week earlier in terms of status when you consider descriptions such as, 'The Scottish League team came out onto the field with a much greater show of life than their confreres at Liverpool.' To all intents and purposes this was England v Scotland the rematch, or the away leg, if you will.

Having been thrashed in Liverpool, the Scots made six changes in personnel. Surprisingly the English line-up saw seven changes including Devey, Hodgetts and Athersmith joining Smith in the team. Both sides could have picked foreigners playing in their league but declined to in order that the match would be as close as possible to an England/Scotland international (plus the English had no need of any Scot who'd been thumped the previous week). Yet only four men kept their place from the Goodison game, two of those were 'Baldy' Reynolds and Stephen Smith. And once again 'England beat Scotland in the League International'.

If the Scots who still believed themselves superior to England in football despite the previous week's defeat were still in denial, a thrashing on home soil had them in no doubt who were the top players in world football in 1895. The start of the game, on a windy day, got spectators thinking perhaps the last match had been an aberration. The Scottish fans had only heard of Hodgetts in the English front line and perhaps the sprightly start by the Scots against a team with some unknowns gave the crowd confidence as they urged the Scotsmen on.[14]

After just four minutes Scotland were ahead, the Scotland player McMahon ran through the English defence and fed Oswald who put the Scots ahead. Celtic Park went wild, last week was definitely a fluke it seemed to the locals. Unfortunately for the Scots, within four minutes England were level in an end to end contest. Smith was left unmarked and he was sent clear down the left wing, 'and a clever pass to Devey gave that player an opportunity of scoring, of which he availed himself, the opening stages were as exciting as one could wish for'. Stephen and John Devey shook hands and Athersmith and Hodgetts trotted over to offer congratulations to their fellow club mates.

The rest of the game belonged to England and in particular, Liverpool striker Frank Becton who smashed home a hat-trick as England won the game 4-1. Hodgetts was the pick of the Villa players that day. Hodgetts 'single-handedly carried the ball quite fifty yards, winding up with a rattling shot that hit the crossbar'. The game did not hit the heights of the British Championship match of the previous week according to the reports, 'it was nothing like the exhibition at Liverpool last Saturday'. Nevertheless over a fortnight period the best English players, professional and amateur, had bested their Scots counterparts by an aggregate of 7-1.

Stephen Smith had played in both games, something only four players that year could claim. He had scored a screamer in the first game and claimed an assist in the second, but that did not preclude him from criticism after the second game, however mild it was, it was unexpected and Hodgetts told him to ignore it. The *Athletic News* stated that, 'Smith seems to have his off days, like most players. It must be taken into account (though) that the Scottish half-back division at Liverpool was a puny force compared with (today), and doubtless on that account the Aston Villa player had less scope for the display of his talents.' As a player though, you can only beat what is put in front of you and Smith and his teammates had beaten the best opponents the world could provide in 1895, two weeks running. Expectations are always high for the players at the top level of the game whatever the era. Stephen Smith knew that.

Chapter 11

'For Archie'

There was now only the small matter of the English Cup Final before Stephen Smith's stellar second season in professional football would be almost complete. Cup fever was high in the week before the event. The *Sportsman* newspaper offered the following services for those desperate to find out the score as quickly as possible:

> RESULTS! RESULTS! FOOTBALL ASSOCIATION CUP FINAL TIE. WEST BROMWICH V ASTON VILLA.
>
> SATURDAY APRIL 20, The result of the match telegraphed immediately upon conclusion for One Shilling. (Half-time, One Shilling extra.) Send name and address and enclose Postal Order to RESULTS DEPARTMENT,
>
> 'SPORTSMAN OFFICE', 139 AND 140 FLEET STREET.[1]

Even neutral fans were targeted by train companies confident the lure of an English Cup final could make them some money judging by adverts in the *Maidstone Advertiser*:

> LONDON, CHATHAM AND DOVER RAILWAY. CHEAP EXCURSION TO LONDON. FOOTBALL ASSOCIATION CUP FINAL TIE AT THE CRYSTAL PALACE. Fares there and back:- Third class including admission to Crystal Palace. 3 shillings.[2]

Back then tickets were sold to whoever would buy a job lot in advance, which included train companies, not like now when both sides would be given carefully considered allocations based on the strength of their average support. Back in 1895 it was basically first come, first serve.

The *Manchester Evening News* comments on the final shows what a household name Stephen and his colleagues had become:

> There is yet a good deal of interest, even in the North over tomorrow's tussle between Aston Villa and West Bromwich Albion, for both teams have been such frequent visitors to these parts that every real footballer knows the players almost as well as he does those in his own town.[3]

It can be seen then that even in 1895 footballers, whilst ostensibly local heroes, were fast becoming national ones although it was not really until the advent of television sets being a regular feature of all English households in the 1970s that they would become international stars. Interest in the English Cup was also evidenced from North of the border in the *Scottish Referee*. It explained Villa's cup final preparations and gave a match prediction:

> After their match with the Wolves on Monday, the Aston Villa players dined together at the clubhouse (in Albert Road, Aston by Aston Hall) and went to Holt Fleet, where they will remain in training until Friday. The men are all fit and well and are quietly confident of proving victorious on Saturday although there is none of the cocksureness which was such a feature of the last few days before the final in 1892. That unexpected 3 to 0 defeat by the Albion has not yet been forgotten and it will be a long time before the memory is effaced; but a victory on Saturday will do a great deal to make their supporters forgive and forget that great disappointment. And now for the winner. For once in a while I have an absolute certainty...ASTON VILLA WILL WIN THE ENGLISH CUP![4]

On the day of the game all roads from the West Midlands led to the Crystal Palace stadium. The Crystal Palace was a cast iron and plate glass structure originally built in Hyde Park, London, to house the Great Exhibition of 1851. The exhibition took place from 1 May to 15 October 1851, and more than 14,000 exhibitors from around the world gathered in its 990,000 square feet (92,000m^2) exhibition space to display examples of technology developed in the Industrial Revolution. Designed by Joseph Paxton, the Great Exhibition building was 1,851 feet (564m) long, with an interior height of 128 feet (39m). It was three times the size of St Paul's Cathedral. After the exhibition, the Palace was relocated to an area of South London known as Penge Common. It was rebuilt at the top of Penge Peak next to Sydenham Hill, an affluent suburb of large villas.[5]

The FA was resolute in its view that staging the cup final in London gave the event the national importance it deserved. It argued that supporters from the north and the midlands would much rather enjoy a day trip out in the capital than in another city. Whether this really was the case is a moot point. The 1895 final was moved to Crystal Palace park for the first time, meaning those arriving at Euston then faced another train ride across London. This supposed, pleasurable outing, must have felt like an everlasting rush hour commute. In his excellent book on football stadiums, Simon Inglis quotes former FA administrator William Pickford describing a typical cup final day: 'The Crystal Palace era was more than a venue for a football match; it took on the character of a picnic.'[6]

The *Penny Illustrated Paper*, described the new venue for the English Cup final as 'The grand Crystal Palace Athletic Arena'. It was described as a place worthy of such a grand occasion and sporting prestige. The paper went onto detail the following:

> The scene of the encounter is our old friend the Crystal Palace, which has risen with the times, and provided a wonderful arena for the decision of field games. For some time past, extensive alterations have been in progress, antiquated fountain basins being filled in and the space covered with turf. Londoners have to congratulate themselves upon the fact that one of the finest arenas in the world has been the result.
>
> Here, many, many thousands of spectators can be accommodated, and while there are a large number of high priced seats, the spectator who pays his humble shilling will also have a view. Some years ago now Crystal Palace owned a very fast cycling track and the view of the racing that could be obtained from the slopes was unrivalled. Something of

the kind is possible in connection with the new turf arena. The prospect of combining a day at Sydenham with the match should prove alluring to our country cousins, who will find very superior covered seating accomodation in case of rain although the weather prophets say that it is to be fine.[7]

Judging by the cup final preview in *Sporting Life* newspaper, Stephen Smith was now a player of national and international import. Smith and the rest of the line-up for the final stare back at you from the front cover of this newspaper. The portraits of Smith, Athersmith, Chatt, Devey, Hodgetts, Cowan, Reynolds, Russell, Welford, Spencer and Wilkes were sketched alongside the men from West Bromwich Albion. Stephen's family, his community, his colliery and, of course, his fiancee Susan must have been brimming with pride that a son of Staffordshire and resident of Hazel Slade had risen to such national prominence. It had been a meteoric rise and Smith was one match away from adding an English Cup medal to his league winners medal, his England cap and his feats of world domination that had seen Celtic and Rangers fall at club level and Scotland and the Scottish Football League reel in the face of his powers internationally, all at the tender age of 21.

The *Sporting Life* showed all due deference to Smith in their description of him stating that, 'Smith the Villa outside left got his cap against Scotland this season and a rare good man he is. One of the best of the season.' The paper followed that up by explaining that, 'he is fast, exceedingly tricky and his centres are famed. Fed and protected by Hodgetts' burly form he is a most dangerous player, and his shooting is very deadly.'

And so the big day had arrived – the showpiece event in the English calendar. Aston Villa versus West Bromwich Albion playing each other in the final for a third time. Football had changed dramatically since 1871 when the first FA Cup competition had been contested. The privileged amateurs representing public schools or public school clubs had been dominant in the years before professionalism, five times the cup had been won by the Wanderers (made up of public school old boys), twice by Old Etonians, once by Old Carthusians and once by Oxford University at a time when only the upper classes could afford to pay for college tuition. These organisations faded into obscurity as professional football clubs were formed in the 1870s and 1880s and by 1895 the game was now one for the masses and Blackburn Rovers had won the cup for a record equalling fifth time in 1891, West Brom had won it twice, Villa, Wolves, Notts County and Preston once each.[8]

The fans swelled the arena having taken specially arranged trains put on by the Football Association as part of the travel packages sold to supporters, from Euston to south London before making their way to the Crystal Palace grounds.[9] Thousands of Villa fans travelled down to London early on the morning of the game from Snow Hill and New Street stations just as they would today and many supporters from the midlands were present in the crowd. A bell was rung at three o'clock to get the pitch clear of all the pre-match marching bands that had been there for the supporters' amusement.[10] Amazingly fans were also allowed on the pitch before the game until of course, the bell tolled. Groundsmen of the twenty-first century would have been very upset at such a scene.[11]

Stephen Smith was feeling nervous in the dressing room underneath the main pavilion of the stadium. Each man had a little compartment to himself to keep him in a state of tranquility.[12] Smith's nervous peace and quiet was shattered by Denny Hodgetts bursting into Stephen's quarters. The legendary Villa hero told him it was going to be a great day, 'you'll win the cup for Archie, Steve,' he said. Smith bucked up as he realised what was at stake for his great friend. As the players made ready to enter the field of play, the captain John Devey addressed his players saying only one single phrase before leading them out, 'this is all for Archie lads, get it done'.

Full of emotion and with his zeal renewed, Smith filed out with his compatriots onto the pitch. The weather was warm and uncomfortable, and Hodgetts opined that it was 'a trifle warm'. Smith gasped as he took in the scenes around the stadium. The ground was packed to the rafters with supporters. The more affluent spectators in their silk hats, spotless ties, frock coats and evident grooming, took up positions in the reserved seats.[13] Aristocratic types in military uniforms and women dressed in the finest fashions of the day could be seen in the covered Pavilion on one side of the ground or the uncovered stand (behind which was a roller coaster ride called 'The Switchback') running alongside the opposite side of the pitch. There was also covered accommodation at one end of the pitch. From the press stand right around the enclosures the stadium was well filled with human activity and presence.

At the other end, behind the northern facing goal post was a huge sloping earthen enclosed embankment. It was packed full of over 20,000 supporters and was a truly imposing sight. Smith had never seen anything like it before in his life as he picked out muffler-throated Midlanders in the crowd with Aston Villa banners and rosettes. Stephen thought these people, with their rough features and cheaply tailored clothing must have been uncomfortable in that hill-like enclosure and had probably spent more than they could afford getting to London to support the Villa – to support him. He realised he wasn't just trying to win for Archie but also the people as well as his family and community back home who read about his exploits in the papers and today were seeing his portrait in the national press.

As a footballer it has always been the case that you are playing for so many more people than you ever thought was humanly possible. A footballer is never just playing for himself whether he likes it or not. It was on this day that Stephen Smith truly finally realised this; realised his responsibility to a community of people, most of whom he would never ever meet. But that didn't matter, they needed him to win so they could live and glory vicariously through his deeds and claim their local pride in their local team's victory. That is ultimately what football has always been about. Primeval, tribal victory over your nearest rivals.

The referee blew the whistle for the kick-off at half-past three and those on the concourses dispersed to their seats or viewing areas. Hodgetts, the man who had played in the 1887 and 1892 finals shouted, 'don't be complacent like in '92 lads!' The crowd roared its approval that the game was about to start before complete silence fell as Villa kicked off.[14]

There were 40,000 people inside the ground, the largest crowd that had ever witnessed a cup final.[15] Many of the players were quite overwhelmed by the sheer volume of people present. Instantly Villa were on the attack as fans and press men were still coming into the stadium, Hodgetts hit a beautiful diagonal ball with his left boot out to Athersmith on the right flank and he centred to Chatt.[16] Chatt was through on goal, bearing down on the keeper 'quite close to the touchline' and Chatt 'shot the ball towards Reader', the Albion keeper.[17]

The ball 'rebounded from Reader' and as John Devey 'rushing up, the ball caught his right knee and shot into the top right hand of the net, a big fluke as Devey made no effort for the ball'. The ball was in the net before anyone could comprehend what had happened. Chatt ran away celebrating as he thought the ball was over the line before Devey arrived, Smith and Athersmith thought Horton, the Albion defender, had scored an own goal as he was next to Devey as the ball bobbled home and he sank to his knees as it went in.[18] Devey also claimed the goal and other Villa players chased him to celebrate while Smith and Hodgetts approached the jubilant Chatt to celebrate. Stephen had no idea who had scored and frankly didn't care. Forty seconds in and his team were already ahead in the English Cup final.

The Villa fans roared with delight and threw their hats into the air as they got caught up in the moment. The noise was deafening and the crazed celebrations were vociferous and the spectators were still dancing with delight and yelling as the Villa players stopped congratulating Chatt and Devey. Smith thought more than one hat would have been lost by those in the contingent from Birmingham and the noise that greeted the goal made him feel like the fate of the nation depended on that successful shot Stephen had never been a part of anything like the 1895 cup final.

The game continued at a terrific pace as both sides blocked, and tackled and harried each other in a very tight game. Smith just couldn't get away from Albion's defenders who were paying him special attention. Hodgetts kept trying to protect his young team mate and set him up with the ball wherever possible, he did all he could to protect 'the little man', as he was termed all around the ground. Stephen was under constant pressure from defenders but 'Smith, of whom great things were expected, failed to make such an amount of headway, time after time Higgins robbed him'. Smith's new found reputation was making him a marked man, it was a compliment of sorts, but one Stephen felt he could do without. At various points in the game Hodgetts told Smith he just needed to keep going when it looked like his head might drop. Stephen was so relieved Denny Hodgetts was his friend.[19]

Bassett, the Albion forward, hit a shot just 'a foot or two wide of the post' as the Throstles looked to equalise. In reply, Charlie Athersmith went close for Villa before Smith finally got clear of his markers and he cleverly slipped through on goal to receive the ball and smash it into the net.[20] The Villa fans cheered themselves 'hoarse' and Smith felt elation like he'd never felt before when scoring a goal, seconds later he felt more deflated than ever after scoring a goal, the cheers 'died away at the provoking news that he had been given offside'. What a game he was having, Higgins and Perry dogging him at every turn and now this, one of the greatest moments in any player's career seemingly achieved and then chalked off. Smith though was a resilient character, and his side were still ahead, just.

Albion forced the issue with two corners that came to nothing as the game slowed slightly as half-time approached. Devey and Higgins clashed heads and a couple of doctors dashed onto the pitch from the pavilion. After a short stoppage the interval was reached 'and the usual breathing space was afforded'. Bassett hit the upright for Albion with Wilkes helpless in the Villa goal, before Higgins returned late to the fray to great cheers with his head bandaged and was much needed in defence as Villa pressed forward. Smith himself was trying his damnedest to score and hit a long range effort that was easily stopped by Reader. As the game wore on the pace slowed. Villa were comfortable but a one goal lead is always fragile and out of desperation Smith hit a weak shot straight at the keeper. He was struggling to make his mark and so was Hodgetts who also sent in a weak unsatisfactory effort on goal.[21]

Villa had evidently the larger following in the ground, but near the end of the game the neutrals were all rooting for Albion to equalise 'in the hope that the game would become more exciting'.[22] But the game was on a knife edge with West Bromwich pressing for an equaliser and Villa nervously playing on the break. They had not been able to get a decisive second goal when in the ascendency and now although they had one hand on the cup, it was not a firm grip by any means.

Billy Bassett, Albion's England international forward, was now causing Villa serious problems. Smith knew him well from playing with him in the recent destruction of Scotland in Liverpool and knew he was a man to be feared. Whenever he had the ball it invariably spelt danger for the opposition. Bassett 'raced off like a greyhound' through Villa's defence and it took Welford, Russell and Spencer to take the ball from him and clear the danger; this event was greeted with loud applause, no doubt with relief that the danger had been temporarily averted.

There was about ten minutes to go and Stephen Smith was getting increasingly anxious. He was so close to completing a dream season with England and Villa that he hoped would finish with the ending of Villa's barren run in the English cup and the gaining of his first ever cup winner's medal. He thought of the great Archie Hunter and how his death had hit the club hard. He thought of Denny who looked after him all the time and how he desperately wanted to help him honour his friend and also become the only Villa man to win the cup twice. And now he thought of Billy Bassett, the brilliant Albion winger who hadn't had a kick all game as Villa dominated, but now was threatening to equalise as Villa tired at the end of a long arduous season. Extra-time could kill them off, thought Stephen. Even after this match there were more fixtures to fulfil.

Smith felt tired, he looked at his teammates, they looked tired. They had put everything into this and had been the better team – until now. Albion's McLeod sent the ball forward with a punt, and suddenly Bassett was clear bearing down on Wilkes' goal in a foot race to reach the ball first. Wilkes rushed out of his goal to challenge Bassett, but as the two players tried to get the ball they slipped and the ball went past both of them and it bounced apologetically towards the goal line. It seemed as though Albion's hopes of an equaliser would come to pass and Villa's second victory in the English Challenge Cup tournament might not be achieved in 1895. An entire season's efforts thwarted by the old enemy and downright bad luck.

From nowhere, at the last second, Howard Spencer, Villa's young full back slid in and hacked the ball clear for a corner. The crowd went wild and it was becoming all too much for Smith. Large swathes of a tight, tactical game had seen his influence limited, especially as he always had two men on him whenever he received the ball.

Top players can often drift in and out of games and yet when it really matters they can come up with a crucial piece of play to take the game away from the opposition. And that is what Smith tried to do in the dying embers of the game. Hodgetts had a word with Stephen telling him to whip any ball he received into the box quickly. The idea being that Devey or Chatt might get on the end of it, or if nothing else, the ball would be kept at the other end of the pitch.

Smith only touched the ball once more in the match. With around five minutes to go he picked the ball up very wide on the left and did as he was told, hit a long, deep cross into the box. The ball missed all the Albion defenders but also Bob Chatt as he arrived in the box, it did however fall to Devey who from his 'grand opening' hit a fierce shot at goal and it hit the net, with the crowd cheering jubilantly.

The ball had hit the net, the crowd had celebrated a goal. But it was the side netting the ball had hit. No goal. Still only 1-0. After his disallowed goal and then this occurrence, Smith once more cursed his luck. The pressure was intense and Albion were not dead yet. Basset went down the left and lashed a cross 'across the goal mouth but he had outstripped all his companions and his efforts were to no avail'. At the other end as both sides tired, the game became an end to end free for all Chatt and Cowan were both denied by the Albion keeper, Reader.

Bassett ran at Villa again as the clock ticked down into the last minute of the ninety, Welford again got in his way and slashed the ball clear and into touch. Albion fans and neutrals alike 'hooted' with derision at what they saw as negative play but Welford and Villa could not have cared less. Russell and Welford laughed with each other at the crowd reaction, Russell had been on a 'special mission to watch Bassett' all game and he often crowded out the Albion player before Spencer and Welford then cleared the ball.[23]

A moment later the final whistle blew and the crowd roared its approval. Aston Villa had won the cup, 'the national trophy of English football'.[24] Smith embraced Hodgetts. Devey beamed at him. Athersmith hugged him shouting, 'we did it Tich!' The two teams exhaustedly shook hands and took the applause of the spectators. By now tears were in Denny Hodgetts' eyes and Smith himself was incredibly moved by what they had achieved in the memory of the club's greatest captain. Typically, Smith was not thinking about all he had achieved in the recent whirlwind months of his career. The quiet boy from Staffordshire who competed in the world of men had once more achieved greatness but was too busy thinking about Hunter, Hodgetts et al.

John Devey then shouted, 'c'mon lads!' and led the players up the steps to where the tall, thick-set frame and bearded face of Lord Kinnaird was waiting to present the trophy from the reserved area viewing gallery in the middle of the main covered stand. Devey took the trophy from the President of the Football Association who remembered Stephen from the England banquet after the Scotland game.[25] He presented Stephen with his gleaming gold medal in a thin square leather box. It made Smith's heart sing. It said 1895 in huge numbers at the top of the medal – 1895 had been one hell of a year for FA Cup winner, England international and International League champion, Stephen Smith.

Devey lifted the English Cup trophy before the London crowd who cheered with admiration and respect for the famous Villa captain and his team. Devey then made a victory speech, described in the *Athletic News* as a 'good speech'. Devey thanked the organisers, the Football Association, the spectators, commiserated with the Albion players and raised the cup once more and hollered, 'for Archie Hunter, God rest his soul!' Smith and Hodgetts hugged once more, the players slapped each other's backs, shook hands with each other as well as Grierson and the Committee members.

'Baldy' Reynolds started drumming up support amongst the players for the celebratory night-time excursion around London town and as the spectators thinned out in the ground, Smith and Hodgetts were the last players to leave the field. Denny turned to Stephen and said, 'we did it then Steve, didn't we?' Smith replied, 'Yes mate, Archie will be looking down on you with pride.' Hodgetts chuckled and said, 'Stop it, you will set me off again.' Smith laughed. He knew he had been part of something very great on that day at Crystal Palace in 1895.

The Aston Villa players remained in London all weekend and did not return to Birmingham until the 12.42 to Snow Hill Station arrived in the city on Monday, 22 April 1895. Stephen and his victorious comrades lost the rest of the weekend to wine, but mostly beer, women in the case of Jack Reynolds, and song in the hotels and entertainment establishments of the capital city. The players smoked and gambled with gay abandon and Hodgetts, Devey and Reynolds all agreed that it needed to be a last weekend of true bachelordom and revelry for Stephen with his wedding to Susan in the offing that June.[26]

Stephen was still rather the worse for wear as the train bound for Birmingham pulled in at Snow Hill. As the Great Western train pulled in the crowds that had gathered around the station were evident from the train's approach, Smith couldn't believe how many people were there on a Monday lunchtime instead of being at work! He looked out of the carriage windows to see a large body of police guarding the entrances to Snow Hill. Only prominent members of the football club were allowed on the platform as far as Stephen could see from inside the train. He could also see and hear a band had arrived and was playing, 'See the Conquering Hero Comes'.[27]

The scenes were raucous as Devey led the players out onto the platform, trophy in hand, to shake hands with Villa's President Joseph Ansell and Secretary George Ramsay with whom all the players shook hands. It was impossible for Stephen to concentrate fully on these pleasantries or even hear himself think as supporters held back by the Police cheered loud enough to shake the rafters and nearly lift the roof off the station. A shiver went down his spine. The crowd was so happy, the cheers so loud. Their victory meant so much to the people, more than Smith thought possible.

As the team made its way outside the station there must have been 6,000 or 7,000 people in Livery Street shouting like mad and stopping the traffic, and vociferous cheering greeted the players as the trophy was raised by Devey to the crowd. The team entered a charabanc decorated with the Villa colours and, accompanied in a second vehicle by the band of musicians, the players wended their way around the principal streets of Birmingham on the way to the club house in Aston on Albert Road next to the Grammar school. A huge crowd of cheering supporters followed them wherever they went. The players thought it was hilarious seeing grown men chase after them begging to touch the cup. Wherever they went the streets were lined with cheering supporters. Smith was exhilarated by it all and he felt immense pride that he had helped people of Birmingham feel as happy and proud as he was, if not more.

Despite being still terribly hung-over, Stephen and his colleagues now had to keep down a huge celebratory dinner put on by the club President. In the clubhouse sitting around the top end of a huge dining table, were all the great and good of the club's committee and leadership. The President sat with Rinder, Cooper, Whitehouse, William McGregor, Lees and vice-president Jones as well as Secretary Ramsay and Grierson the trainer. The playing squad sat around the middle and bottom end of the table and, having finished their meal, respectfully stopped their conversations as the President rose to give his end of season speech.

Joseph Ansell proposed a toast to 'the team!' with which everyone joined in heartily. He thanked the players for their efforts and was so proud of their achievement in bringing back the cup. He then reminded the players of his promise to award them a guinea piece each if they won the cup; this was met with great approval from the players for it was a healthy bonus, what most working men in England would only get after six days work in a week. Stephen, with wedding costs to consider and a new house to pay for, was absolutely chuffed with this news.

Ansell then praised all the players before singling out John Devey for his play and leadership. This brought a resounding 'hear, hear' from the players for a captain, Steve and company would do anything for. Devey was toasted with champagne by everyone in the room as Stephen's head started to throb as more alcohol went into his body.

John Devey stood up as the pressmen present scribbled more notes in their pads and waited for a quote from the great man himself. He politely thanked the President for his bonus, the Committee for their input and care and said he could not really find the words he needed to express how much pleasure he felt that the team had won the English cup again at long last. He could not be more proud of his team who did everything they could for the cause and made his job as captain an easy one. 'Good old Jack,' shouted Denny Hodgetts as loud applause rang out from the players.

The players then took a back seat as the President and Committee toasted each other for good politics. But there was still time, as the night became morning, for the tactics of Grierson to be toasted as well as the efforts of George Russell for stopping Billy Bassett in the final. Smith could barely stand when the final toast was made to him and all the other Villa players who had played for their country that year and as William McGregor banged on about beating Albion again in the Birmingham Senior Cup, the players stumbled out into the dawn-drenched early morning.

Smith headed for Aston station and the northerly route home to the bosom of his proud family. He thought only of his tiny, delicate fiancée and showing her his cup medal. He would also go to the Slade pub with his father and brothers, but he doubted whether he would drink anything alcoholic ever again. Besides, his next big match would be his wedding and he could ill afford to get entangled in the antics of Reynolds, Athersmith and Hodgetts now that he would soon be a married man.

Stephen Smith had done it all in his first two years as a professional footballer. The FA Cup had topped off an amazing rise to the top of the ranks of world football.

The *Athletic News* said of Smith two days after the cup final that:

> Smith, who comes from Hednesford, has been with the Villa two seasons, (came into) the League team last year, and now he has secured his Scotch Cap. He was little thought of outside the midlands until the semi-final of the English Cup, but his display against Sunderland went a long way to gaining his place in the Scotch team.

Smith then was now a well-known national sporting figure. His wedding would even be reported in the newspapers, although in a much more low key way than modern footballers' nuptials are presented. On 3 June, 1895, Stephen waited outside St Peter's Church in Hednesford for Susan Blastock to arrive. He stood in his black suit and white shirt with black tie next to his best man, younger brother William and father Stephen Senior. The Reverend Collett opened the doors to the church and let the men in as guests from both sides of the family began to arrive. After the ceremony and reception, he took his bride to bed above the Slade Pub in a special honeymoon suite laid out in the guest quarters by Susan's family. Stephen made love to his new wife for the very first time. He had never been happier, 1895 had been the greatest year of his life.

The local paper the *Lichfield Mercury* documented the events of the Smith's wedding, the report helps show how far Smith had come in terms of invading the national consciousness:

The Nuptials of a well-known football player

The marriage of Mr Stephen Smith and Miss Blastock, both natives of Hazel Slade, Hednesford took place in St. Peter's Church. The ceremony, which was performed by the Rev. W. Collett, was witnessed by a number of residents who are naturally proud of the success the bridegroom has achieved on the football field and who only two seasons played with the Hednesford Town's team. Mr Smith (Steve Smith to his many admirers) is the well known outside left of the Aston Villa Football Team and during the past season won golden opinions in the International League.

It was proof positive that as the new couple moved into a new terraced house in Chapel Street, Hazel Slade, Stephen Smith had become a minor celebrity in his own community, admired by many locally and nationally for his footballing prowess and amazing achievements in such a short period of time. It was to be only the beginning.

Chapter 12

William Smith

Despite winning an FA Cup, Steve Smith still had to work in the colliery during the summer months. This was common amongst most footballers, John Devey played cricket and George Russell part of the 1895 cup winning team left for Glasgow Rangers 'to combine work at his trade as a tailor with football'.[1] Smith's first job was still seen to be a miner and Russell's, a tailor. Footballers may have been professional but it was not always clear during these years which job was their main one and which one supplemented their primary wages. Only the very top players were paid more for football than their other, usually, manual job or trade.

The part-time miner joined up with his team-mates once more in the summer of 1895. The *Scottish Referee* gloried in the club during the pre-season period and on the eve of the campaign in late August wrote:

> The Aston Villa practice matches continue to draw large crowds to the Perry Barr enclosure twice weekly to see the 'Champions' perform. Where can you find better men in England than Athersmith, Cowan, Devey, Campbell, Steve Smith and Dennis Hodgetts? The last-named has been playing brilliantly in all the practice games and is sure of a place in the eleven once again.

Steve Smith, described as one of the best players in England, was ready for the new season, and once again would have his closest team-mate by his side. The pressure would be more intense than ever on Stephen and his colleagues, with the new additions to the squad. The *Athletic News* described Villa as 'a most expensive and supposed to be a very "class" team, and it goes without saying that if they fail it will not be because they have not the talent, money, or the opportunities'. Villa were the best team in the world, they were expected to win the title with ease. If not, questions would be asked, and players' futures and livelihoods would be on the line.

Villa romped to the title in the 1895/96 season and despite a serious injury in that year Smith was a League Champion for a second time. Cartilage injuries in the twenty-first century are relatively easy to recover from nowadays but back in 1895 treatments available were limited. The cartilage injury did not heal by itself and in March, Smith was sent to Manchester for a surgical procedure to cure his problem. It was a success, but the operation was not effective enough to get him back on the pitch before the end of the season.[2] Smith had more than played his part in Villa's second title victory, but he had to watch his team's procession to the title from the stands.

He had claimed another league medal but that was tempered by his injury which had also stopped him adding to his England cap. He had also been unable to supplement his football wages by returning to the colliery due to his lameness. He was such a valuable commodity in the footballing world by this time however that Villa had been happy to pay for surgical procedures to get him back to full fitness and more than happy to offer him a new contract for the 1896/7 season, one that would be the most momentous in the club's history. And on top of all this 1896, in Hazel Slade his first son was born, named Stephen Charles Smith Junior – a greater prize to Smith than any he had or would win on the football pitch.

At the end of the season, when the title was being celebrated, there were tears in the eyes of many players, including Smith, when it was confirmed Denny Hodgetts would not get a new contract. It all felt very much like the end of an era for Stephen Smith, but the legend would rise again. Denny went on to become a publican, and in 1930 was elected Aston Villa's vice-president, a position he held until his death, aged 81, in March 1945.

Smith's injury gave him time to take stock of life in the summer of 1896. He now had two Football League Championship medals, an FA Cup winner's medal, an England cap, a Football League cap, he'd got married and had his first child all by the age of 22. Things felt like they were going in slow motion compared to the previous three years. But they were to soon speed up.

His younger brother, William Smith, was now 20 years of age and had been earning rave reviews for Willenhall Town. In May of that year

Stephen and his father had been present in his father's house in Hazel Slade when William signed his professional forms and first contract with Wolverhampton Wanderers, he too was an outside left like his brother. He was listed in the *Birmingham Mail* on Thursday, 7 May 1896 as one 'of the following players signed on for next season with Wolverhampton Wanderers'.

Billy and Stephen were goaded by their father saying he could not wait to see how they would cope playing against each other in First Division. The Smith family would have two sons in the topflight of English football in 1896, what a sporting brood the Smiths were turning out to be. Billy expected to play only a few games in his first season as a professional footballer, but with six defeats and just two wins in their first ten games Wolves thrust William Smith into the first team on 21 November 1896, at home to Burnley.

Wolves won 2-0 and Smith was described as 'constantly hovering around the Burnley goal and promising additional scores'.[3] A 'splendid centre' from Smith led to Wolves getting the second through Nicholls. His debut was well received in the press as well, Billy being described as 'a rattling good wing, and ought not on this display to be moved, being speedy and clever and knowing how to shoot'.

Billy would not lose his place for the rest of the season scoring 5 goals in 20 appearances in a successful first season in professional football.[4] Wolves finished comfortably in midtable in tenth place out of 16 teams and just three points off the top six. A year later in the 1897/98 season, Wolves finished above Villa and the bragging rights went to William in the Smith household as Wolves ended the season in third place whilst Villa finished sixth. William played twenty-three times scoring 8 goals in what was by far his most successful season in old gold. The following season he managed to play just 14 times in a 34 game season scoring 3 goals.

In three seasons in the top flight with Wolverhampton Wanderers, Billy Smith made 57 league appearances, scoring 16 goals. In that three season period, Steve Smith's Aston Villa played Billy Smith's Wolves six times. Villa won twice, Wolves twice and there were two draws, thus honours were even when the two brothers' clubs faced each other.

At the start of the 1896/7 season, while William Smith was waiting patiently until Wolves' eleventh game of the season to make his debut, his brother Stephen was slowly recuperating from ligament injury that had curtailed his previous season. He would have to wait until Villa's tenth game of the season himself in order to pull his boots back on once more. John Cowan who had made the left wing berth his own during Smith's absence was injured a week previously and this occurrence finally let Smith back in. But with typical Stephen Smith timing he returned with a big game performance.[5]

Villa won comfortably at Stoke in front of 8,000 fans in the Potteries, Smith securing the win by passing the ball into the net through the goal keeper's legs.[6] Smith had not played for ten months and watched himself being usurped by John Cowan on the left flank, while he sat idly by as Aston Villa's dominance of English football continued unabated but at the same time passing him by. But now he was back. Smith and his team drew this comment from the *Athletic News* after their performance, 'It is fully early to talk of champions, but I believe the veritable top-sawyers of the League for 1896/97 were seen at the Victoria grounds on Saturday.'

Smith had played well enough to hold his place for some time.[7] Specifically, Smith played the next eighteen matches in a row scoring four goals as Villa marched towards the top of the league and the English Cup quarter finals.[8] Back in October 1896, however, having beaten Stoke, Villa were in third place one point off the top spot held by Bolton Wanderers.

When the two clubs met on Boxing Day 1896, Villa were clear at the top whilst Wolves were languishing fourth from bottom.[9] The bravado of his siblings had totally subsided, and Steve and William had not seen each other over Christmas as both men had played for their clubs on Christmas Day. They would see each other on Boxing Day – on the pitch.

A heavy downpour in the morning had apparently adversely affected the size of the crowd, but that said, 18,000 saw Villa start the game strongly. The game was scheduled at 11am so that spectators could take in the horse racing at nearby Dunstall Park in the afternoon. Stephen and William were close, but were also competitive sportsmen who wanted to win, and get their win bonuses. That meant getting one over on each other. They gave each other a brief handshake and nod just before the kick-off. But then it was time for business. They were enemies trying to claim the bragging rights for the Black Country and Birmingham.

Villa started strongly, 'the ground was on the heavy side, and the ball was greasy and the pace, as set by the visitors was a cracker and the excursions of Captain Devey and his merry men to the terrace end were frequent and dangerous'. Wheldon the new Villa centre-forward forced the Wolves keeper into three saves, Reynolds hit a shot just over the bar, it seemed like, 'Villa meant business of the 18 carat order'.[10]

Stephen was getting lots of the ball, but not as much as Charlie Athersmith who was praised for his crosses, he produced 'a trio of real beasties' early on and Stephen felt sorry for his brother as his esteemed team-mate kept leaving William trailing in his wake. Steve had seen it all before, William unfortunately hadn't. Villa's attacks eventually broke through the Wolves rearguard. Chatt hit a shot that deflected a Wolves defender's leg from long range and Villa led. The 'contingent from the hardware capital went wild as the rest of the ground fell silent'. Steve was elated but avoided William's sullen gaze as the ball was returned for the kick off.

Wolves attacked straight away striking forward as Villa's complacency saw them miss challenges and Steve looked on in horror as Jay Tonks, who he should have been marking, waltzed through the Villa defence and squared for William in the six yard box. Steve's heart sank as he realised what was about to happen and the grief he would get when he got home.

The ball fell for William who swung his left boot. He was about to score against his brother's team, the League Champions. But somehow, he missed his kick, the ball went past him and was cleared. Villa survived and Steve was relieved and sorry for his brother at the same time. The mixture of emotions confused him. The miss confused the reporter too who wrote that, 'there ought to have been an equalisation of the scores almost immediately, but Smith missed his kick when he had no one but Whitehouse to beat, the leather having been put grandly across by Tonks'.

What on earth will I say about that miss to Billy, thought Stephen in the moments after it had happened. But that would have to wait, Athersmith was still beating Billy down the right flank for Villa. Another one of Athersmith's centres was put through his own net by Wood, the Wolves back, and Villa were now two up inside the first half an hour of the game.

Stephen Smith was going to get the family bragging rights when they headed home to celebrate Christmas belatedly that evening. The worry was now how much of a humiliation for Billy the score line was going to be. But this was the top division of the Football League, Steve and his teammates were expected by the committee, the fans, their city and even the nation to win the title and win well, even if that meant upsetting members of your own family.

Villa were overrunning Billy and his team mates on Wolves' left flank, Campbell and Athersmith on the right wing both hit the woodwork. The game was heading towards half-time with Villa comfortably in the ascendancy, but they slackened off as they had after scoring the first goal and Malpass the Wolves forward hit a shot into the top corner from range to half the deficit just before the players headed to the changing rooms.

Villa began the second half poorly and Wolves were 'more than holding their own'. Tonks and Lyden then both went close for Wolves and it seemed like Steve just couldn't get hold of the ball anymore and neither could Athersmith who had dominated proceedings. Villa though were the superior team and Cowan and Reynolds made the Wolves keeper make fine saves before Wheldon hit the post, the third time Villa had done that in the match.

In the final few minutes, Wolves had possession and pressure but could not make chances with it, and then suddenly Villa broke clear. Stephen Smith was sent clear down the right flank and bore down on goal, no one was near him and glory beckoned. The game would be sealed and siblings silenced. Steve only had Tennant in goal to beat as the Wolves defenders tried in vain to catch him. Smith shot for goal and his shot hit the keeper but bounced straight to 'Baldy' Reynolds who also amazingly hit the now prone keeper and the chance went awry.

Much to their father's and older brother Charles' amusement both Smith brothers had missed sitters. Ammunition for the Christmas dinner table had been noted and stored away for the next family footballing debate. William finally managed to get the ball in an attacking situation in the final minute of the game. He went past full back Spencer in the penalty area and was brought down with a challenge. Billy thought he'd won a penalty, so did Steve, but just like the previous year the referee gave Villa the benefit of the doubt with a controversial decision. As reported, 'there were loud calls for a penalty'.

The referee waved away the home side's penalty claims and as a result was faced with heavy criticism from the black country supporters.[11] The final whistle blew, and William continued to argue with the referee, as did many of his colleagues. Stephen left him to it. He'd done what he'd needed to do and was happy to let his younger, louder brother let off steam before their family Christmas together.

It was a quiet train journey back to Hednesford station as the four Smith men kept their thoughts mostly to themselves, such was the controversial nature of the game and the fact neither brother had managed to miss gilt-edged opportunities to score that they both should have taken. The rest of the family lay in wait back at Chapel Street in Hazel Slade. Steve knew that Susan and his mother would countenance no footballing talk at the table and so that was the end of it.

Billy was glum but felt better after reading the match report in the paper the next day. It stated that 'every man on the winning side played well' but that, 'W. Smith also did well' and 'a draw would have afforded an accurate representation of the play'. Stephen was just relieved it was all over and thankful his team had won. The pressure on him and his fellow squad members was intense. But Stephen was confident that another trophy-laden season was on the cards, as the *Athletic News* explained Villa 'would require a lot of catching'.

Chapter 13

Celebrity, Superstar, 'Double Winner'

As winter turned to spring Villa marched further and further clear of their rivals at the top of the table once more. There was even a trip to the Grand Theatre in Blackpool before a cup quarter-final away at Preston. Stephen dug out his club suit and tie as he and the squad were invited to attend a performance at the one of most prestigious theatres in the land. Stephen Page details Stephen Smith's status in Victorian society in 1897:

> Thursday evening saw an example of how Aston Villa players enjoyed celebrity status throughout the country. The manager of the Grand Theatre invited the team to watch a performance of *The Geisha* – and ensured the local press and any potential ticket purchasers knew that the world-famous football club's star names would be in attendance. The 'superstars' then spent their last day in Blackpool taking more seafront walks and discussing the slaughter of the Preston lambs.

Unfortunately, after the victory over Preston in the quarter-finals Stephen lost his place in the side after being bed ridden with influenza for a number of weeks. It cost him a place in the FA Cup final that year. The day before the cup final Villa were as good as champions again.

Preston in fifth place could in theory finish above Villa by winning the six games they had left. That would leave them with 41 points but they would need to improve their goal average dramatically. Derby could still get to 42 points, so Villa needed 43 points to regain their title, with three games to spare providing Derby and Preston won all their games, they already had 41.

On the evening of 3 April 1897, Stephen Smith accepted what he already knew in his heart of hearts. He was not going to be picked for the FA Cup final. Villa had sent a mixed bag of first teamers and reserves to play in a warm-up friendly at Bristol Rovers. Steve was made to play in it but then so was John Cowan as well as Wheldon and Campbell. Villa still won 5-0 and Smith scored two and made one other. But he had been asked to play right wing, Cowan got to play left. He felt like he was being asked to make up the numbers and was only playing because Charlie Athersmith was on England duty. What happened in that game was of little consequence to management in a game that was just a fitness exercise.

Devey, Reynolds and Athersmith patted him on the shoulder in consolation as they left their base and made their way to the Crystal Palace stadium on Cup Final day. Smith sat forlornly in the main stand with his other unpicked teammates and took in the scene.

Smith watched spectators enter the arena:

> There was a record number of them, 65,891 people packed the stands. At that time they represented the largest Cup Final crowd ever and possibly the biggest attendance at any football match played anywhere in the world. The stands appeared to fill slowly, but by three o'clock the ground was bursting at the seams. Everton exited the pavilion first to be greeted by an incredible roar. The Brummie voices showed Crystal Palace that they too could belt out their support as the Villa hit the field. In the Pavilion stand, former Prime Minister Lord Rosebery and his two sons were joined by Lord Kinnaird.[1]

Kinnaird remembered Smith from his England exploits and nodded towards him, expressing surprise Steve wasn't playing. Smith merely smiled politely and shrugged his shoulders apologetically. John Devey won the toss and chose to defend the north-east goal with the declining sun in the Villa players' faces. Whatever Stephen's personal disappointment, he knew that he was the part of a squad that was close to achieving immortality and with it £34 in winnings. No one he knew back in Hazel Slade would have ever even dreamed of getting close to that sort of money. For Smith, who had done much in the earlier rounds to get Villa to the precipice of glory, financial security for him and his entire extended family was within touching distance.

The game that unfolded in front of him, one of the greatest cup finals of all time, would have him sweating and biting his nails until the very last second. Villa won an end-to-end contest 3-2. As referee John Lewis blew the final whistle, Smith and the other squad members embraced in the stands and the crowd surged on to the pitch and carried their heroes shoulder high to the pavilion. John Devey walked up the steps to be greeted by Lord Rosebery and unlike today there was no swift handshake and mumble of congratulations. The noble Lord delivered a long speech praising both teams before he handed the trophy to John Devey who returned thanks on behalf of Aston Villa and proudly held aloft the cup to the cheers of the deliriously happy Villa supporters.

Steve Smith cheered as loudly as any fan from his vantage point in the pavilion. Yes, he wanted to play, but his job was to help this club be successful and yet again they had done that. He would be rewarded for the part he had played throughout the season accordingly. He was a professional and as long as he was remunerated fairly by his employers he would always do as they saw fit. He was a quiet and modest man, a team player, and enjoyed others' success as much as his own.

After the stadium had emptied, about an hour after the final whistle, Steve and his teammates partied through the night in Upper Norwood. And what a night it was. A telegram came into the Villa director's possession explaining that the last team that could stop Villa winning the league, Derby, had lost at Bury. With three games remaining, Villa were confirmed as champions. More than that, they had become the first – and only – club to win the FA Cup and League title on the same day. The celebrations at Upper Norwood were described as 'the party of the year'. By the next morning Steve and his teammates couldn't remember their own names, but for Steve, the party at Norwood was about to be dwarfed by the celebrations held on Villa's return to Brum.

The players staggered slowly on to the train for players and officials at ten past ten on the morning of Monday, 12 April. Stephen and his teammates were still feeling very fuzzy around the edges as the train arrived around one o'clock at Birmingham New Street Station. Just as in 1895, Stephen witnessed the totally chaotic scenes, from the window of his train carriage with a mixture of happiness, amusement and confusion. The city's pride in its football club never ceased to amaze him:

> By the time the train was due in, the City Centre was at a standstill. The Birmingham Constabulary attempted to keep the platform clear but hundreds of fans swamped

New Street Station taking up every available vantage point. A massive cheer went up along with numerous hats as the train pulled into sight. A band struck up a rendition of 'See the Conquering Hero Comes' as the claret and blue covered carriages screeched to a halt by the Queen Street exit. The committee and wives had to retreat back to their retreat back to their carriage from where Fred Rinder held aloft the English Cup to deafening cheers.

He had finished the 1896/7 season, on top of the world once more and entered history as one of those rarest of footballing specimens, a 'Double Winner'.

Chapter 14

Champion Again

From a personal perspective 1897 had been the year when Steve Smith had become well enough off to finally not need to supplement his income by mining. As well as the generous bonuses from winning league and cup, all the first team players had been awarded a wage of £4 per week all year round, then a very generous payment in football, most players needed alternative employment in the summer months.[1] Stephen had already achieved so much in his first four years as a professional footballer but coming from such humble beginnings, for him to no longer have to work two jobs to secure the short and medium-term financial future of his family was an almost incomprehensible triumph, when you consider how the social class he had come from was faring at this time.

The procession of league titles and cup wins didn't continue during the 1897/98 season. Smith played in both defeats to Derby in late January 1898 in League and Cup that saw Villa's defence of the English Cup over at the first hurdle and the club way off the pace in the title race. Aston Villa faded alarmingly in the defence of their title to finish in sixth place, eleven points behind champions Sheffield United. Villa's problems had been a lot to do with the departures of Reynolds and Campbell, who had been such vital cogs in the previous seasons.[2]

While Villa's form that season had been inconsistent, Smith's had been good enough to gain a second Football League XI cap against the Scottish League. He didn't have to travel too far to join up with the Football League squad that would take on the Scottish League as the match was to take place at Villa Park. As explained previously, this game was ranked on a par with the England vs Scotland international. To be picked against the Scots was always a great honour, whether in the International or League representative contest.

The League contest was always a week after the international clash. After the first few Inter-League matches, the two Leagues had a gentleman's agreement to only pick players who were from the country in which the league was situated. Scots were not selected for the Football League again until the 1960s, by which time the match was declining in importance.[3] Smith had a good record against the Scots thanks to his two victories against them in the international and in the inter-league meetings. He couldn't wait to play against them again.

Despite England winning the international title in 1898, it had been their first title since Smith inspired them to victory in 1895. Scotland had nine championship titles to England's eight, including shared crowns. The previous year in 1897, the Scottish Football League had thumped their English counterparts 3-0 at Ibrox. This game was truly up there in terms of importance to the footballers of the Victorian age and Smith was as proud as the next man to be involved.

In the dressing room he once again rubbed shoulders with the stars of the Victorian game. Smith himself was far too modest and quiet in character to see himself as a star, but he was, otherwise he wouldn't have been picked. In goal for the English was William Foulke who had just won the League title with Sheffield United. In 1895 Foulke only weighed 12st 10lb but over the next few years he put on a lot of weight and was nicknamed Fatty or Colossus by the fans. Foulke was 6ft 2ins tall. At the time the average height for an adult male was only 5ft 5ins and therefore he towered over most of the players.

Steve was dwarfed by Foulke and a little bit intimidated by him until he started to chat to all and sundry as they changed for the match. Smith had a chuckle when Foulkes quipped, 'these Scots will give me some stick today, but I don't mind what they call me as long as they don't call me late for my lunch'.[4] The English team roared with laughter at this and many other jokes from the larger-than-life character. He was great for morale and eased the tension before they took on the Scots.

'Aye up Tich,' said a voice behind Stephen as he changed into his football kit. Smith recognised the Potteries accent immediately; it was Billy Beats, the great Wolves striker and teammate of his brother William. Beats was a legend in Wolverhampton, he had joined two years ago from Port Vale in his native North Staffordshire and had been top scorer in both seasons and fired Wolves to the 1896 Cup final. It was from Beats that Steve would ascertain that his brother William was getting a rough ride from some of the more critical Wolves supporters, but that he was sticking at it and trying to win them over.[5] Billy wasn't doing too badly, having scored 8 times in 23 league games as the Wanderers finished third in 1897/98.

Steve could hear the crowd roar from inside the changing rooms as the referee told the players to get ready to leave their inner sanctums. The *Sheffield Daily Telegraph* explained the high-status nature of the fixture stating that, 'the match which the English League thought fit to allot to the ground of Aston Villa Club was a big one in that it brought together what was generally looked upon as the cream of players in English and Scottish Leagues, and as such proved a very attractive fixture'. Despite the fact that the early rainstorms that day petered out, there was a chill wind in the air that blew across the pitch as the players entered the field and continued throughout the game.

Despite the damp weather in the morning leading to a slippery pitch on which to play, the rains had not dampened the enthusiasm of the crowd, with 20,000 fans in attendance. It was the type of attendance that was regularly gathering at Villa Park and doubtless many of the locals had come to shout for Charlie Athersmith, Fred Wheldon and Steve, three of their own. Ernest Needham, whom Steve had played with for England twice in 1895, was the skipper and having won the toss made the Scots face the wind.

The English started well, and so did Stephen, desperate to impress both his home supporters and English selectors. Smith danced down the left and fed Wheldon but his shot went just wide. Stephen felt good; that first run at the Scottish defence had left him full of confidence.

The Scots then attacked twice in quick succession and Foulkes made two brilliant stops to keep the scores level. Then the English, 'besieged their opponent's goal' and Athersmith, Needham and Morren all went close. But then disaster struck for the English, and the Scots caught their opponents on the break and Hamilton put through on the right silenced the crowd scoring, 'the first goal for Scotland with a beautiful shot, the ball passing over Foulke's head' into the net.

Stephen was very disappointed. It had all been going so well, but things change very quickly in football, sometimes extremely quickly. From the restart the ball was sent straight to Charlie Athersmith who whipped in a ball that Wheldon smashed towards goal. The Scottish keeper, Dickie, could only parry the ball to Billy Beats who tapped in the equaliser. Smith congratulated all the players involved in a goal made

Champion Again

totally by men from the Midlands. Smith was happy too. It had seemed at one point all his team's good work would come to nought.

The Scots came again. Needham headed a Scottish attempt off the line from underneath his own crossbar. The English had been caught cold and had only just got away with it. Once they had steadied themselves the Football League went on the attack. The problem was the Englishmen were very wasteful. Beats missed from yards out, Wheldon had a fizzing shot tipped just wide and the ball just would not go in the Scottish net.

Just before half-time there was a moment of controversy that had Foulkes in the English goal apoplectic with rage. Scottish striker Hamilton bundled over Thickett in the English defence and went through on goal, Foulkes stopped, expecting the referee to blow his whistle, but he didn't and Hamilton smashed home his and his side's second. The giant Foulkes stood over the referee and questioned the decision but to no avail. Foulkes was still complaining about the goal at half-time but no one had the gumption to question why the giant keeper hadn't played to the whistle. After the way he had harangued the referee it didn't seem a wise policy.

The English were under the pump at the start of the second half with McPherson and Hamilton missing good opportunities. Thickett of England was constantly mentioned in the match reports due to the defensive work he was forced to do as the Scots pressed. After Beats and Wheldon both went close again, 'further pressure on the home goal followed and Foulkes was again called upon to save from Hamilton'.[6]

As the game reached its final quarter, Steve Smith was feeling increasingly frustrated as the Scottish domination continued and he was starved of any possession. In the end he came in field and claimed the ball himself before setting off down the left flank with his home crowd cheering him on. He sped clear of the Scottish defence and was about to shoot when his namesake Nicol Smith managed to block him and the chance was gone. Smith was crestfallen; it had been three years since his last call up and he had been desperate to make his mark again at this level but to no avail.

In truth the Scots were much better on the day and there was only one further incident of note. Foulkes had continued to air his thoughts on Hamilton's second goal in the second half's final moments. This led to Hamilton 'directing a piece of bad temper' towards Foulkes who did not take kindly to this and players and supporters watched aghast as the two players squared up to each other. Unsporting behaviour on the football field was not uncommon even in an era perceived as a bastion of fair play in the game's history.

Eventually the players were separated 'though it led to a stoppage until peace was restored'. Smith thought Hamilton was very brave to go toe to toe with the famous William 'Fatty' Foulkes; he wasn't sure he would do the same. From this point to the end the Scotsmen did all the pressing, and when the whistle blew were deserved winners. Smith trudged off forlorn as the Scots took the applause of the Villa Park crowd. He was disappointed his winning run against Scotland was over. 'Cheer up mate,' said Billy Beats, 'it's not every day you meet the great Fatty Foulkes!' he added as they left Villa Park together with Athersmith and Wheldon.

And it was true, it had been a good day, he had met a national celebrity and played on the same team as him, a man whose mythical status in English footballing folklore has stood the test of time whereas others' fame, Smith's included, have largely faded, save for the interest of football club historians. What was even more important for Steve to hold on to was that he was rubbing shoulders with the best footballers in the land once more. He was where he wanted to be, playing football at the highest level.

In April 1898, as the season ended and the dust settled on a disappointing defence of The Double, Stephen and his friends Charlie Athersmith and Fred Wheldon felt dissatisfied with the Villa committee. Two of Villa's star players and legends of the club, captain John Devey and Howard Spencer were forced to renegotiate aggressively with the board in order to get new deals. The way these two men were dealt with by the club made Steve, Charlie and Fred realise that if Devey and Spencer were expendable then anyone was expendable.

Charlie and Fred were regular England internationals and Football League XI players, Stephen had played for England and represented the Football League twice. They felt they were worth better contracts than they were currently getting and realised with what had happened to Devey and Spencer, that as professional footballers they had to get the best deal possible for themselves as they did not know when they might be deemed surplus to requirements. On top of this was the awareness that the fledgling Southern League was paying big wages and signing on fees to attract top professionals down south. The newly formed Portsmouth

FC (who had been admitted into the Southern League) had approached Stephen and his brother to play for them already. Billy had been tempted but signed on for another year at Wolves after their third place finish, three positions ahead of Villa, as Billy had gleefully pointed out to Stephen.

Tensions surfaced in the Villa camp due to Devey's and Spencer's injuries the previous season and how insensitively it seemed the board dealt with others. As John Lerwill explains:

> For the new season, the Board had to consider very seriously the situation concerning two of the club's stalwarts during the 'double' campaign, Devey and Spencer and also had to negotiate quite hard to keep the services of Athersmith and Wheldon, amongst other players (Smith and Whitehouse). The keeper Whitehouse refused to sign.

Regarding the matter of John Devey and his unavailability through a good part of the previous season, the Board discussed his matter at length on 21 April, and determined that if his leg broke down, he would be required to help the club in other matters. The club was determined to get its money's worth out of Devey if they had to sign him up again as they were not convinced his rheumatism would improve. The rest of the players were amazed at the lack of trust and empathy for a club legend and team captain. No matter what you have done in the past, in football, now and then, if you are perceived as not contributing, the knives are quickly out and assessments about your worth to your club and whether you deserve the financial investment placed on your shoulders will abound. As ever in football, money talks.

There was also a significant lack of financial faith placed in Howard Spencer, which, as with all the other Villa players angling for better terms, would be played out in the newspapers. Like many players after him, Spencer used the media to explain his points of view, show the fans how he was being treated and ultimately strengthen his bargaining position. Lerwill explains the Spencer negotiations:

> There was an astonishing stand-off situation that occurred between the Villa and their great full back. When the season started, he still had not signed on. It had been reported in the *Sports Argus*, 6 August 1898, that because of last

season's lengthy incapacity of Spencer through injury, and although pronounced fit by a specialist, he was to be given two months trial by the Villa. If the trial was successful the re-engagement would be at the usual rate.

At this stage, there was a cloud between Spencer – who wanted an unconditional agreement – and the directorate. The matter had still not been cleared prior to the start of the season and the *Sports Argus* sent a reporter to Spencer's home. Spencer said, 'In the first place, I should like to say that my disagreement with the Villa board is not now a question of terms. Some of the statements that have been made about me are sheer nonsense, and the information Mr Ramsay gave you is not quite correct.'[7]

Athersmith, Smith, Wheldon and Whitehouse had also seen their contract negotiations reported in the press where their contractual demands were criticised. Their demands were likely leaked to the press to gain sympathy for the directors and perhaps cow them into agreeing terms for fear of being seen as money grabbers by the paying public.

In the *Sports Argus* of 23 April, 1898 it was detailed that Villa had not managed to sign up all the players they had required yet:

> The work of signing men and coaxing them to sign for the next season is engaging the attention of the Villa directorate. Such players as Athersmith, Wheldon, Smith, Whitehouse and the two Sharps are still 'hanging fire'.
>
> Athersmith, Wheldon, Smith, Whitehouse, I am told, are asking for £5 a week all year round. Good players as they are, I must say, that if true, this is a most exorbitant estimate which these young men put upon their exorbitant abilities. Of course, they may trot out the old argument that, as they make the money for the club, so they ought to share in the spoils. But there is reason in all things.
>
> Rumour is abroad that Southern baits are being held out to one or two of the men of £5 10s a week. Well, if that be the case, let them go. They will be silly if they don't, for football is a business nowadays in which sentiment goes clattering against the wall. What is very clear is that

the Villa directors may find themselves in anything but a pleasant position in regard to this signing-on business.

Whilst it is unclear what wages Stephen Smith eventually negotiated, he did not go south but also did not get the £6 a week awarded to Athersmith and Wheldon. That was probably because he was not a regular England international like his two friends. Smith did sign on again with Villa and turned down the offers from Southern League clubs. The press reported he wanted £5 a week, a £1 increase on the previous year's deal. There were offers of around £5 10s from down south. He was first choice for his club again and had been called up for the Football League and while there is no evidence he was paid £6 a week, it is clear he got a deal he was happy with – £5 probably – a decent pay rise and one that would be in line with a player of Smith's repute.

Howard Spencer eventually negotiated terms agreeable to himself early in the new season. And so, whilst the age old, preconceived notions from the media and the footballing establishment alike, that it was quite outrageous for working class men to dare to think they deserved a pay rise of any sorts, regularly, as would be expected in middle- and upper-class professions such as teaching, law, medicine and government, the men of Aston Villa were happy. They were all signed up on better financial terms than the previous year and ready for the season ahead.

With no player adequately replacing Johnny Campbell after he left, the centre forward slot was going to be contested by George Johnson, signed after a trial from Walsall, and 20-year-old Billy Garratty who had made his debut at the end of the previous season.[8] Garraty, great-great grandfather of recent Villa captain Jack Grealish, was tall, thin and wiry with a big, waxed moustache and would eventually become a Villa legend thanks to his exploits in the early twentieth century. These two young men were not without talent but filling the void left by the mercurial Campbell would take some doing. The previous season had shown that.

By the end of the 1898/99 season the remoulded Villa side that had surrendered the League and Cup so meekly the previous year were again in the hunt for the title of Champions of England. Come the final day of the season Villa and Liverpool were level on points but Villa had a superior goal average. The Villa just needed a draw to regain the title. Stephen Smith was once again in touching distance of the title and making history. No club had won the title four times before. Victory would see them eclipse Sunderland's 'Team of all Talents' and cement Villa and Stephen's place in history. A great player in the greatest team in the world. A fourth title in just eleven years of the league. It seemed incomprehensible to Stephen. He had been playing professional football for just seven years.

So, on 29 April 1899, Aston Villa faced Liverpool at the Aston Lower Grounds. Whichever team won this match was to win the championship. The gate for this match stood as a new League record: the receipts were £1,558 1s 6d.[9] Everyone wanted to see this match, and Villa were inundated with requests for tickets. The *Athletic News* gave context to the huge attendance in Aston that day:

> The Aston Villa Club will undoubtedly have the best return of gate receipts of any club in the League this season, for Saturday's match augmented the amount by a matter of £1,558 while 41,357 paid for admission. In point of attendance this is a matter of about 15,000 ahead of the international match, and it is evident that Birmingham people, like the residents of Liverpool, prefer to see their own team [something that has stood the test of time for supporters of most clubs to this day – author's note].

As Stephen and his teammates waited to get the game underway the crowds outside in the arena amassed in huge proportions. The crowd was so big that the *Athletic News* reporter had concerns over crowd safety as the match built up to its frenzied kick-off. There was a cup final feel to proceedings:

> The Football League has now been established a matter of eleven years, but never previous to this has the destination of the Cup been in doubt until the last Saturday. Not only so, but the deciding battle between the two clubs (had the records of), Aston Villa 43 points, 1.77 goals to 1, Liverpool 43 points, 1.75 goals to 1. This was a nice state of affairs and the league decided to hand over the cup at the conclusion of the game. I should imagine there were 43,000 present. The sixpenny patrons on the city side of the ground experienced much amusement apart from the match, for they swayed to

and fro in a manner that suggested switchback (rollercoaster) enjoyments, although it struck most folks that a sudden fall of the packed crowd would prove disastrous. I do think the Villa committee might erect a few more barriers.

The monstrous crowd roared on the players as they entered the field of play. There were people everywhere, they were doing their best not to spill onto the pitch. He looked down the line at kick off and saw Wheldon, Devey and Athersmith as well as Billy Garraty. He looked back and saw the legendary Howard Spencer and James Cowan. He was ready for this moment.

The game was played in April showers with intermittent warm sunlight shining on the ground that at the end of a long season could be forgiven for lacking much grass. The days of undersoil heating and hydroponic lights were generations away. Liverpool kicked off the match and pressed immediately. Villa were rocked back on their heels and in the early play Crabtree was twice cheered for especially good defensive work.

Villa had started badly, but they always seemed to these days, thought Smith. He needed to get on the ball and make something happen. About four minutes in, Smith managed to get hold of the ball and took it down the wing, he could see John Devey in the box and whipped in a 'grand centre' that his captain rushed towards and headed Villa in front to 'tremendous cheering'. Liverpool steadied themselves and got a foothold in the game once more. The game settled down and remained tight.

After about twenty minutes, Crabtree ran through Liverpool's midfield and laid the ball wide to Smith, 'when it seemed a hundred to one against his doing so'.[10] Smith went down the left again and once more whipped in a cross that Devey smashed home. Villa then ran amok, Wheldon hit two more and Crabtree added a fifth before half time. The noise as the players walked off for refreshments was deafening.

As Smith got into the changing room he and Charlie Athersmith were in a jovial mood. John Devey was not. 'We haven't won yet lads,' he shouted. 'They will have the wind behind them in the second half, we will defend well and win the trophy.' Devey and Grierson explained that Fred Wheldon would drop back into midfield to help the half backs. The second half saw Villa let Liverpool have a lot of the ball. Stephen watched on as his defenders and midfielders kept their opponents in check and he had time to think about what he had achieved.

George, Villa's keeper had very little to do as the afternoon whiled away. The crowd, impatient for the end of the game, sometimes strayed onto the pitch but not too far and not very often. The final whistle went and the supporters could not resist spilling onto the pitch en masse and assembled in front of the grandstand. They were desperate to pat the players on the back and witness the presentation of the trophy. Stephen and his teammates managed to get to the grandstand and walk up the steps eventually after many a back slap and pat on the head.

Smith looked out onto the field in wonder from the grandstand where a huge crowd had assembled. Everyone was cheering and shouting and when the trophy was handed to Devey there was applause that was almost deafening. Devey tried to give a speech that sympathised with the losers and expressed gratification at being the captain of the winners. Unfortunately much of it was drowned out by the great crowd on the pitch that stood cheering and shouting for some minutes until it dispersed with the consciousness that a brilliant victory had been duly honoured.

Stephen felt elated but exhausted. He had never known so much pressure in a league season. His team had looked odds on to win the league, then odds on to blow their lead at the top before scoring 18 goals in a week to claim the title with three back-to-back wins. It had been a relief in the end when it was all over.

What was also clear was that Stephen Smith had returned to the heights of his earlier successes of 1894 and 1895. He had battled back from injury and fought off all competition for the left wing berth for the best club side in the world. He had won four league titles in seven seasons as well as an FA Cup and The Double. He had fought off his injury problems that had cost him his place for long periods between 1895 and 1897. He was once again at the top of his game, playing for the top team in the world in the top league in the world.

He would once again be able to command a £5 a weekly wage due to his exploits as on 24 March 1899 Villa decided that a wage of £5 per week should be offered to ten 'first teamers' with the exception that Athersmith and Wheldon should continue to receive £6. 10s. John Lerwill explained how well thought of Smith was in 1899 in footballing circles:

In terms of personnel, it had in the end been proven that the old guard of the 1890s – principally Devey, James Cowan, Crabtree, Athersmith, Smith (who had re-found his old form), and the finds of the 1896-7 season, Spencer, Evans and Wheldon, had yet again shown they were the best players on the Villa's books. John Cowan left and returned to Scotland. His form came to its peak in time for the final of the Double season, replacing Smith, but in the past season the reverse had taken place, so that Smith was now the recognised left-winger. At his best, 'Tich' Smith was simply the better player.

Smith would never again encounter the injury problems that had dogged him in the past, although he would always feel his knee ligaments until he retired, from time to time. He managed to play in 29 of Villa's 35 League and cup games in 1898–99, 36 out of 40 games in 1899–1900 and 33 out of 41 games in 1900–01.[11] Smith would win the League title again in the 1899–1900 season and gain another call up for the England team against Wales on 18 March 1901. His bad knee forced him to miss out, which was both unfortunate and somewhat ironic during this period of his career where he appeared most consistently in claret and blue.

In the summer of 1899, his brother Billy left Wolves to join Portsmouth. The newly formed club appointed Frank Brettell as manager in February 1899. On 6 May 1899 Brettell confirmed the first ever players to be signed for Pompey. William Smith was one of those first eleven players.[12] He signed up for £4 a week and played at inside left in Portsmouth's first ever competitive match. The *Portsmouth Evening News* declared that on 2 September 1899, 'the new Portsmouth Football Club made its debut in the football world, being entertained by Chatham in the Southern league'.

In 1899, despite Billy's jokes to the contrary, Stephen Smith would have never contemplated leaving Aston Villa. But he was interested in how things turned out for Billy. He was a quiet man of simple needs and pleasures. Life with Aston Villa was always anything but quiet. In another pressure cooker season, Villa jousted at the top of the league with the previous side to hold the championship crown Sheffield United. Once again the title race went to the final game of the season. But this was not before his benefit game with Wolves was played (a 2-2 draw at

Villa Park) and the announcement of the game detailed in *The Athletic News* showed that while he was seen as a great player, he was not quite an A-list celebrity due to his placid personality and avoidance of the limelight in comparison to his pals, Hodgetts, Athersmith, Devey and Wheldon:

> With all the pleasure imaginable I would direct attention to the match to be played this evening between Aston Villa and Wolverhampton Wanderers for the benefit of Steve Smith, who in his day has been one of the very best outside lefts that the Villa have ever possessed. Of a singularly modest and retiring temperament in these go-ahead days, he has never gained the recognition from the crowd to which his sterling services have entitled him. Now, however, there is a chance for all to show their appreciation of one of the Villa's international players.[13]

The 1899-1900 season started well with two straight wins, including a 9-0 win over Glossop. Smith scored twice and assisted many of the goals in a game where Billy Garraty scored four. Villa won seven of the first nine games of the season before losing to main rivals Sheffield 2-1 despite a Smith goal in the second half. Villa then went on a run of losing just two of their next 17 games to go to the top of the table. During that run Steve Smith scored his only Villa hat-trick in a 5-0 win at Preston North End.

Not only did he score a hat-trick but also one of the goals of the season. Smith was in imperious form. After Billy Garratty had put Villa one up, a second goal came when Smith picked the ball up in his own half and 'ran half the length of the field' past both full backs Dunn and Holmes.[14] When close to the left touch line, Holmes dived in as he scrambled back but slipped as Smith turned him inside out and cut across the goalmouth, he dribbled close in beating the keeper and smashing home. The goal was greeted with a 'rousing cheer'.[15]

Smith was elated with his wonder goal and with confidence surging through him he ripped Preston apart. Smith smashed in his second goal and Villa's third just before half-time. Late on, with Villa four-up, Smith 'again raced clear and scored the fifth goal, which was apparently quite enough for many of the on-lookers, who began to leave the enclosure in hundreds'.

Game after game Smith excelled and as usual Villa marched on. In a 4-2 win over Sunderland, another of Smith's favourite opponents the *Sports Argus* reported that Smith, 'was earning thunderous applause for his clever wing play and accurate centres'. It was from a Smith corner that Johnson made it 4-1.

Argus Junior in the *Sports Argus* of February 1900 opined that:

> Steve Smith is showing his best form for four or five seasons in his sharp sudden dashes. The pace he develops the moment he gets the ball is surprising.

Smith's form helped Villa to their fifth title in seven seasons, they had won almost half of the first twelve championship seasons since league football began. Villa finished the season with 50 points from 34 games. They then had to wait for Sheffield United to win their two games in hand. It was not as dramatic as the last day of the previous season's title win but still as satisfying for a player at the top of his game at the top club in the game.

The *Sports Argus* explains how victory and Steve's fifth League winner's medal had to be waited upon:

> The Villa's programme having completed, Sheffield United were left with needing to win their last two matches, and then the last of these 9-0 (due to goal average thus making the title as good as Villa's with a game to go), to win the championship. They lost their last match, in fact 0-1 – a goal in the last minute.

The players were invited for a celebratory dinner at the Holte Hotel on 4 September, four months after the title was won, where they finally got their championship medals.[16]

In the 1900–01 season, the bumps and strains, knocks and kicks were starting to catch up with the core of Villa's team that had dominated English football for so long. Howard Spencer missed the last nine games of his last season in a villa shirt through injury.[17] The other full back Albert Evans missed ten league matches through injury, James Cowan missed twelve games, while Charlie Athersmith missed nine games.

Villa bumbled along inconsistently in the league in mid table until a run of one win in their last nine games saw them drop fourth from bottom. They were never in a relegation battle but finishing 15th out of 18 teams was a big shock to the system after such a period of success. Smith however, continued to flourish, playing another 33 games, scoring 5 goals and gaining another England call up for the squad to face Wales.

Despite injury robbing him of another cap against Wales, Smith was a Villa regular, an England and Football League international, a man with five league medals and a cup winner's medal, as well as being a man earning sizeable wages, closely comparable with the biggest hitters in English football. Stephen was in a very healthy position in 1901, he had no worries that his family, that now included baby William Smith, named after his brother, would live very comfortably indeed. In fact, as his form improved, he hoped he would earn bigger wages to secure his family's future even further.

Stephen felt that he was settled and that he would be at Aston Villa forever. In 1901 even as he trudged off the pitch at Derby's baseball ground following his last game of the season on the 22 April, a disappointing 3-0 defeat, he felt he could get even better and play for England again. He and Charlie Athersmith believed Villa would regenerate and return to the top just as they had after the disappointing 1897–98 season. Unfortunately, the FA and the Football League had other ideas.

Chapter 15

Portsmouth

Villa's title defence of 1900–01 had been a disaster, the club that had dominated English football, and were the pre-eminent team in world football had finished just two places and four points clear of the relegation places. The club needed rebuilding, and investment, something the club had always had, they along with Sunderland and Liverpool paid the best wages and attracted the best footballers. In terms of wages and bonuses, players at the champion teams mentioned above like Stephen Smith were on very good money compared to the ordinary working man. By the early 1890s leading clubs such as Aston Villa, Newcastle United and Sunderland were paying their best players £5 a week and by the turn of the century players at the top teams could earn £10 including bonuses.[1]

Stephen Smith as a Villa regular and England international player expected a certain level of pay. Despite his working class origins he was a valuable commodity in the sporting world and while perhaps no longer at his peak in terms of performance, was a player with vast experience, pedigree and ability. A player Aston Villa Football Club and its supporters valued highly, he expected to be paid accordingly. Footballers were the higher earning members of the working class, by comparison, at the turn of the century, casual dockers earned between 5s 6d and £1 2s 7d for a 44-hour week. Tram drivers made £2 3s for a 60-hour week and men employed in the building trades averaged £2 8s for a 44-hour week. But Stephen and Aston Villa's world was about to change dramatically and not necessarily for the better.

The problem was that the Football Association which had been formed in 1863 had always been particularly averse to professionalism. People like Arthur Kinnaird could, as land owning aristocrats, play the game for free as amateurs. The FA was a group of men from the upper echelons of British society, men of prejudice, seeing themselves as patricians, heirs to the doctrine of leadership and so law-givers by at least semi-divine right.

They wanted to control the game and the working-class men who played it, to do that they needed to control the players and, thus also the clubs. They could not do this if clubs could pay players what they liked because the players could then demand what they wanted and would have too much leverage in negotiating contracts at a time when the FA compelled all professional players to register annually with the organisation. No player was allowed to play until he was registered, nor was he free to change clubs during the same season without the FA's permission.

Smaller clubs with lesser attendances than Villa, Liverpool, Sunderland and Newcastle and who could not pay the biggest wages had proposed a cap on wages as early as 1893. Stephen on £2 a week in his debut season in professional football wasn't even aware the motion had been tabled. The wage cap was £4, and as he was no Denny Hodgetts or John Devey back then, his wages were half the cap proposed and he needed a second job in the Colliery to make ends meet. As previously mentioned at the time most players were only part-time professionals and still had other jobs. These players did not receive as much as £4 a week and therefore the matter did not greatly concern them. However, a minority of players were so good they were able to obtain as much as £10 a week. This proposal posed a serious threat to their income.

The proposal never came to fruition but the Football League introduced a rule that bound football players to their club and without the chance to negotiate their own transfer deal and terms of pay. It seemed like another situation where the young men who had made a life through their sporting skills were being prevented from making their fortune by those who still believed sport was an amateur enterprise played best by those who could afford to play it for free. Obtaining a comfortable way of life off the back of the gains of sport was seen as vulgar and beneath the ideals of the aristocrats and higher classes administering the game.

As John Simkin explains:

> The Football League introduced a new rule that stated that any professional player who wished to move on to another club had to obtain the permission of his present club. The Football League also insisted that once signed, a player was tied to his team for as long as the club wanted him.

Therefore, if a player refused to sign a new contract at the beginning of the season, he could not sign for anyone else unless the club gave permission.

In February 1898, the top earning players, including Steve Smith's captain John Devey, announced the formation of the Association Footballers Union (AFU). Devey himself came out in the press stating that, 'we're not taking up the question of wages and we are not talking any strike business'. The secretary of the AFU, John Cameron, announced that the union had 250 members and pointed out that their main objective was that they wanted any negotiations regarding transfers to be between the interested club and the player concerned – not between club and club with the player excluded.

Simkin goes on to explain how the AFU was successful in fighting for players' wage rights until the turn of the century when things changed drastically for Football League players and clubs alike. He states:

> The AFU managed to persuade the Football Association and the Football League not to introduce maximum wages. When Liverpool won the First division championship in the 1900-01 season their players were on £7, which with bonuses could reach £10.
>
> The Football Association passed a rule at its AGM that set the maximum wage of professional footballers playing in the Football League at £4 a week. This was double what a skilled tradesman received at this time. At the same meeting they also voted to outlaw match bonuses. To encourage men to play for clubs for some time, players were to be awarded a benefit after five years. It was claimed at the time that this was an attempt to curb the power of the wealthier clubs. This new rule was brought in at the beginning of the 1901–02 season.

As some players had been earning as much as £10, they decided to join Southern League clubs where there were no restrictions on wages. As John Harding pointed out in *For the Good of the Game: The Official History of the Professional Footballers*: in effect, the Football League abolished the free market where players' wages and conditions were concerned... there were escape routes to clubs and countries where a player could ply his trade freely and earn a reasonable (indeed, where some Southern League clubs were concerned, highly lucrative) wage... Southern League clubs began enticing Football League stars to defect with promises of up to £100 signing-on fees.

Stephen Smith and his good friend Charlie Athersmith were not happy. Their wages were about to be reduced at a time when they had finally been able to play football for a living without an extra job on the side. Smith's family was growing and he had a lifestyle and outgoings that reflected his healthy wages. The wage cap was going to be a problem for both of them. 'What will you do Steve, you've got a big extended family to look after?' enquired Charlie. 'I don't know what to do Charlie, I never thought I would play for anyone else but the Villa but they haven't said anything about what they will do about our wages yet. Maybe I'll get into the pub game with you, Charles!' he replied.

Charlie dabbled in running a pub every now and then, such was his erratic lifestyle and the hours he kept outside of football. He was a very social creature and it suited him. He was always looking for a profitable pub to run and was always getting offers. But he never seemed to stick at it for very long, in Smith's opinion. Soon though, Stephen Smith was to get an offer of his own when brother William returned to Staffordshire over the summer. He was visiting, up from Portsmouth in the Southern League as it was pre-season. After Billy's tough exit from Wolves he was having a great time down south. In his first season in the Southern League, Portsmouth had finished second only to Tottenham Hotspur, a much more established team and above pedigree sides in southern circles such as Southampton, Queens Park Rangers, Reading, Bristol Rovers, Bristol City and Millwall Athletic who had knocked League Champions Aston Villa out of the English Cup in 1900.[2]

The season that had just finished had seen Portsmouth finish third ahead of Tottenham, West Ham, QPR, Luton and Watford. It was a new up and coming club that was making a name for itself and wanted to invest in more players to finally win the Southern League title. '£10 a week, Tich £100 sign on fee, no need for a second job, I will show you the ropes, family will love it, little house on the shore in Southsea, walk to the ground for training and matches, chairman and gaffer want you,' blethered Billy as soon as he got inside the front door.

'Football League are fools Stephen! £4 a week for an England international and five times league champion. Come and play with me. It will be capital!' Billy continued. 'I don't know, I don't know Billy, I love the Villa, our whole family is here, it would be a big wrench,' rejoindered Smith. There was much for Steve Smith to think about. He loved the Midlands, he loved Hazel Slade, he loved Birmingham, but he couldn't bear to work down a mine again. He saw how it crippled people's health, he couldn't do it anymore, but he would have to, now the wage cap was happening.

Susan told him they should go, a new life, fresh air, stable income. But still he couldn't bear the thought of it. What about Charlie? What about Villa Park or Rinder who found him at the coal face? The love of the people of Brum and Hednesford and Hazel Slade? All that would be in the past. He did not think he would play football for anyone else. He played for the best team in the world. All that would be over. Just as Denny Hodgetts' negotiations every summer before his retirement ended up in the press, so too did those of Stephen Smith and Charlie Athersmith. Their futures were the subject of intense scrutiny in the local Midland press. It was also clear Aston Villa were not going to lose their top players without a fight. Villa and Liverpool, at the very next Football Association meeting after the wage cap was introduced proposed that the following rules be deleted from the new laws:

> At the annual general meeting of the Football Association on Friday 24th, the following amendments to the rules of the association will be proposed by members ... that the whole of rule 32 be and is hereby rescinded ... Clubs shall not pay any player more than £10 as a consideration of signing his professional form ... a bonus cannot be paid to a player on resigning for his own club ... the maximum wage which may be paid to any player shall be £4 per week, or £208 per annum, and the payment of bonuses dependent on the result of any match shall not be allowed.[3]

Villa and Liverpool's amendments were unanimously dismissed. This left a lot of players with big decisions to be made during the summer of 1901. As explained earlier, the press had got wind of Smith's proposal from Portsmouth. The *Nottingham Evening Post* reported that, 'Steve

Smith the Aston Villa International, has not yet re-engaged for next season, but rumour has it that he is contemplating going to Portsmouth'.

Smith was in turmoil about what to do and that led to a very rare public outburst in the papers. As speculation reached fever pitch that he was to leave the Villa the *Sports Argus* sent him a telegram asking if it was true he had signed for Portsmouth. He was stressed out, he realised how much the Villa supporters valued him and that the people of Birmingham and the wider Midlands would be very sad to see him go, but he also realised the money on offer was huge to a man like him, a man who was always trying to earn money for his family due to the insecurity of employment that had always run in his family through their background of itinerant work and low wages. Smith was always fighting to stay as far away economically from his old life as was financially possible.

'Its none of their bloody business Stephen, ignore them', suggested Susan 'I can't, love, the Villa fans will want to know what's going on.' He went straight to the Post Office in Hednesford and telegraphed back. His reply was printed in the *Birmingham Sports Argus* the very next day, but it just made Smith feel worse, as the way the article was written suggested Smith was probably staying:

> It was rumoured during the week that Portsmouth had been fortunate in obtaining the signature of Steve Smith. This we learn is incorrect. Smith wired us, in answer to the query as to whether he had signed for the club mentioned as follows: 'No, I have not signed on for anyone yet.'

Susan suggested unsympathetically that she had told him to keep quiet but he hadn't listened. Smith felt he owed the Villa supporting public an explanation, which shows how highly he knew that he was thought of by the supporters, that he felt they had a right to know as to whether he was leaving or not. His wife disagreed. Aston Villa had treated him very well. He did not want to leave, but he did not want to take a pay cut either. That the *Sports Argus* said Smith hadn't signed for Portsmouth was unfortunate when it was clear he couldn't stay at Villa on reduced terms if a good offer came in. As Smith had said, he had not signed 'for anyone yet'. His attempt to set the record straight only increased the speculation in the newspapers. Charlie Athersmith was also keeping his cards and his public house venture plans close to his chest. The *Athletic News* reported that 'after due consideration George, Evans and Crabtree have signed again for Aston Villa but I understand that Steve Smith and Athersmith are a little coy at present'. In an article entitled, 'The signing of players' the *Lancashire Evening Post* detailed that 'Wilkes yesterday resigned for the Villa next season.' But in a nod toward Smith and Athersmith's situation continued that, 'the older players do not like being forced to sign at a reduced figure'.

As the pre-season wore on Villa started to lose players to the bigger wages on offer in the Southern League. The talk was also that the older players were considering their options due to the new limitations placed on their earnings by the FA and the Football League. The press were not far off the mark if Smith and Athersmith's dilemma was echoed around the world of professional football in England. It certainly seemed to be the case. The *Nottingham Evening Post* reported that:

> Bowman and Brown, two of Aston Villa's players, will probably play for Southampton next season, and several of the old 'Villans' do not care to re engage at reduced wages necessitated by the £208 limit imposed by the Football Association. (Especially when the) Villa club has had a splendid season financially, the total receipts being £12,000 and the profit being £2,500 on the year.

It didn't seem fair that the clubs and the League were getting richer and the players who made them so, would be losing money if they re-signed. Britain and its Empire made its wealth from free trade wherever possible; capitalism was king, unless you were a top international footballer. Then despite your ability you were facing a severe loss of income. In some cases over a 50 per cent loss of wages per week. Stephen and many of his colleagues just couldn't get their heads around it.

As the impasse continued the *Sports Argus* of Birmingham described the situation at Aston Villa as a lamentable one. By 18 May, over a month since the previous season had ended, Stephen Smith still hadn't made a decision on his future. The *Argus* asked the question:

> What is the mystery about Steve Smith? Surely he is the last man to leave Aston Villa. The Villa are determined

not to pay more than the legal wage. The men don't like it. But they have had to put up with it. Let their Union get the minimum wage rule rescinded. But the Union does nothing. And never will do anything. Johnson, Athersmith and Steve Smith are still unsigned. The Villa will have largely a new team this season.

William Smith was still bending his brother's ear as they kept fit running on Cannock Chase. 'The men in charge of Pompey have got big plans, Steve, and they want you to be part of it,' said William. 'We've got a new player manager who is great, Robert Blyth, he's a top player as well and before him we had the Spurs boss, Brettell, they get the best because they can pay the best. We can win the league this year. And you will get the pay you deserve.'

'But what about the Villa, all the trophies, we are the best?' muttered Smith. 'Exactly Tich, you are the best and they want to lower your wages!' shouted William. 'As it stands I will be earning more than you, and I've won nothing, never played for England, chased out of Wolves by the fans, come on Steve,' he continued getting heated. 'It's not their fault, Villa's hands are tied,' offered Stephen unconvincingly. 'And now, so are yours mate,' finished William. They carried on running down the Rugeley road with Stephen deep in thought.

Portsmouth Football Club had come a long way very quickly as Graham Dubber explains:

> When, in 1898, a handful of Portsmouth businessmen announced their plans to form a professional football club in the town, it is unlikely that the local residents anticipated the speed and success with which the ambitious scheme was rolled out. Within little more than a year, land was purchased, Fratton Park was built, club officials were appointed and players were signed up. In their first season, 1899/1900, Pompey finished as runners-up to Tottenham in the Southern League.

The following year they were third, fully justifying the League's decision to allow the fledgling club direct entry into the First Division, without the need to prove its worth further down the ladder. Frank Brettell, whose appointment as the south coast outfit's first manager had stunned the football world, made his name as boss at Bolton before joining Tottenham, where he built another force to be reckoned with. It was a major surprise when he quit White Hart Lane with no explanation offered, but all became clear just a few days later when he was unveiled by Pompey. But Brettell left the club by mutual consent in June 1901 after he and the directors failed to agree on one or two fundamental matters. The team's regular right-half, Robert Blyth, was promoted from within to become Pompey's first player/manager. He immediately set about preparing the club for the 1901/02 campaign.'[4]

Robert Blyth thought that Stephen Smith could be the missing piece in the jigsaw. He knew Stephen would need some persuading. William had done his bit and done it well, he invited Stephen and his family down to Portsmouth where he could introduce Smith to the Pompey directors and to show him where he and his family could live. The directors were keen to interview 'well known players' who could improve the club and win the Southern League.[5]

Stephen, William and Susan got the train from the Midlands to Portsmouth Town train station. The station is now called Portsmouth and Southsea and was close to Southsea beach. At the platform was a tall, thin, dark-haired man with a thick moustache in his early thirties. The man would one day be the uncle of the great Bill Shankly. In a thick Ayrshire Scottish accent he addressed Stephen. 'Hello, Mr Smith, it is indeed an honour to finally meet you,' said Robert Blyth.

'Hello Mr Blyth,' replied Stephen. 'Please, call me Bob,' replied Blyth before introducing three generic officious looking types in suits and bowler hats – Portsmouth directors no less. Bob exchanged pleasantries with his team-mate William Smith and gave Susan his compliments. They then took the branch line train to Fratton station. From there they took a horse and carriage to Portsmouth's football ground. The ground was built in 1899 on the site of a potato field in Milton, a Portsea Island farming village which later became a residential suburb of Portsmouth, as the city expanded across the island during the twentieth century. Fratton Park is named after the nearby Fratton railway station (which is in Fratton) and not the geographic area of Fratton of Portsmouth. This peculiar misnaming has caused many of Portsmouth's residents and football fans to incorrectly assume that Fratton Park is located in Fratton, and not in Milton.

Fratton Park was built in 1899 on a plot of land in Milton, which at the time was a small rural village on the east side of Portsea Island. The land was purchased by Portsmouth FC from the Goldsmith farming family in the autumn of 1898. At the time, the late nineteenth century village of Milton still retained a remote, rural and isolated feeling from the busy town of Portsmouth, and had no railway station of its own, the nearest being located one mile to the west in Fratton, in the centre of Portsea Island along the south coast of England.

Fratton railway station – in a nineteenth century Victorian era before mass car ownership – was seen as key to attracting supporters to the early Portsmouth FC football ground in rural Milton. It was decided by the club that the Fratton part of the Fratton railway station name was to be for the naming of the football ground, to deliberately understate the actual one mile travel distance from Fratton railway station to the newly built Fratton Park football ground – in Milton.

Stephen loved the idea of playing football in this place. It was almost like having Villa Park picked up from Birmingham and put smack bang next to Hazel Slade village, where Portsea Island juts out into the Solent is Southsea beach. This was the next destination arrived at by the horse and carriage hired by Portsmouth FC. Stephen discussed terms with the directors of the club whilst walking along the promenade as Blyth and William showed Susan the sights of Southsea.

Southsea was always busy in the spring and summer months and the weather that day was lovely. If Susan hadn't been sold on the move before, she was now. Southsea, which got its name from the sixteenth century Southsea Castle, which became a fashionable destination for bathing and other seaside leisure activities in the early nineteenth century. In 1901 it remained a vibrant, traditional resort town with plenty of visitor attractions. The Southsea beach stretched from Old Portsmouth to Eastney. The beach itself was made up mainly of flinty shingle, although a stretch of sand was exposed at low tide. The beach, which sloped fairly rapidly into the sea, was backed by a promenade and children enjoyed dangling bacon tied with pieces of string into the water to see what creatures would take the bait. From the beach there were views out across the Solent towards the Isle of Wight. Also visible out to sea was Palmerston's Folly, a series of four large forts built in the 1860s to defend against the risk of an invasion from Napoleonic France which never happened.[6]

The Smiths loved everything that they saw in Portsmouth that day but still Smith's loyalty to the club that had plucked him from the coal face at 19 years of age tugged at his heart strings. He didn't know what to do. But there was no let up in the Portsmouth FC charm offensive. The directors took the Smiths to 141 Fawcett Road, Southsea, and the Victorian redbrick terrace house there was to be Stephen's if he signed on.

Inside the house, the directors clearly star struck by Smith and his reputation, made their last play to the now seriously wavering Stephen. They offered him a three year deal, no longer would he have to renegotiate and sign on every year or worry if he would be kept on, not for another three years anyway and on these wages he would certainly not need a second job.[7] Smith could continue to earn £10 a week plus a £100 signing on fee and his wages would be guaranteed for the next three years by which time he would be 30 years of age and close to retirement.[8]

Bob Blyth chimed in as well to add his two penn'orth into the argument, 'all the top players are coming south Steve, John Cameron and Tom Bradshaw are at Spurs, Harry Wood and Abe Hartley are down the road at Southampton, Johnny Holt is at Reading. There's no money in the Football League and they will lose their best players trying to get you lads to play for a pittance. Jack Bell and David Storrier are off to Celtic. This new rule has ruined the League. The Southern League is the future and we intend to be at the front and winning, and you Stephen are the icing on the cake.'

Susan looked at him, William gave him a pen, Stephen Smith signed the forms. After five league titles, an FA Cup and International recognition, Smith was a player in great demand. A man who could demand top dollar for his services and, after his financially insecure past growing up in the mines of the Black Country, he could now leave that all behind. He would work two jobs no more and be able to provide financially for his family with a considerable amount of luxury into the bargain. His Aston Villa adventure was over, the local hero was moving on to pastures new. He was now a Portsmouth Football Club player and as wealthy as anyone from a working class background could be as the Victorian era ended and the Edwardian period commenced.

Before he left for Portsmouth that summer, Smith met up once again with his great friends Charlie Athersmith and the long-retired Denny Hodgetts. The 38-year-old Hodgetts was a publican himself now and still larger than life. He was beaming at seeing his former protégé again. 'Here he is, the man the city of Birmingham is in mourning about!' blustered Hodgetts. Steve felt embarrassed and amused as he often did in conversation with his mentor.

Charlie Athersmith bounded into the pub where they were all meeting. He was in high dudgeon having signed a new professional contract with Small Heath and the pub they were meeting in was now his. With the wage cap and an unwillingness to leave the area, Charlie needed a second income and this was it.

'I have got adverts in the local press for this place lads, look!, Athersmith boomed as the ales and cheroots were consumed. Athersmith opened a page of the *Walsall Observer and South Staffordshire Chronicle*. Denny and Steve read the advert and loved what they saw.

> CHARLIE ATHERSMITH OF ASTON VILLA, IS NOW MINE HOST OF THE RED LION, BLOXWICH ROAD, BLOXWICH. TRAMS PASS THE HOUSE EVERY FEW MINUTES, HE WOULD BE GLAD TO SEE ALL OF HIS OLD FRIENDS.'

'But Charlie you've signed for Small Heath,' said Steve. 'Yes, but I'm famous for playing for the Villa, it's all about advertising,' Charlie rejoindered. Hodgetts interjected saying, 'yep, we need to be associated with our best days Steve in order to attract the punters, we are not like you, Tich making the big money down south!' Hodgetts and Athersmith proceeded to gently josh Smith about his move and the reactions in the press to his departure for Portsmouth. The pressure would be on at Fratton Park as well with Smith and the other signings Pompey had made making the favourites for the Southern League title.

The *Birmingham Mail* reported Smith's transfer in very dramatic terms:

> The Southern clubs have had their attention turned towards the League clubs and late last evening they, according to information received from a reliable source, succeeded in capturing three of the Villa's men. Steve Smith, who has

> never played for any other League club but Aston Villa, signed on for Portsmouth, on a three years' engagement, while Bowman of the first eleven and Brown of the reserves signed for Southampton. Crabtree will also go southwards…

The exodus south was in full swing as footballers kicked back at the unfair working restrictions imposed on them. But in this new age the working man no longer had to accept the wages of his overlord, those with a trade or a skill now had opportunities and fortunes to be made. No longer would the Smiths have to accept their lot as they had done during the mining strikes and famines of the 1890s. England was changing, it was becoming, in a small way, if not by class but by sheer economics, a more equal place to live.

The *Portsmouth Evening News* explained that Smith had better seasons than the 1900–01 campaign, as Villa tumbled down the league, but he was still putting in top level performances on a regular basis that led to another England call up and his big money move south. Aston Villa were also very upset at his departure:

> Steve Smith's secession from the Aston Villa ranks to join Portsmouth has created some amount of regret in Birmingham football circles. Although by no means at his best last season, this gentlemanly Hednesford player displayed very good form as a rule, maintaining his old-time high speed in fine fashion. In fact, so satisfactory was Smith's work that he was selected for England's international event at Newcastle, illness however preventing him from winning his second cap. Smith has been with the Villa for eight seasons. His brother W. Smith, will partner the ex-Villan on Portsmouth's left wing.

Hodgetts and Athersmith jested about the need for Steve to win the title straight away. The press in the south had big expectations. None more so than the *Berkshire Chronicle*:

> The Portsmouth FC should be a power in the land next season, and it will not be surprising to see the club make a bold bid for the Southern League shield. Seven new players, all of

them good class men, have been engaged. These include Steve Smith of the Villa, Arthur Chadwick of Southampton, Dan Cunliffe (New Brighton), Charles Burgess (Newcastle and ex-Millwall), Harry Turner (New Brighton), McAulay (Aston Villa), and T. Conran (Everton).

The great friends joked that even Charlie Athersmith's new pub venture made the news and that it was amazing what football fans found interesting. They were often confused about how much they meant to the supporters, but they also appreciated it. They also agreed that people would be shocked when it came out that Athersmith had crossed the Birmingham divide to Small Heath. On the eve of the new season with captain John Devey also not yet signed on (though he would eventually). The *Birmingham Mail* was suitably maudlin:

> What are the Villa going to do this year? It is a question that cannot be answered. It will seem strange to see the Villa enter the arena without such favourites as John Devey, Charlie Athersmith, Steve Smith and Tom Bowman, but the ex-captain has not yet been signed on, Athersmith has taken on a public house, and if he plays at all it will be under another banner and Smith, Bowman and Brown have been attracted south.

Aston Villa Football Club had been decimated by the knock-on effects of the wage cap and would not win the title for another decade. The hegemony of Villa, Liverpool and Sunderland was broken by the wage cap as players voted with their feet and found other streams of revenue, sporting or otherwise. It was the end of the Victorian era, the end of free trade in the Football League and the end of Aston Villa's dominance of the national game. It ended with the wage cap and the departure of their star players like Stephen Smith who became a trail blazer as a top athlete in the first-class game who went to the fledgling Southern League.

It was the biggest shake up in professional football until the advent of the Premier League in 1992. The Southern League made players richer than they had ever been before in a way the Premier League era has done in modern times although on a much grander scale. Stephen Smith played a big part in this seismic shift of the footballing landscape. Socially and financially, people could be much more upwardly mobile in an era where people now had skills and those skills were in demand and they could sell those skills to the highest bidder whether the establishment liked it or not.

The three friends bade each other farewell as they went on with their new ventures. The three men had contributed to Aston Villa's greatest period in domestic history, feats the like of which would not be equalled for almost 100 years. It was an emotional parting of the waves. All three men realised a part of their lives was now over forever, parts of their youth, never to be recovered. But Stephen knew the pressure was on for him to justify his new salary and bumper three-year contract on the south coast.

The *Portsmouth Evening News* declared his signing as important as that of Dan Cunliffe, a man who had also won his international cap with England and was returning to Portsmouth after a year with New Brighton. That Smith's signing was seen as equal to Cunliffe, who was a veritable goal machine showed how highly Stephen was regarded in footballing circles and that much was expected of him. The article read as follows: 'Equal in importance is the capture of the famous old "Villan" Steve Smith. With the two brothers Smith playing together, the left wing should be as near perfect as possible.'

The *Athletic News* was also interested to see if Portsmouth's heavy investment would pay off and if the crowds would get larger:

> Portsmouth seem stronger than last year, and nearly all the men are, to use the words of a club official, a steady well-behaved lot. They also have several good reserves. During the close season Portsmouth have improved the banking arrangement at the ground and have provided accommodation for an additional 10,000 spectators.

The stage was set for Stephen Smith's first season with his new club.

Despite all the fanfare surrounding Smith's arrival in Portsmouth his first game for the club was reasonably low key. They would play local rivals Southampton in a Western League match, it was a nine club competition played mainly on mid-week afternoons. Portsmouth would win the competition for a third time that season and retain the shield. It was a league used mainly to blood reserves and trialists but many of the Southern league teams were involved. Tottenham took the competition seriously, Southampton, West Ham and Queens Park Rangers less so. The Southern League was the senior competition and the one the new signings had been hired for. However, at the start of the season line-ups tended to be strong as they were used as a warm up for the main competition. Mid-week afternoon matches obviously tended to be less well attended, but this first meeting between local rivals of the new season brought out a decent crowd for a second-class tournament fixture.

Both sides were taking it seriously as the *Portsmouth Evening News* explained: 'Portsmouth and Southampton open their season tomorrow evening in a Western League match at Fratton Park (4 Sept 1901), both teams will be at full strength' with Smith making his debut alongside his brother and Cunliffe as well. Stephen remembered his debuts for Hednesford and Villa and felt the same nerves he had in his youth. This time though, people knew who he was and expected instant results. Pompey and The Saints faced off, 'Portsmouth the holders of the shield, opposed their old neighbours and rivals, Southampton, the Champions of the Southern League'. Smith might be over a hundred miles from his roots in the West Midlands but wherever you play as a footballer, local bragging rights are what are most important to football fans and key for a new player trying to make a good first impression with his new employees and supporters.

Portsmouth had never yet been beaten in a 'league engagement at Fratton Park'. The kick off had also been put back until 5.30, 'to give the working classes an opportunity of being present'. On a beautiful summer's evening, with a strong breeze to help the players in their endeavours, 5,000 fans packed the ground to see Portsmouth's new line-up.

'We look like fucking shrimps in these tops Steve,' barked William as Blyth led the team out in the salmon pink shirts that they would wear that season. Indeed, that was the nickname the team earned careering about in those colours. Steve didn't care what colour they played in and from the off picked up the ball down the left wing and swung in a trademark centre that was cleared by Molyneux the Saints' back.[9]

Steve Smith had started well, determined to make a good impression. Smith swung in another centre for Arthur Chadwick but his shot was blocked, once again by Molyneux. Lancastrian Chadwick, a tall balding centre half was another player who was an example of Portsmouth's playing strength and financial muscle. He had two caps for England and had played in an FA Cup final as well as two Southern League medals with the team he'd just defected from, he also had the dubious distinction of being the first Saints player ever to be sent off.[10]

Smith and Chadwick were beginning to control the game and after Smith's fine run led to a corner, the ball fell to Cunliffe who hit the post. The game was played at a feverish pace and Southampton had a goal disallowed before the Southampton keeper saved 'grandly from Cunliffe'. Amazingly just before half time Southampton had another goal disallowed, 'McDonald got right away and beat Reilly at close quarters but was given offside.'

What was clear was that although Southampton had a team of some repute, Portsmouth were matching them toe to toe. Steve knew from the many big matches that he had played in, that his team had to stay in the game and take any chance they could to nick the game. He and his brother William were having very good games. William and Stephen both went close with shots on goal and nine minutes from time they combined decisively.[11]

Steve dribbled down the wing to great effect before feeding William and he gave 'Cunliffe a splendid opening', making no mistake 'Danny' let fly the ball entering the net in an oblique direction well out of Robinson's reach. Cunliffe raced towards the Smith brothers in jubilation as the crowd erupted in unison. Southampton had another goal disallowed as tempers frayed amongst players and fans alike, but as the final whistle blew Stephen knew he'd done it again, Villa, England and Pompey, he'd won and either scored or made a goal on debut.[12]

The fans were in a raucous mood as the players walked off the field. The upstarts challenging the traditional giants. It was Villa versus Sunderland all over again, thought Stephen. Danny Cunliffe, the match winner, put his arms around Steve and William as they left the field. He had been impressed with the service they had given him and bought them both ales in the club house after they had all changed. Steve eyed up Cunliffe as he spoke, he didn't know of him but it was clear he was a lethal finisher and a top player. He also liked anyone who offered to buy him a beer. Cunliffe from Bolton was another tall fellow, though most were taller than Stephen anyway. He had black hair with a side parting and sometimes Lancastrian and Black Country dialects had to be slowed down so each man could understand one another, especially when Stephen offered to 'boi him a point'.

Cunliffe was another England international added to the ranks. As explained in 'Vintage Footballers':

> He joined Pompey before their first season, 1899–1900, helping Portsmouth to finish runners-up in the Southern League and impressed so much that he was chosen to represent England in a 2-0 victory against Ireland in his only international at Lansdowne Road, Dublin on 17 March 1900. He returned, however, to Merseyside in May 1900 and re-joined New Brighton Tower for a second season, scoring 12 goals in 30 appearances before re-joining Portsmouth in the summer of 1901.

Stephen Smith was excited by the possibilities of success with his new team. Stephen, Cunliffe and Chadwick were internationals, William had played First Division football for Wolves, Cunliffe for Liverpool, Chadwick was a two-time Southern League champion, Blyth had played for the mighty Glasgow Rangers. They all had pedigree. Added to that Smith's five Football League Championship medals, the English Cup medal, his achievement of being a 'Double winner' in 1897 and the international success against Scottish clubs as well as defeating Scotland to claim the title of top footballing nation as part of the England side of 1895 meant that Portsmouth FC, a very expensively assembled 'dream team' of Edwardian football, would take some stopping in the 1901-02 season.

Before the much anticipated Southern League season got underway the return match with Southampton took place at The Dell. Once again with local pride at stake and players needing to build up match fitness, both sides fielded strong teams for another early Wednesday evening kick off. Stephen was able to catch up with ex-Villa man Bowman before the game and reminisced about old times in Birmingham and Smith was able to inform him of Athersmith's and Hodgetts' public houses.

The Southampton public, much like their own side, took the Western League a lot less seriously than in Portsmouth with just 2,000 fans inside the ground at kick-off.[13] The Portsmouth players however were desperate to keep up their recent successes against their more illustrious opponents and once again started brightly. Steve Smith 'brought Robinson (the Saints keeper) to his knees' with a powerful shot early on. Bowman cleared several Portsmouth crosses into the box before Harrison of Southampton forced Reilly the Pompey keeper to save.

Steve who had been hacked at by lesser players all his career then got his first thumping challenge in a Portsmouth shirt. He raced down the left flank 'but Henderson checked his progress' as Smith ended up off the pitch. Welcome to the south, Steve. As ever Smith got up and went again. Yet again Southampton had a goal disallowed for offside from a free-kick with the crowd in uproar before Arthur Chadwick hit the post for Portsmouth. The South Coast derby was once again getting heated and Henderson's next victim was William Smith who was knocked out by his challenge. There were no checks for concussion in 1901 and William just lay in a heap as the rest of the players waited for him to come round. Arthur Chadwick was not happy with what had taken place and remonstrated with the referee. The referee let the challenges continue unchecked when the players resumed after William had recovered.

Arthur Chadwick then smashed into Henderson exacting revenge for his team mate as 'the players resumed with rather too much energy'. Chadwick 'was cautioned for fouling Henderson and then just before the break Cunliffe hit the post. At half-time there were a few cross words as both sets of players made for the changing rooms.

One and a half games in and Stephen Smith was starting to wonder what he'd signed up for. Hampshire was supposed to be genteel in comparison to the industrial West Midlands. The rivalry on the south coast was every bit as wild as Villa/West Brom, just on a smaller scale. Supporters and players alike were consumed by the local rivalry and Smith was quite shocked by it all.

The chaos continued into the second half. Two minutes after the resumption Edgar Chadwick completely baffled the Portsmouth defence with a tricky run and screwed the ball against the inside of the upright. The ball rebounded off the post into the keeper's arms but the referee 'after inspecting the upright gave the goal'. 'What on earth was happening?' thought Smith. This was ridiculous, just ridiculous. Football in the south was very different to what he was used to. The referees were awful. The Portsmouth players were incensed and once again this derby match was threatening to boil over.

Portsmouth looked like they were going to fall apart as Edgar Chadwick missed two more chances for the Saints. The game was stopped again for an injury to Portsmouth's Wilkie and a few minutes later Molyneux of Southampton needed treatment as the reckless challenges continued. Danny Cunliffe had not been able to affect the game up to that point, but he gained a measure of revenge against Southampton's Henderson for his earlier chances, wriggling past him in the box to equalise. William Smith and Arthur Chadwick, who had the most to be annoyed about with regards to Henderson were delighted.

Stephen Smith and Bob Blyth calmed their troops. They sensed a double over their bitter rivals could be completed with a bit of composure. The crowd was at fever pitch and the supporters of both teams demanded victory but sweeter revenge was to come Pompey's way. The ball kept being loaded into the Southampton area but then being cleared until Molyneux's latest clearance fell straight to William Smith. He smashed the ball home with delight on his face, Stephen laughed out loud and ran after him to congratulate him as nearly everyone in the ground fell silent. Stephen had not even scored the goal, but seeing his brother flat on his back unconscious in one moment and a goal scorer an hour later aroused his passions to fever pitch. Rarely the hero in Wolverhampton while Stephen's career reached its zenith, William was very much the star man in Portsmouth and Stephen loved it.

With five minutes to go and no floodlights in football grounds in 1901 'the players could hardly be distinguished'. Steve Smith fed Marshall who made it 3-1 to Portsmouth and then had to tell the reporter after the game it was definitely Marshall who had scored, such was the failing light as the game ended. Another fine victory over their arch rivals had been achieved. The gloom at the final whistle seemed to dampen the bitterness in the contest but make no mistake about it Southampton were now very aware of the coming threat of Portsmouth and the likes of Arthur Chadwick, Danny Cunliffe and Stephen Smith.

Finally, in mid-September the Southern League began in earnest. Portsmouth's opponents home and away, would be Brentford, Bristol Rovers, Kettering, Luton, Millwall Athletic, New Brompton, Northampton, Queens Park Rangers, Reading, Southampton, Swindon, Tottenham, Watford, Wellingborough and West Ham.[14]

Portsmouth began their campaign away in Northamptonshire to Kettering Town. Five thousand spectators were in attendance for this fixture with Portsmouth the heavy favourites.[15] Kettering's ground had a steep slope to it and after winning the toss and attacking down hill Portsmouth laid siege to their opponents' goal, but try as they might they just could not score. Smith and his team mates could not get any sort of rhythm in the second half and Reilly saved twice in quick succession from Kettering forwards Worrall and Winterhalder. Portsmouth believed they could just attack at will and a goal would eventually come, and even when Worrall broke through and was denied only by the linesman, they continued to be careless at the back.[16] A few minutes later and Winterhalder broke the same Portsmouth offside trap and, unlike all the recent goals chalked off against The Shrimps, this one was not and the expensively assembled superstars had started the season with an embarrassing defeat.

The two matches with Southampton had been insane in terms of player, spectator and referee behaviour. On a boggy, third rate pitch against semi-professional nobodies, a team full of England internationals had been defeated quite easily. Stephen Smith, however, had made a career out of not knowing when to quit and vowed to give all his help to his new player manager and make his controversial move a success.

Things did change considerably for the better as the season got going as Graham Dubber explains:

> Pompey supporters were upbeat about the prospects for the new season, but the outcome of the opening day fixture at Kettering may have taken the edge off their bullishness. The Shrimps, as the pink-shirted team had become known, lost 1-0, although the inauspicious start was soon forgotten as Blyth's men embarked on what remains the most sparkling run of form in the club's history. Four straight wins were followed by two draws before seven more victories followed.

Portsmouth were clear at the top of the table and were in a four way fight with Tottenham Hotspur, old rivals Southampton and West Ham United. On 2 November 1901 they travelled to The Dell to renew hostilities with the Saints. In October they had drawn 2-2 at Fratton Park in another epic south coast contest. Ten thousand fans had packed into the ground that day for another controversial and bad tempered free for all where goals from William Smith and Bedingfield looked to be sending Pompey to a 2-1 victory before a late penalty was awarded to Southampton and Brown beat Reilly to safe some local face.[17]

The atmosphere was intense. Portsmouth were desperate to wrestle the Hampshire bragging rights from the well established Saints and win the Southern League for the first time. Southampton having been champions in four out of the last five of the seven Southern League seasons to date and FA Cup finalists in 1900, were desperate not to be knocked off their perch and certainly not by the local upstarts who had become their bitterest rivals. The towns of Southampton and Portsmouth had always been civic rivals, now they were sporting rivals too.

The *Bournemouth Daily Echo*, a local but neutral bystander, summed up the rivalry brilliantly:

> The Dell, Southampton was on Saturday a veritable battle of the giants. Whenever the Saints and Portsmouth oppose each other sparks fly. With these two the only senior teams in Hampshire a spirit of keen rivalry must ensue. Portsmouth is a football nut the saints have tried hard to crack. In their first season the representatives of the great naval port succeeded in beating the Saints no less than four times, once even at Southampton. Since then Pompey has held the upper hand and have in fact whipped the Saints in every Western League match they have played. But in the Southern League Southampton have done a little better, although not so well as one would have expected from a side that has four times held the championship.[18]

In the warm-up disaster struck when Reilly, the first team goalkeeper, went down injured. Darling 'the substitute was practically an untried man'. The experienced men in the dressing room such as the Smiths and Blyth made sure the defenders knew they must protect the young keeper at all costs. The weather was fine and crisp and only a moderate breeze blew across the finely cut Southampton pitch.

Stephen filed out onto the pitch with his teammates as the Southampton Town band 'played lively airs at frequent intervals' with the 12,000 plus crowd swelled by 3,000 supporters from Portsmouth, who had been in the ground long before anyone else in order to make sure they got the best possible view of the encounter. Stephen and many of the

Portsmouth players were fascinated to be once again playing football on the same pitch as C.B. Fry. Stephen could not get over the fact that he had shaken the hand and shared an ale with the English sportsman, politician, diplomat, academic, teacher, writer, editor and publisher, who is best remembered for his career as a cricketer.[19]

Fry's achievements extended to association football. A defender with exceptional pace, Fry learned his football at Repton School, where he played for and captained the school team.[20] While still at school he also played for the famous amateur club the Casuals, for whom he found himself turning out in an FA Cup tie at the age of sixteen. Fry went on to win Blues in each of his four years at Oxford University captaining the side in his third year.

In 1891, he joined another famous amateur club, the Corinthians, going on to make a total of 74 appearances for them between 1891 and 1903 scoring four goals. Although extremely proud of his amateur status, he decided that entering the professional game would enhance his chance of international honours. He chose Southampton F.C., as the leading lights in the Southern League, and also because The Dell was conveniently close to his home. He made his debut for Southampton (as an amateur) on 26 December 1900, against Tottenham Hotspur and went on to help them win the Southern League title during that 1900–01 season. He was picked to play as a full-back for England in the match against Ireland on 9 March 1901 (played in Southampton).[21]

The famous Fry played at right back and thus was in direct opposition with the Smith brothers. The men from the coal mines pitted against the student of Repton and Oxford and batsmen for the England cricket team since 1896, a man who could class W.G. Grace as a personal friend. Fifty years previously these people would not have been anywhere near each other's orbit but England had changed irrevocably between 1850 and 1900. Football truly was the game of the people for all of the people.

The shouting started before Bedingfield kicked off, but it was Southampton who had the first attempt on goal, Darling saving from Joe Turner. Steve Smith picked up the ball as ever on the left flank and bore down on Fry's area of the pitch but Fry was able to kick the ball clear and stop Steve's charge. Smith was impressed with Fry just as he had been in their previous encounters. But although he respected his opponent, he was desperate to get the better of him, he was a professional footballer, Fry was an amateur. In this sphere, Stephen Smith was the man at the top, expected to best his lessers. Fry had the upper hand socially in civilian life but the football field was Smith's domain.

Southampton started to press forward more consistently. They went close from a free-kick, then from a corner and finally a long shot from Fry that Darling nearly fumbled over the line. Danny Cunliffe had terrorised Molyneux during the Western League matches and now he burst past his opponent and found the centre forward Bedingfield who tapped the ball into the net to give Portsmouth the lead. Portsmouth were beating Southampton again and The Dell faithful were not impressed. Portsmouth were truly in the ascendancy and William Smith shot over the bar and Stephen Smith dribbled through the Southampton defence but couldn't get a shot away. The Portsmouth forwards, 'frequently brought off dangerous bursts' and from one such burst Chadwick intercepted a loose pass and pushed the ball forward down the left where, 'Fry lunged at the ball and missed and Steve Smith nipping in scored'. Stephen hadn't expected the ball to come to him but when it did he realised he was through on goal and burst forward with pace to send Portsmouth 2-0 up. He was elated, and was constantly striving to challenge himself, to prove that he was a success and could now add the high society celebrity footballer, cricketer and dyed-in-the-wool member of an establishment he would never know, as another one of his sporting victims. Stephen Smith was an extreme example of what a working man could achieve in the brave new world of Edwardian England.

If they hadn't fallen in love with him already, the Portsmouth supporters – certainly the three thousand there that day to see him put their beloved Pompey two up against the old enemy in their own backyard – did that day. He looked back after celebrating with his brother to see a disconsolate C.B. Fry taking a lecture from his teammates. He did feel sympathy, but Fry had no real business in Smith's sphere of sporting influence. That Fry played for England was due to the desperate notion of amateurism still being clung to by the dinosaurs at the FA who always have seemed behind the footballing times in any era.

Southampton rallied for a time, Meston shooting over after a fine run by Arthur Turner, at the other end Stephen was well supplied down the left but couldn't get the better of Fry and his fellow backs. Darling was forced to save three times in quick succession from Saints forwards as the helterskelter, end-to-end pace continued in a breathless fashion.[22]

As ever controversy was never far away in this fixture and as the ball bobbled around in the Portsmouth box a melée ensued. The ball was nowhere to be seen as Portsmouth players stopped what they were doing to remonstrate with the referee who had awarded Southampton a penalty. Arthur Chadwick and William were in the thick of it until Blyth and Stephen pulled them away, 'Edgar Chadwick was entrusted with the kick and he scored'. Stephen told his men not to panic despite the crowd's decibel level rising as they sensed a Southampton comeback. But Smith had dealt with partisan away crowds before and was not unduly unsettled.

Steve Smith was determined to get Portsmouth back up and running. He fed his brother who 'made a fine attempt to score with Robinson saving brilliantly. Then, 'Steve Smith, with the other forwards well up, middled, and the ball cannoned off Bedingfield's head into goal, but Robinson caught it and threw away'.

C.B. Fry, up from defence, hit a great shot that the keeper, Darling, could only parry to Joe Turner who was almost under the bar; the ground held its collective breath as the equaliser presented itself, 'but the winger aimed wildly and sent over missing the chance of a lifetime'. No one could believe it. Southampton should have been level and then been ready to end their Pompey hoodoo. It remained 2-1 at half time as the players walked off, all except Saints' captain Brown who limped off after a heavy challenge from Arthur Chadwick, who else.

The second half had barely begun when Arthur Turner crossed to Joe Turner at the far post to level the match at 2-2, redemption for the winger had been mercifully swift. Bedlam engulfed The Dell 'amid a scene of indescribable enthusiasm, hats, sticks and umbrellas being frantically waved'. The fervour inside the stadium was electric and it seemed as though Portsmouth would now be rolled over as Southampton attacked at will. Shots were rained upon Darling, but inexperienced as the custodian was, he showed remarkable coolness and fisted away splendidly.

Another melée in the Portsmouth box led to Wilkie laid out on the ground and a stoppage was needed until he recovered. It was again turning nasty on the South coast. Portsmouth managed to clear their lines and regroup as the Saints fans roared louder. A Pompey throw-in was missed by everyone in midfield and through pure luck the ball went straight through to Bedingfield 'who put the visitors ahead with a clinking shot'. As the ball clinked in off the post you could hear a pin drop around The Dell as Portsmouth were in the lead once more.

Stephen Smith and Bob Blyth conversed agreeing that if they could hold their nerve the victory would be theirs. But Blyth had problems of his own as an Arthur Turner cross went over his head to the far post and Wilson equalised – except he didn't. The linesman's flag had gone up. No goal. Another set of footballers argued with the referee. Blyth continued to be terrorised by Arthur Turner and his next cross again fell at the far post. This time, however, it was not off side, Edgar Chadwick made it 3-3 and The Dell nearly took off in the excitement.

The game was nearly over, Stephen was dog tired, both teams seemed out on their feet, the noise of the crowd was deafening. He sent a lazy lobbed pass into the path of Bedingfield hoping he would hold up the ball and ease the pressure on the defence. Bedingfield found a burst of energy from somewhere and raced forward before shooting at goal, the shot hit a defender before bobbling up and wriggling out of the hands of the keeper Robinson and ran clear where 'Cunliffe gained possession and promptly netted placing Portsmouth ahead once more'. Stephen let out a cry of delight, as did 3,000 men of Portsmouth as The Dell crowd finally admitted defeat.

Soon after the whistle blew and all the players slumped to the ground. Blyth shook all his players' hands in jubilation. Portsmouth were still top of the league, their unbeaten run was continuing. The Smith brothers couldn't believe what they had been involved in. They joked about how they had bested the toff England cricketer with the posh voice. Then after the match they went into the Southampton club bar and took an ale each from the round of drinks bought for the Portsmouth players to congratulate them on their victory. 'Who bought the round for us?' asked William. 'C.B. Fry,' explained Blyth. The brothers Smith looked at each other sheepishly and then went and thanked the man in person and congratulated him on a game well played.

By the turn of the year, Pompey had been beaten just once. They celebrated Christmas Day with a 2-1 win at Tottenham Hotspur.[23] The *Portsmouth Evening News* explained the importance of this game and the value of the victory:

> So close a race are these teams running in the Southern League Championship that it was felt that the victors would be considered the eventual winners of the competition.

> Consequently, although Christmas morning is not an ideal day for football, over 13,000 spectators were present. A grand game, one of the best ever seen on the Tottenham ground, was the result of the meeting.

Players with big game experience like Chadwick, Cunliffe and Smith were making a real difference turning Portsmouth from also-rans into Champions elect. In the winter mud and rain a William Smith shot slipped through the Spurs' keeper's grasp over the line to give Pompey the lead.[24] William Smith was making a habit of scoring crucial goals at crucial times for his club. He had been taught well by his brother. They were certainly a formidable duo causing havoc for their opponents. The *Sporting Life* remarked that, 'the brothers Smith on the left wing set up a bombardment of the Spurs goal' after Tottenham had equalised, and this pressure led to Bedingfield hitting the winning goal. Another rival for the title had been vanquished as Portsmouth marched on.

The first three matches of 1902 finished all square, but there was little cause for concern. That was followed by eight wins and two draws in a run that took the club to the top of the table and in touching distance of the title by the end of March. The main delay in Portsmouth taking the title was the successful FA Cup run in January and February of 1902. Steve Smith missed these two months due to injuries sustained as always from the merciless hackings he had from full backs and half backs throughout his career. First Division Grimsby Town were knocked out after a replay, then after knocking out Reading they took First Division Derby County to a replay in the quarter-finals.

The country was realising that Portsmouth Football Club was now truly a force to be reckoned with. Portsmouth had wowed the country with their remorseless advance towards the Southern League title and their English Cup exploits. Augmented by names familiar to the public such as Stephen and William Smith as well as Danny Cunliffe, they were becoming a side of great interest to the football community which has always been a small world. A player may be transferred halfway across the country but they will still regularly meet the same players and teams on the league and cup circuit. A familiar face or blast from the past from a previous footballing life was never too far away. Football is a game for the community that has its own layer of community inside of that.

Although Smith was injured for the majority of the matches on Portsmouth's epic run to the cup quarter-finals, he was in the line-up that started the entire cup odyssey off in the qualifying round of the competition against Small Heath on 14 December 1901.[25] William Smith beamed as he heard who Portsmouth were playing when the draw had been made. He gave Stephen a look of satisfaction as he could see how happy his older brother would be to welcome his great friend, ex-Villa teammate and now Small Heath player and famous publican, Charlie Athersmith. It had been seven months since Stephen had seen his friend and that was all he could think about at the complimentary dinner put on by the Mayor of Portsmouth in recognition of Portsmouth's pre-Christmas surge to the top of the Southern League, and the furthering of Portsmouth's civic pride thanks to the club's recent and many victories over arch rivals Southampton.[26]

'Upon the result of Saturday's match depends the future of the club,' bellowed Chairman of Directors, Mr John Brickwood, as he began his speech on how Portsmouth would come to dominate English football. The FA Cup brought big crowds and thus big money for a club that had spent and spent and spent in recent seasons. He was basically telling the players they needed to keep winning or lose their lucrative contracts. Stephen and Bob Blyth accepted the money men's rights to spout off like this as they bankrolled the club and kept silent.

The men that put up the money have to be paid homage to by football players, have their opinions heard and their egos massaged thanks to their association with the local football club and the local celebrity footballers. The players do as they're told and pretend to like it in return for a big signing on fee and a fat contract. Stephen Smith accepted that this was the way and let the rest of the speech wash over him as he thought of things to say to Charlie Athersmith to wind him up during the game.

Brickwood continued to explain that at Portsmouth FC, 'the directors of the concern, but the players and supporters alike, fully recognised the great importance of the match against Small Heath at home before their own crowd, was in itself a stroke of good fortune'. Brickwood was basically saying, 'home match, big crowd, big money, win and get another big pay day, and another etc'. Football is not always as easy as that but people were beginning to expect a lot from the new Pompey.

Stephen Smith had been used to pressure from football club directors throughout his career. Portsmouth were expected to win, Small Heath were fourth from bottom in Division One of the Football League and had lost four games in a row. Athersmith and the Smith brothers met before the game and joked about how the great England player had left the famous Villa for their local rivals. It had caused quite the stir. 'Not as much as leaving the city entirely for Portsmouth, people still haven't got over it!' chortled Athersmith. 'Not used to losing all the time, Tich, I can tell you kid, I miss you and Denny and Devey, Small Heath are awful, I won't play for England again!' Athersmith only half laughed, but he was right. He finished up by saying, 'I spend most of my time in my pub anyway, makes more money.' Athersmith walked back to the hotel where Small Heath were staying. 'You'll be staying at my house tonight Charlie, after the game, Susan's making dinner and then we'll go into Southsea to keep Billy out of trouble.' Athersmith waved in agreement and walked away.

The *Portsmouth Evening News* set the scene for the match:

> The gates were thrown open at 12 o'clock and directly afterwards a steady stream of people commenced to flow into the ground and by the time of the kick-off there were about ten thousand present. Those who arrived early were chilled to the bone by the strong cold wind which blew directly across the ground.

At kick off, William and Stephen on the left wing looked directly across to Charlie Athersmith on Small Heath's right wing. 'It's fucking freezing round here Tich, fuck's sake!' Like Charlie Athersmith, the rest of his team mates didn't seem to like the south coast winter of December 1901 and were on the back foot as Bedingfield twice and Cunliffe also twice went close early on.

Steve Smith tormented his old rivals down the left flank, the man who scored Villa's first ever league goal in the Second City derby was too fast and too brave for the men from Birmingham. Adey, the Small Heath defender smashed into him and Smith was 'laid out in the collision'. Smith did what he always did after one of these crude challenges, he got back up and ran at the defenders again, 'able to resume after a temporary stoppage'. The Small Heath players saw Smith as a scalp, a player who had dominated them in the past. They were out for revenge.

William Smith went close with a 'fast drive' and 'Steve Smith put in one of his characteristic runs and forced a corner off Adey'. Smith didn't want Athersmith to think he'd faded as a force, he wanted the Small Heath team to go back home and say he was still the player he'd always been for the Villa; the rivalry ran deep and so did local pride. Charlie Athersmith didn't enjoy playing for his new team as much as his old one, but he still had professional pride, he still wanted to play for England again, and didn't want Steve to think he'd given up on the game. He sprinted past Blyth but his whipped cross into the box was cleared by Wilkie.

Stephen 'dodged and tricked at least three of the opposing defenders and fed Bedingfield whose shot was blocked, and then just before the interval Cunliffe found Bedingfield who finally scored and put Portsmouth ahead.' Steve Smith was delighted to have got one over old adversaries and even his old buddy Athersmith. He had a job to do and expectations were high. He could have no sympathy for his old team mate under the pressure that he was under to deliver success at Portsmouth.

Stephen, having been clattered by an old foe from Birmingham in the first half, was right up for the game in the second half and from William's cross-field ball he shot just wide. Athersmith was sprinting down the wing with alarming regularity and rapid speed but being crowded out by the Pompey defence at all costs, but there was nothing anyone could do when McRoberts 'scored one of the best goals ever obtained on the ground, from thirty yards range' and equalised for Small Heath.

Steve Smith fluffed two chances late on as Portsmouth looked for the winning goal with Small Heath seemingly content for a replay. Late in the game Smith was able to find Bedingfield in the box and the ball was crossed in for Cunliffe to smash home, leading to 'a perfect frenzy of delight and regardless of the high wind, hundreds of hats were thrown high into the air only to be carried on to neighbouring buildings'.

After the final whistle the Portsmouth directors crowed with delight and mingled with the players. They bought them drinks and tried to schmooze a disconsolate Athersmith. Stephen was glad his team had won, it was another sign of the club's strength to beat a Football League club from the First Division, but he felt bad for his good friend. Athersmith would be criticised for the defeat to a Southern League club, even one with Smith in it. For that Stephen felt bad. In the footballing community, whether you were a hero or a villain to your public, you were just a fellow player and professional inside the game. Smith was the hero today, but as he told Charlie later as they drank in the public houses of Southsea, Athersmith would always be his hero.

As explained above, Smith's constant clatterings, such as against Small Heath in the FA Cup, meant he was often side-lined for a time. He missed January and February through injuries related to his old ligament damage as a Villa man in the mid-1890s, something he never totally recovered from. He didn't play again until early March of 1902 when the small world of the professional footballer once again conspired to see him reconnect with old friends.

On Saturday, 1 March 1902, with Portsmouth's Western League game with Spurs postponed due to their involvement in the Dewar shield competition, Stephen Smith returned to Birmingham and to Villa Park after a hastily arranged friendly with Aston Villa was fixed up thanks to his links with his old club. He had thought it would be a long time before he visited the Aston Lower Grounds again and he felt a tinge of regret that he had been forced to leave the club that had been his home for eight years.

Villa Park had been a huge stadium when Villa moved there from Perry Barr in 1897 but it had increased in capacity so much so that 50,000 supporters had witnessed the derby with Small Heath on Boxing Day 1901. Before the match, Stephen wandered contemplatively round the cycling track of the huge bowl-shaped stadium.[27] His teammates were wowed by the size of the stadium and the purpose built grandstand on the Witton Lane side of the ground. To the north of the stadium you could see the large imposing Aston church as the large terraced bank behind the goal known as the Holte End was uncovered. This also offered an unimpeded view of the higher ground where the Jacobean stately home of Aston Hall was situated.

The picturesque view belied the gravity of situations often felt by Stephen as a Villa player as titles were chased and expected to be captured, such were the expectations at the most successful club in England in 1901. With the wage cap and loss of players like Smith and Athersmith meant the Villa were treading water in mid-table and the natives were restless. When Stephen was at the club they had won five league titles and two English cups in eight seasons.

Unfortunately, Stephen was still injured and would not be playing in the fixture despite being instrumental in arranging it. He was however looking forward to looking up some old faces during the ensuing afternoon. James Cowan and John Devey, his fellow double winners from 1897, greeted him warmly with firm handshakes all round. They were both injured themselves and envisaged an afternoon reminiscing about the glory days that were not that long ago, but did seem were sliding from view as 1902 would be the second year in a row that Villa would be nowhere near the title.

Then as 8,000 supporters were in the process of flowing through the turnstiles the news broke that one of the linesmen would not be able to make the game. Stephen was too polite to turn down Villa and Portsmouth's request to run the line and found himself once more back on the pitch of his old stomping ground.[28] It was not quite in the manner he had hoped for but even so he took the adulation of the crowd for the entire ninety minutes. The crowd shouted for Smith to come home, 'we need you back, Steve, we need your pace', 'we need your crossing and shooting Tich!', 'I was at Ewood against Sunderland in 1895 Steve!', 'come home!'

Players who give their all whether they excel or not, are always remembered by supporters no matter what. This will never change. Smith might no longer have been a local hero in Birmingham and had become the pride of the South Coast footballing community instead, but as someone who had both excelled and grafted for Villa in equal measure, to the generations of fans who had watched Villa in the Victorian and Edwardian period, he was immortal.

With Blyth, Smith and Bedingfield all absent and Villa at pretty much full strength, Portsmouth were thumped 6-0 and showed what a great achievement it had been to take so many Football League scalps on the way to the cup quarter finals.[29] It had actually been 0-0 at half-time before Jack Grealish's great-great grandad inspired Villa to victory with an avalanche of second half goals. Smith's moonlighting as a linesman was reported all across the press that week: 'Portsmouth's outside left, walked the line against Aston Villa last Saturday and proved a big favourite with the crowd, who called on him to come back to Aston. They evidently remembered the many grand games Smith played at outside left for Aston Villa.'

Smith left Birmingham that evening with a heavy heart, full of emotion after his day in Aston. He felt immense pride at the reception he had received, and his brother William jested that he thought he saw him crying at one point. But this was Edwardian England and stiff upper lips were the order of the day. Anyway, thought Smith, enough of Aston Villa. Portsmouth had a history of their own to make.

The Southern League title race had now reached a fever pitch level and with Portsmouth and Tottenham's cup commitments out of the way they were now ready to slug it out at the top. William Smith's form had been even more impressive than his brother Stephen's and he had filled the goal scoring breach left by his injured sibling with many wonderful and crucial goals up to this point. Even in Scotland his form had been noticed and it was pointed out in the *Scottish Referee* that perhaps Wolves fans were regretting their treatment of William Smith at the end of his time there:

> In the Southern League Portsmouth and Tottenham are running a neck and neck race, with Reading and Southampton in close attendance. The spectators at Wolverhampton are earning an unenviable notoriety for barracking players. If they take a dislike to a man he has to leave. As an instance of this Steve Smith's younger brother was practically jeered out of town by them some seasons ago and he is at present time one of the most brilliant forwards in the south. The Wolves could do with him now.[30]

This shows that players who get on the bad side of supporters at a club often know their days are numbered. This has never changed. The article above also documented how tight the title race was and that poor old William, despite his excellent season was still referred to as the brother of Steve Smith rather than by his own name such was Stephen's fame at this time. Nonetheless it was sporting redemption for William Smith who doubtless will have seen how his older brother repeatedly came again after numerous setbacks and took inspiration from it.

Good Friday, 28 March 1902, was the start of a pivotal weekend in the championship race as it entered its final straight. Level on points at the top, Portsmouth took on Watford at Vicarage Road whilst Tottenham travelled to The Dell to third placed Southampton. Four thousand spectators entered the stadium as fine sunny weather swept over Hertfordshire and the crowd waited expectantly for the players to arrive. Watford were desperately fighting relegation and their supporters were right behind them from the off. But Steve Smith, a man of many title run-ins, knew that one of Spurs and the Saints would take a dent to their challenge that day and so anything Pompey could get on their travels could be vital in the final analysis. He made this abundantly clear to his team mates beforehand and when the quiet man spoke, people tended to listen.

Portsmouth were in no mood to be complacent and attacked from the off and 'Watford found themselves practically unable to stop the onslaughts'.[31] After ten minutes and countless balls loaded into Watford's box the ball fell to Stephen Smith who smashed home from close in to give his team a priceless lead. Smith was then tripped in the area and a penalty was awarded. Smith gave the ball to Danny Cunliffe and the crowd was in total silence as he gave Portsmouth a 2-0 half-time lead.

At half-time Bob Blyth made sure the players knew in no uncertain terms how crucial it was not to let up. 'Let's make history lads and take the shield for Pompey,' he barked in his thick and aggressive Ayrshire accent. The team heeded their player manager's words and completely demolished Watford in the second half. William and Stephen were merciless, cutting through the opposition defence and laying on three more goals for Danny Cunliffe who ended up with four on the day.

Victory at Watford was only part of Stephen Smith's concerns, however, and he and Bob Blyth hurried off at the end to find any journalist who could get the Spurs-Southampton result telegraphed to them. When Smith and Blyth relayed the news of a 2-2 draw at The Dell to the away dressing room there were roars of delight. Thanks to the day's results Portsmouth were a point clear of Tottenham and with a much better goal average to boot.

A 4-1 win for Portsmouth over Brentford and a 0-0 draw away at Luton for Tottenham meant that the lead over Spurs crept up to two points. With four games to play and Tottenham Hotspur next up at Fratton Park the destiny of the Southern League Championship was very much in Portsmouth's own hands. But the game against Spurs was one game too many for Stephen Smith's long standing ligament injury. He had to watch from the sidelines as the top two sides clashed in front of over 18,000 supporters at Fratton Park.[32] The ground was heaving with supporters from early afternoon as people were determined to make sure they didn't miss out on this potential title decider. Tottenham had been champions before and had pipped Portsmouth to the title in

1900 in Pompey's first season as a Southern League club.[33] Portsmouth had a poor record against Tottenham as well including an 8-1 defeat in the Western League and 4-1 in the Southern League in the previous season. To say there was recent history between the two clubs was an understatement.

The crowd that had assembled faced the wind as ever along the south coast. The sun shone despite the blustery conditions and Stephen nervously paced around the side of the pitch with the Pompey committee men. He felt helpless, he couldn't help his team mates and he couldn't help his brother. They were within touching distance of glory and he was invalided on the sidelines with the faceless suits who only thought of the financial situation and the reflective glory in running a football club. He was in a terrible funk.

The match was tense and cagey, Tottenham needed to win to have any real chance of winning the title, they had 38 points from 26 games while Portsmouth had 40 points from 24 games, for Spurs the games were running out. The sides tried to keep things as tight as possible and chances were few and far between. Smith, despite all his experience, was getting nervous, they were so close to the title. No sooner had these doubts crept in than a crossed ball into the Tottenham box fell to Stephen's little brother William. The ball had bobbled to him through sheer luck, but being lucky is part of being successful and Billy Smith didn't hesitate to thump the ball home from close range.[34]

As the crowd lost its collective mind inside Fratton Park, Smith jumped for joy in the main stand and watched his little brother wheel away in celebration and take the congratulations of his teammates. Billy Smith had been ground down and demoralised by the Molineux boo-boys and told he was surplus to requirements, had gone away to the then relative obscurity of the south coast of England to play football for a team barely one year old and was now on the cusp of becoming a league champion and emulating his exalted older brother.

Portsmouth proceeded to dig in for the rest of the half as the game got bogged down in a scrappy midfield tussle. The interval arrived with no further score and Smith could relax a while and congratulate his brother and team mates on a first half job well done. But it was a tense dressing room nonetheless as the Portsmouth players discussed how they could finish the job. Tottenham Hotspur knew that a victory over Portsmouth was pretty much their last chance at the title and defeat would leave West

Ham as the south coast club's nearest challengers. The nerves on both sides were evident with a lot of scrappy and poor play apparent. Spurs continued to press but were reduced to shots from range until Arthur Chadwick, beaten to the ball in defence, cleaned out two Tottenham players at once as they went through on goal and received his marching orders. The only fortune for Portsmouth was that there was less than ten minutes to play when it happened.

Stephen winced on the side-lines as Chadwick trudged off, the previously buoyant Fratton Park crowd seemed to hold its collective breath. They were edgy as Tottenham pressed further. Shots went wide of both posts and over the bar. In the last seconds of the match the ball bobbled around in the box and looked certain to end in the back of the net of the team with ten men. Somehow the ball was lifted over the bar and after what had seemed like an eternal amount of football played with one man less than the opposition, finally ended.

Smith embraced his brother, then Blyth, Chadwick came out from the changing rooms and hugged everyone in his team while simultaneously apologising and Cunliffe and Bedingfield also did the rounds hugging all and sundry as they left the pitch to a tumultuous round of applause. Tottenham were as good as out of the running now, Portsmouth had lost just one of 25 games with 42 points on the board, West Ham were now in second place with 39 points from 29 games and could not now actually win the title having drawn that day. Tottenham sat in third with 38 points from 27 games and they could in theory get to 44 points as could Southampton who had the same record as Spurs. Portsmouth needed just three points from their last five games to be champions. So near and still yet so far.

On Saturday, 5 April 1902 Portsmouth Football Club travelled to Northampton Town knowing a win would clinch the Southern League Championship. The problem was that William Smith and Stephen Smith were out with knee injuries, Bedingfield through sickness and Chadwick because of suspension, it wasn't going to be easy. For Northampton, safely ensconced in mid table with no threat of relegation, there would be no pressure whatsoever, for Portsmouth the pressure would be on and they would be going for glory with 'five reserves doing duty'.

So with half their first team absent and in 'soft and slippery conditions' with players struggling to 'maintain a foothold', after finding their feet, Portsmouth set about their opponents but they couldn't find a way through, 'Bullimer (the Northampton keeper) was having to dispose of some decent, though not dangerous shots'. As the players slogged it out in the mud and sopping wet grass for half an hour the ball fell in the penalty area to McAuley who 'popped the ball into the net from a scrimmage in the goal mouth'. The Northampton supporters fell silent, the only noise came from Portsmouth officials and staff that included the Smith brothers who were now hoping against hope that this very low key arena with hardly any Portsmouth supporters present would be the scene of the club's first ever title triumph.

As rain started to fall things got even better for the away team. In the thirty-third minute McAuley 'utilized a weak clearance by Dilkes and steered the ball past Bullimer, with a beautiful shot'. William turned to Stephen as they stood behind the railings surrounding the pitch and said with glee, 'we are going to be champions Tich!' If they were going to be champions it was going to take longer than they first thought however, 'as a few minutes before the interval rain descended so heavily that play had to be suspended for a few minutes, and when it was resumed [the pitch] was like a quagmire'.

In the second half the conditions got even worse, almost farcical in fact, and was reported as such in the press. The game was reported as 'more like mud larking than football'. The chaos that ensued threatened to derail Portsmouth's title bid. A minute after the restart the ball was bundled home for Northampton as players fell in the mud and sludge. Just five minutes later Portsmouth reserve Corrin centred the ball into the area which Bullimer 'fumbled' and then 'beat himself'. The spectators were agog as soon after that Portsmouth's 3-1 lead was reduced to 3-2 with 'Reilly being beaten by Lawrence while floundering in the mud'.[35]

The Smith brothers looked at each other in panic, before the rains had come Pompey were headed for a routine win over an average mid table outfit with nothing to play for. Now Northampton were within a goal and in the current conditions anything could happen. And they did. And it was not good. Corrin's goal-bound shot stuck in the mud on the line in the final few minutes of the game before the ball was launched to the other end of the pitch where Northampton forward Lawrence scored again with a shot that managed to limp over the line in the sludge to equalise the game at 3-3. Stephen's heart sank, he couldn't bring himself to look at the boisterous celebrations on the part of the Northampton spectators and players. They'd blown it. They would not be champions, it seemed. At least not that day.

Time ticked on, Portsmouth and Northampton players got stuck in the mud. Blyth urged his men on, but he was without the Smiths, without Chadwick, without Bedingfield, but Portsmouth still had Danny Cunliffe, the only England international left standing. But if you pay the money needed to get quality players, then you get the best outcomes. That is football now, then and forever, and Cunliffe was the best forward in the division and from McAuley's through ball he scrambled the ball past the keeper and scuffed it through the mud towards the goal line. It slid, and rolled and crept obediently towards its target. But it didn't go over the line.

And then Danny Cunliffe slid through the mud and took the ball with him via his right foot into the net, 4-3. The Portsmouth players and those connected with the club on the sidelines whooped and hollered with delight. The ground fell silent and the referee blew for full time. Applause then rang out from around the whole ground. The Northampton players shook the Portsmouth players by the hands and in the style of what happens at the end of a rugby match had a guard of honour of Northampton players, patting the new Southern League Champions on their backs as they made for the changing rooms. Stephen Smith had seen his reserves do the trick that day, but the groundwork had been laid by he and his brother and Bedingfield and all the other England players in the squad throughout the season. Once again in his first season at a new club he was a champion. But what meant most to him was the fact that his brother was now a champion too.

The *Bournemouth Daily Echo* explained the magnitude of the victory at Northampton stating that, 'by their fine win at Northampton, Portsmouth have now made certain of the Southern League Championship, which is thus retained in Hampshire, and a fortnight hence we are hoping to welcome the cup to this side of the county as well'. Portsmouth had beaten Southampton to the title, a Southampton side who had reached the FA Cup final beating league title rivals Tottenham Hotspur and Football league First Division sides Liverpool, Bury and Nottingham Forest. Portsmouth and Southampton could match the very best of the Football League but this year Portsmouth were the ones who had also topped the efforts of the best teams in the Southern League.

Portsmouth also won the Southern League that year with a record points total. As *Lloyd's Weekly* pointed out, 'Portsmouth won the competition with a score that is without precedent in the history of the league'. Stephen Smith's Portsmouth were the best Southern League team in the history of the competition. Smith finally felt vindicated about his decision to leave his beloved Aston Villa, and from an Aston Villa point of view, he was sorely missed and never forgotten. Not in his own lifetime at least.

Portsmouth's final home game of the season would see the Southern League Championship shield presented to the team at the end of the match. Portsmouth had not lost a single game at home all season and as the *Middlesex Independent* explained had a formidable home record that they were anxious to keep hold of, 'Few teams can boast that for the first three seasons of their existence they have not lost a single Southern League match at home, and Portsmouth could not afford to part with it without a big struggle'. Portsmouth were in no mood to let Brentford spoil their celebrations even though Brentford needed the points to avoid the dreaded relegation test matches.

Unfortunately, despite the fact Portsmouth had just been crowned Champions the gate was just 4,593 due to the game being played on a Tuesday afternoon. There were no floodlights at the ground yet and midweek games often started while most people were still at work due to fading light even in the Spring. It was a far cry from the 18,000 who had crammed into Fratton Park two weekends before to witness the victory over Tottenham, nonetheless the coronation of the Southern League kings would be celebrated with a royal performance masterminded by the footballing aristocrat Stephen Smith.

Unlike William he was fighting fit once more, though there were still injury problems to contend with. The *Middlesex Independent* explained that: 'The Pompey defence was an uncertain quantity, it not being decided until the last minute which of the trio of backs would play. Both Burgess and Wilkie were suffering from injuries.' Corrin continued in place of William occupying the outside left role, Stephen came to inside left and McDonald continued in the absence of Bedingfield.

It was a hot day and unusually with no breeze from the coast, 'there was scarcely any wind and the ground was in a very baked condition'. Virtually from kick-off Cunliffe raced forward, and 'after a dashing dribble he transferred the ball to Steve Smith and the latter passing to McDonald, the centre forward had an open goal, and beat Spicer (the Brentford keeper) before the game was a minute old.' It was an unbelievable start for the champions and as ever Stephen was in the thick of it. He was glad to be back; it had been horrendous watching the drama unfold from the side-lines.

The crowd was in high spirits throughout as the Portsmouth onslaught continued. Portsmouth were quickly on the move again and from a pass by Steve Smith, Corrin went close to a second. Soon Portsmouth were two up however, from a Corrin corner McDonald was able to 'rush the ball into the net' for 2-0. McEleny, the Brentford half-back who had left the field for ten minutes after the second goal, was able to return 'and for a time Brentford held their own much better, although their forwards were always kept at a respectful distance by the Portsmouth defence'.

That was about as good as it got for Brentford and just before halftime the roof fell in. Smith found Cunliffe who placed a shot past the keeper for 3-0, and seven minutes before the interval Cunliffe scored again 'with a beautiful shot following some clever play'.[36] At half-time the Pompey players headed for the dressing room with the game pretty much won and Cunliffe and McDonald arguing about who would score a hat-trick first.

Three minutes into the second half McDonald won the race with Cunliffe to get his hat-trick first and thus claim the match ball. As the sun continued to beat down as the evening wore on McDonald scored with a 'lovely shot' to make it 5-0 with just 48 minutes on the clock. The atmosphere in the stadium was electric as the Pompey team continued to dominate. The reporter described the following scene, 'Portsmouth were now playing in irresistible style, and created a lot of enthusiasm amongst the spectators. Marshall had a lovely straight shot punched away by Spicer, who was, however, beaten after ten minutes by McDonald'.

McDonald had now bagged four goals in the game and Portsmouth were 6-0 up with thirty-five minutes still to play. A veritable cricket score was on the cards and Stephen Smith was determined to get in on the act. Brentford managed to hold off Portsmouth and frustrated Smith until ten minutes from the end when a real collector's item of a goal was scored with Stephen as the main protagonist. As the reporter for the *Middlesex Independent* explained, 'thirty-five minutes from the start (of the second half) Marshall went through on his own and centring beautifully, Steve Smith, who was well placed, was able to head the ball into the corner of the net, thereby placing Portsmouth seven goals to the good'.

In truth Smith couldn't miss and he chuckled to himself that a player as small as him could score so easily with a headed goal, but he had so much space. Brentford were demoralised and beaten, Portsmouth players and fans alike were exultant. Brentford pulled a goal back late on but a 7-1 score line was a fair outcome based on Pompey's dominance. It had been one hell of a way to bring down the curtain on the season in front of their home crowd. It was the third straight season in which Portsmouth had avoided defeat at home in the Southern League. Portsmouth had not lost at home in the Southern League since the club had been formed. It was some record.

Stephen and William had achieved the objective set when the younger brother persuaded the elder to travel south to Portsmouth to avoid the Football League wage cap and blaze a trail in the financially unconstrained Southern League. They had broken the hegemony of Southampton and Tottenham Hotspur and had done it in fine style to boot. They had finished five points clear of Spurs and the Saints and been unbeaten in the four matches against them.[37]

Stephen Smith's debut season could not have gone any better. Yet despite setting a new record for points to win the title there was anxiety for the players due to the bold actions of some of the only southern-based club in the Football League, second division Woolwich Arsenal. A reconstruction of the league would lead to Stephen Smith, his brother and his colleagues once again under the yoke of the Football League's wage cap. Arsenal wanted less travelling away from their London home with a regionally divided second division (north and south) for more local games, leading to more money made from healthier gates from more local derbies. Members of the Arsenal management committee were also members of the Football League management committee and wanted to absorb the Southern League into their organisation to increase their reach and control over professional football in England. If this happened Stephen would have uprooted his family for nothing and once again his wages were at risk of being cut. The *Leeds Mercury* explained the situation:

RECONSTRUCTION OF THE FOOTBALL LEAGUE – IMPORTANT PROPOSALS.

With a view to enabling the Southern clubs, which would then include all the leading professional clubs in England, Mr G.H. Leavey (Woolwich Arsenal), a member of the Management Committee, will submit a scheme at the meeting of the League in London on the 16th, for an increase in the number of clubs to 54, the First Division remaining as it is at present and the other 36 clubs to be divided into Northern and Southern sections, the top two clubs would automatically replace the last four in the First Division at the end of the season. [Author's note – the southern section was basically Leicester Fosse and the Southern League Division One clubs.]

The proposal, which may meet with opposition, is that no transfer fees would be paid by clubs of the Southern League, or any other club not a member of the Football League, for League players now in their service.[38]

Portsmouth Football Club had invested big money in wages and fees on players to help secure their first ever Southern League title. They did not want to be financially capped which would be the case in the Football League. However, to be seen as a truly credible club, testing yourself against the best, you needed to be in the Football League. But without the ability to finance yourself you could not be competitive; therefore, it was a real Catch 22 situation. A footballing impasse ensued.

It was an impasse that would continue beyond the First World War and long after the end of Stephen Smith's career. Portsmouth would be the last winners of the Southern League Championship in 1919/20. In 1920 the Southern League was finally absorbed into the Football League. This expanded the League's operational radius all the way to the south coast of England, as the number of member clubs increased from 44 to 66. The new Third Division was formed by clubs of the Southern Football League Division One of the previous season, except for Cardiff City. Portsmouth would finish mid-table in their first season in the football league whilst bitter rivals Southampton finished second.

It all meant that the remaining two years of Steve Smith's initial three-year contract were safe and he was able to see out the remainder of his career in the Southern League without a wage cap. He would in fact play another two years for Portsmouth, such was his impact in the first three years of his Fratton Park career. Portsmouth were now a legitimate force to be reckoned with in the Southern League and challenged at the top of the table in every season bar one that Smith was at the club.

Chapter 16

The Old Warrior's Return

The following season was an anti-climax after the elation of Stephen's first season down south. By late March 1903 Southampton had the title wrapped up. Portsmouth could not live with the form of their arch rivals that year. Southampton smashed Pompey's points record as they got to 48 whilst Portsmouth trailed behind with 41, losing six games compared to just two by the Saints. Portsmouth's title defence had been a disappointment but individually Smith and his brother still continued to receive praise for their performances. *The Sportsman* stated that 'the Smith combination on the left wing (was) especially prominent'.

After the heady days of Portsmouth's big spending early years investment was not as pronounced as in previous years. Portsmouth dropped to fourth in 1903–04 and Southampton did the double over them, home and away.

Unfortunately, the money pumped into Pompey to get them up and running as a force in the Southern League was starting to dry up. The 1904–05 season was a huge disappointment with further defeats home and away to Southampton as Portsmouth fell as low as eighth. In the three years since Pompey had been champions Southampton had won it twice and Bristol Rovers once. The supporters were not happy. The only success was in a couple of epic FA Cup ties which Steve Smith starred in, and on one occasion, most satisfactorily, on the stomping ground of one of his oldest and bitterest of rivals. One was a narrow defeat against Sheffield Wednesday after a fine win at Small Heath. The local hero returned to Birmingham to remind people he was still very much alive and kicking in a footballing sense.

On 4 February 1905, Portsmouth travelled to Birmingham to face the daunting task of Small Heath at their Coventry Road ground in front of over 20,000 spectators.[1] Portsmouth were expected to be lambs to the slaughter. Small Heath were in third position in the league, ahead of bitter rivals Aston Villa in the table whilst Portsmouth were bumbling around in the middle of the Southern League table and would end up losing 14 of their 34 league games that season winning less than half.[2] Small Heath had won 14 and lost just 3 of their previous twenty league games. Only one outcome was expected when a side near the top of the football league was playing a mid-table side from the southern league on their home turf. The game at Small Heath's Coventry Road, or Muntz Street ground as it was also called, would see Steve reunited with his old friend Charlie Athersmith once more. Both Athersmith and Smith were now a long way past their best footballing years and their glory years with Villa were a dimming memory. At the age of 31 Smith was fast approaching retirement. Nowadays footballers through fitness and diet regimes stretch their careers into their late thirties but in the early twentieth century any time on the field after your very early thirties was considered a bonus.

As Portsmouth travelled up to Birmingham by train, the Smith brothers discussed their careers in the Midlands and also reflected on where they were now. Steve had left the Midlands reluctantly but had instant success at Portsmouth and then a couple of years of fruitless challenging at the top, before the disappointing season they were currently in the midst of. Smith and Portsmouth were in decline. It seemed a long time since he had scored the first league goal in the Birmingham derby. He had terrorised these most local of rivals for years, scoring plenty of goals against them, on top of the titles and cups he had won which would have been viewed with envious eyes from those who supported and played for the team from across the city.

They would be waiting for him that day, the supporters of Small Heath. They would remember him and be delighted to let him know that his best days were behind him if he put so much as a foot wrong. The reception would not be as friendly as the one afforded to him when he ran the line at Villa Park on his first return to Brum in 1901. For William the tensions wrapped up in this match were much less fraught, but he also wanted the midland public to see him at his best after the way he had been chased out of Molineux many moons ago. Whatever happened in the match, however heavy the defeat might be, they were determined that their individual performances could not be called into question by followers of their careers, whether they be from the south coast or the industrial West Midlands. The Portsmouth FC entourage arrived at Birmingham New Street in good order and from there they travelled by steam tram down the Coventry Road to a terminus near Dora Road, a few yards from the ground. Steve Smith remembered the ground well from his time as an Aston Villa player. He surveyed the scene on the pitch after the players had been greeted by their hosts and shown to the away dressing room.

It was bordered on two sides by developed streets, Muntz Street on the western side, Wright Street to the south; the other two sides of the enclosure adjoined farmland.[3] Uncovered terracing surrounded the pitch, and a hut acted as the players changing room. A small but well-appointed covered wooden stand was built on the Coventry Road side, and over the years the terracing was enlarged to raise the capacity to around 30,000. Smith chuckled to himself as he gazed over the terrace cover behind the goal at the Muntz Street end. Small Heath had paid £90 to Villa, for an old grandstand from Villa's former Wellington Road ground in Perry Barr in 1895, and transported it piece by piece to its new abode. Smith remembered the episode well and how bemusing it was to all involved.[4]

As Smith and his side filed out onto the pitch to face their in-form opponents the crowd had swelled in the grandstand and terraces to around 25,000 spectators while 'three train loads of enthusiasts made the journey from Portsmouth and the greatest enthusiasm prevailed'.[5]

Portsmouth won the toss and attacked with the breeze behind them, and pressed the Small Heath defence from the off. G. Smith the Small Heath keeper tipped several shots behind as the home crowd were surprised by what was unfolding in front of them.

The First Division side managed to steady themselves after Portsmouth's initial salvo and get a foothold in the game. Portsmouth kept Small Heath's forwards from getting shots in on goal until Glover got free from a corner and headed goalwards.[6] Fortunately for Portsmouth, the ball went just over the bar. Small Heath now seemed to be ready to put Pompey to the sword. Then, eleven minutes into the game Steve Smith exchanged passes with his brother before swinging the ball into the box for Pompey centre forward Lee to give the south coast side a shock lead with 'a terrific drive'. The *Athletic News* described the strike in typically detailed terms reporting that, 'due to a delightful bout of passing between the brothers Smith, Lee shot so high up that the ball caught the inside of the crossbar'. The crowd were shell shocked and continued to be so as Portsmouth marauded forward at will, as 'they continued to play up in great style'. Just before half-time, with only the

Portsmouth supporters making any sort of noise in the large crowd, it looked like the game would be over before it had even really begun as a contest, Lee having gone through and fired towards goal. Wigmore, the Small Heath defender, managed to block the shot just as it seemed to be heading home.

At half-time, Stephen realised he had not had to worry once about any barbed comments from supporters of his old rivals. They had had no cause to get enthused about the possibility of the ex-Villa man slipping up, he and Portsmouth had been that dominant. The second half was very different, Small Heath got their act together. Harris the Portsmouth keeper saved several excellent shots early in the second half, 'he had a wonderful game'. As *The Sportsman* reported, 'The second half was brimful of excitement, both sides infusing plenty of energy into their play. At one time Small Heath seemed certain to draw level but Harris would not be beaten and Walker and Harris were resolute in defence.' Portsmouth were now under increasing pressure and Steve Smith wondered whether his side could hold out for the victory as they entered the final eight minutes. On a rare Portsmouth foray upfield in the second half, Smith was sent clear down the left, one thing that had not deserted him into his thirties was his searing pace. Smith surged down the left flank and shaped to cross the ball to the far post. The keeper expected the cross, the defenders expected the cross, Smith's own teammates expected the cross – instead he hit a curling shot that looked to be going just wide and at the last moment the ball curled into the top corner of the net grazing the post.

The game was won. Not for the first time Stephen Smith had been the match winner in Birmingham. The Portsmouth fans erupted in delirium, Smith ran off in celebration of another goal against the old enemy. He knew his goal would not go down well with the locals as he took the acclaim from his teammates. But while the Small Heath fans did not appreciate the shock defeat to a mid-table Southern League team, they did appreciate the performance of Portsmouth and in particular Steve Smith.

Smith and brother William, were amazed, as he, the ex-Villa man and his team were cheered and applauded by the Small Heath supporters in acknowledgement of their fine performance. The brothers Smith had upset the odds on many occasions in their footballing careers but for a man forever associated with the claret and blue side of Birmingham to be so generously acknowledged by the blue side of the city, was up there with their most unexpected triumphs.

As the final whistle went the *Birmingham Gazette* summed up the local supporters reaction to their defeat:

> Fairly and squarely beaten by the better team. That was the unanimous verdict of the twenty odd thousand people who witnessed the defeat of Small Heath by Portsmouth in the first round of the cup at Coventry Road. Disloyal as it may sound, there was no regret or disappointment on the part of the Heath followers. In genuine sportsmanlike manner they acknowledged in demonstrative terms the fine achievement of the Southern cracks, and the enthusiasm at the conclusion of the game was almost as pronounced as if Wigmore (Small Heath's captain) had added another victory to their already long list.

The local and national press waxed lyrical about Stephen Smith having rolled back the years in such an impressive and unexpected fashion. The local hero's return had been akin to that of the return of the prodigal son. The *Birmingham Daily Gazette* dedicated a full paragraph of the match report entitled 'STEVE SMITH'S BRILLIANT GOAL' to his strike, explaining:

> The two Smiths on the wing came along ominously. The puerile opposition offered by Bird was easily swept away, and then Glover was circumvented and passed. Stephen Smith swung the ball into the centre, and there was a scuttering of the other visiting forwards towards Robinson. There was however no need for them to interfere. Smith's cross twirled under the crossbar and into the net beating Robinson out of house and home.

The *Birmingham Daily Gazette* also described 'the ex-midlanders, the brothers Smith, as quite the best of a smart forward line'. The *Athletic News* was equally gushing in their praise of Smith:

> The second shot which took effect was a wonderful one. Steve Smith came along the wing at top speed, and just when everyone expected him to centre he shot for goal. The ball

looked like going outside when it left Smith's toe, but it unexpectedly curled in, and went between the posts and high up in the far corner. Opinions were divided between Steve Smith and Wilcox as to which was the best forward on the field, as the old Villa man scored one goal and was mainly responsible for the other.

The *London Daily News* headline for the match was, 'STEVE SMITH REDIVIVUS' (reborn), and said the following about this performance:

Steve Smith, although he must now be regarded as having reached the veteran stage, was the best forward on the field. He showed his old capacity for beating the half-back, and even the back, and centring with deadly effect. Smith was largely responsible for the first goal, and he scored the second off his own bat, as it were, shooting when everyone expected that he would merely centre.

Finally, *The Football News* explained that Small Heath were, 'scarcely a match for Steve Smith, the old Villa warrior and his brother W. Smith'. Wigmore, the Small Heath captain, was criticised for letting, 'Steve Smith have a free field', 'the result was that not only did the first goal come from the ex-Villa man's wing, but the international was so far let loose as to score one himself eight minutes or so from the finish'.

It had been a wonderful last hurrah in the city where he had made his name. His performance and goal in particular, a microcosm of his career. Rapid pace down the left flank. Devilishly accurate centres into the box and oblique, ferocious cross shots that found the far corner of the net. If the ball didn't go into the net, it invariably fell to someone who put it in the net. Simple, raw, precocious skill and power. Natural ability that had once again seen him make his mark in the Midlands, his home, where his fame and reputation, now waning, flickered on once more as brightly as it had ever done.

The following year, in the 1905–06 season, Portsmouth were renewed and once again in contention for the Southern League title. They were back doing what they did best, beating Southampton. They defeated the Saints 1-0 in November 1905 and by January 1906 they were disrupting the form of league leaders Fulham with a last gasp victory, also by a goal to nil, scored by Smith. Unfortunately it was to be another false dawn and Pompey's title challenge faded in the New Year and an air of staleness seemed to have set in. Perhaps enthusiasm amongst the players was also in short supply as half the team, including Stephen Smith and Danny Cunliffe had not been able to agree suitable terms to return for another season at Portsmouth although William was still in negotiations.

The day after the last day of the Southern League season Smith was asked to trot out for the final game of the Western League, pretty much a reserve team competition by this time. He did so dutifully in front of just 500 spectators in the final act of his Portsmouth career. Millwall's East Greenwich ground witnessed a 4-0 mauling of Pompey's second string and, despite Cunliffe adding strength to the ranks, the performance left a lot to be desired. Stephen went on a 'nice run' on one occasion 'but shot yards wide'.[7] That was as good as it got and the curtain came down on Steve Smith's Portsmouth career in an obscure and underwhelming fashion. It was a long way from the Southern League Championship and even further away from the FA Cup final and the International Football Championship which now seemed such a very long time ago.

Chapter 17

Gillingham

William Smith sheepishly entered his older brother's home and sat down. 'All right bab,' said Susan Smith. 'Stephen is in the garden, love, go on through,' she instructed warmly. Stephen Smith was in his back garden enjoying the spring sunshine. 'All right mate,' said Steve as his younger brother came and sat down next to him on a wicker chair facing the sun. 'You look nervous Billy, what's up?' continued Steve. Billy felt bad, his older brother had not been kept on by Portsmouth due to his age and the recurring knee injury, but after some negotiation he had secured a new contract with Pompey.

The Portsmouth management wanted to shake up the personnel somewhat, and Stephen and Danny Cunliffe, despite being England internationals were being cleared off the wage bill. A whole raft of the Pompey squad had been let go, the directors were desperate to shake off the tag of nearly men. They were a team that kept getting close after the initial success when Smith first joined. Every season after that had been a vain attempt to replicate the 1902 triumph. Steve had accepted it was time to move on but his little brother was nervous at what his reaction would be to Billy staying on at Pompey.

'I've signed again Steve,' blurted William, 'what are you going to do Steve?' He was hoping to take the conversation away from his good news. 'Ah, that's good to hear Bill, plenty more years in you yet young man,' said Steve. 'I'm not sure yet Billy, my knee gives me some real gip at times, maybe it's time to call it quits. I've been thinking about maybe starting my own business. I love it here by the sea, a shop maybe, sell fish?' he elaborated.

'They should have kept you on, Tich, you're still a great player,' said Billy in that way a person always does when they have kept their job but a friend has lost theirs. Sympathy and platitudes were not needed by Stephen. He had two children and a wife to look after but he had money in the bank and he would find another club or a different job if needed.

Smith was loved in Portsmouth as he had been in the Midlands and that opened doors. He did not want his brother to feel guilty just because he had time on his side in his career.

In football time and sentiment waits for no man and Steve Smith had known towards the end of the previous season it was likely his days were numbered and the speed of the arrival of his replacement on the left wing confirmed this. Less than a week after the end of the season, the *Portsmouth Evening News* revealed that Richard Bonney the Pompey manager had raided Aston Villa for a new left winger:

> (Arthur) Elston is another player, who it was expected, would remain in Birmingham. He is quite a lad, but is fit to take his place in any company. He is exceptionally fast and clever, and is expected to be a worthy successor to Steve Smith.[1]

As the summer wore on Portsmouth remoulded their squad but for Stephen Smith and his old pal Charlie Athersmith uncertainty remained. For the first time in their careers they were unsigned and on the Football League transfer list – the list you were put on when you hadn't impressed your previous club enough to be retained or had enticed another club to apply for your transfer. Charlie Athersmith had told Steve he didn't even know why he was on the list, he had left Small Heath in 1905 and had not played professionally for a year. He'd been concentrating on his publican duties. Steve himself had started to think about alternatives to the game he loved playing. First and foremost, since his earliest days, it had been drummed into him the need to survive, make money and look after your family. If football wasn't going to pay, he needed to find something that would.

The Sportsman newspaper explained the changes at Portsmouth that didn't include Stephen:

> Portsmouth have experienced no difficulty in retaining the players they wished to engage for next season. It was announced that Walker, Bowman, McDonald, Buick, Digweed, Hickleton, Kirby, W.Smith, Hunter and Dix have already appended their signatures for another campaign, and there are likely to be other names shortly, although it is expected that the club next season will contain much new blood.

The *Dundee Evening Telegraph* thought it strange that Athersmith and Smith were on the transfer list at all, 'it is curious to see the retention of Athersmith and Steve Smith (the old England internationalists)' given their recent employment outside of the Football League and also due to their ages (Charlie was 34, Steve 32). Perhaps the paper was insinuating that it thought it was time for Smith to think about calling it a day. Athersmith had retired and Smith had been playing in the Southern League since 1901.

Both players, it seems, by allowing their names to be put on the list were not averse to returning to Football League action despite their absence in recent years. Steve Smith had obviously not ruled out a return to football in the Midlands or perhaps further north. By being on the list, at least it meant clubs from all leagues knew he was available. How likely it was that an offer would be forthcoming though, was another matter entirely. In the summer of 1906, Stephen Smith's footballing career was entirely up in the air.

Steve was not overly concerned about finding a new club. He knew that whatever happened he would only have a few more years left as a footballer. Perhaps it was time to turn his attention towards a new business venture or perhaps use all the experience he'd accrued in his career to become a trainer or part of a football club's management committee. One of his ex-Portsmouth team mates, the former England international Danny Cunliffe, told him he had signed a deal with New Brompton in the Southern League.

Cunliffe said was the plan to get proven Southern League players to the club in a bid to improve its fortunes. New Brompton had won the Southern League division two title in 1895 and had been in the top division ever since. They had never been anywhere near the leading places however and had finished third from bottom in 1904 and second bottom in the season just finished, avoiding relegation due to the expansion of the league to 20 teams.[2] Stephen Smith wasn't convinced that this was the move for him. New Brompton was in Kent, a fair trek from Portsmouth. He would have to uproot his wife and two boys, Stephen and William, to play for a club that was habitually at the bottom end of the table and on the end of plenty of heavy score lines. It was not necessarily the way he wanted to go out.

In the coming weeks, other former members of the Portsmouth team signed on at New Brompton. William Lee who had been Smith's fellow front line forward had also signed and had bent Steve's ear about joining. Smith was still not overly impressed as New Brompton's top striker Barnfather had jumped ship to Southampton for better terms. Interestingly the newspapers said that this was a natural thing to do. Nowadays, with wages much greater, players come in for fearful criticism if they are seen to have moved just for more money but in 1906 it was seen as the natural order of things. For New Brompton though it showed their lack of financial muscle compared to the bigger sides in the league. Smith knew he would not be on the wages he had been at Portsmouth.

In the end, two things swung it for Stephen to make the move to New Brompton, the first being that he was offered a chance to be part of the coaching team, something that intrigued him and gave rise to thoughts of possibly moving into management after retirement.[3] The second thing was Smith's love of the sea; he loved living by the south coast and by open water. The New Brompton football ground was very close to Chatham Dockyard and overlooked the River Medway. This was also how he could sell the move to his wife, Susan. The gravy train wages of the Portsmouth years were over but a two-year arrangement with the possibility of moving into another sphere of football employment offered more regular money and a guaranteed prolonging of his football career until he was 34 without having to work another job. People were now getting to a stage in terms of employment where quality of life and work-life balance were becoming things prospective employees were taking into account before committing to a job. Employers had to make terms and conditions of service desirable or else people could now go elsewhere, as was the case with Barnfather leaving for Southampton. Steve Smith was still a precious enough footballing commodity in 1906 to extract some favourable terms of work and pay in this brave new world of social mobility and more varied job opportunities for the working classes.

On the eve of the 1906-07 season the *Athletic News* previewed all the teams that made up the Southern League:

> Although the New Brompton club did not do nearly as well as was expected last season, the directors have not lost heart. Every effort has been made to secure a strong team for the ensuing season, and judging by the names of the players who have been secured the club will be a force

to be reckoned with this winter. From a financial point of view the results of last year's working was anything but unsatisfactory, but the management are in hopes that they will be able to recoup themselves for their losses.

Failure in front of goal was the reason why several matches were lost last season, and the directors wisely set to work to strengthen the front line. The club would have been glad to retain the services of P. Barnfather who was one of the lightest forwards in the League, but Southampton offered better terms, and naturally enough he accepted them. The Kentish club will have the assistance of no fewer than four of the Portsmouth forwards – Joseph Warrington, outside right, Daniel Cunliffe, inside right, William Lee, centre, and Steve Smith, outside left.

Steve Smith was confused. Steve and his family were going to New Brompton to sign with his new club and see the football ground that he would be playing in, but he was told to get the train for New Brompton and Gillingham station and then he would need to travel to Gillingham to meet officials from New Brompton FC. On no account was he to go to Brompton, because that was actually Old Brompton. He needed to head to Gillingham, which was a village but also part of New Brompton. So he would be playing in Gillingham for New Brompton FC, which wasn't in Brompton because New Brompton and Gillingham were one in the same and soon the whole area would be called Gillingham and Brompton would be called Old Brompton and a part of Gillingham or New Brompton. Steve was still confused but did as he was told.

Brompton dates back to the late seventeenth century, and grew rapidly in the eighteenth century to accommodate the fast-growing dockyard workforce. It was a deliberately planned settlement, laid out by Thomas Rogers, Esquire, the owner of Westcourt Manor on whose demesne lands it was built. In the 1750s, with the building of the Chatham Lines to defend Chatham Dockyard, the village became completely surrounded by military establishments, limiting its ability to expand much beyond its original plan. When war with France recommenced in 1778, it was necessary to strengthen the dockyard defences. Fort Amherst and the Chatham Lines (defensive ditches) were improved and extended, and work was later begun on additional perimeter forts in Chatham and

Rochester. The Barracks – still in existence today – were built to house the soldiers. This, and the expansion of the dockyard, meant that more homes were needed for the workers. The position of the Chatham Lines meant that eventually building could only happen to the east of the defensive ditch, and so New Brompton came into being. The population rose to 9,000 by 1851.

From the 1850s, following the building of New Brompton, Gillingham Station, and the subsequent expansion of the town of New Brompton (Gillingham), the original settlement of Brompton became known as Old Brompton. From the late nineteenth century the importance of Old Brompton as a commercial centre began to decline. Gillingham Green was a small village and eventually it, too, was swallowed up, and the name of the whole settlement changed to Gillingham. Whatever the name of the place he was playing in, Smith loved the history of the town, and he loved the thought of still being paid to play football by the sea.

He had played at New Brompton before and knew the ground was no Fratton Park or Aston Lower Grounds, but the directors had overseen some redevelopments that they were keen to show Stephen and were very proud of their work. The ground on which New Brompton played was called the Priestfield Road Ground due to the piece of land on which the club played, being named after the road on which the land stood.[4] Most spectators would stand on terracing, banked earth, or simply along the perimeter of the pitch.[5] It had a capacity of around 7,000. There was nothing extraordinary about this and the two ends of the ground looked like this. The footballing scene presented to Smith was a modest one.

What the directors were at pains to point out to Steve was that the club had recently purchased an additional acre and three-quarters of ground and had constructed a stand which also contained 500 seats.[6] Add into that a pavilion area next to the stand facing towards New Brompton town centre decorated with black and white stripes from where more salubrious guests who were prepared to pay a bit extra to watch the match, could do so in greater comfort.[7] This was an update to the stand built in 1899 along part of the Gordon Road side of the ground, built by off-duty dock workers in exchange for beer and cigarettes. New Brompton were trying to bring their football enclosure into the twentieth century and Stephen appreciated that. It felt to him like a smaller version of his Portsmouth adventure. His family seemed happy too, Susan knew he loved being a footballer.

What the directors neglected to tell Stephen was that come the winter the Priestfield pitch was horrendous due to the ground being used for other events, such as smoking concerts, fêtes, athletics meetings and a ladies football match. Sheep were allowed to graze on the pitch during the week, a common practice at many grounds at that time. After the season started, however, the state of the pitch would be seen to be the least of Stephen Smith and New Brompton's footballing problems.[8]

New Brompton were still a club set in its ways. Many clubs now, such as Portsmouth and Tottenham in the Southern League had managers in the modern sense of the word, an ex-player with vast footballing experience brought in to take a hands on, individual approach to buying players, training players, imparting tactics and picking the team. If a club was still managed by committee, in that committee there would be directors with specific roles such as at Aston Villa. George Ramsay (a former player) scouted the players and selected them for the team, Fred Rinder organised the transfer deals, Joe Grierson trained the squad and explained the tactics that needed to be implemented.

The fashion was now for a man with a sporting background to have control over team affairs much like the modern day manager. At New Brompton, William Ironside Groombridge, the club secretary was in charge of everything and implemented club policy after discussions with the directors. No one man made unilateral decisions with regards to the team's training and tactics. Although the roles were not as clearly defined in the pre-war era, he is regarded as having carried out the responsibilities of manager since 1896. His uncle, Thomas Saxton, was landlord of the Napier Arms pub where the club was formed in 1893. He also had an influence on the running of the club. They were businessmen with no footballing background and while they had set up and run a club in the Southern League Division One, they were perpetually at the bottom of the league and had never got close to honours.

This was the one worry at the back of Steve Smith's mind as the season got underway against Bristol Rovers at Priestfield Road in front of around 5,000 supporters.[9] Training was not as it had been with Villa and Pompey. The players were pretty much left to their own devices with senior players expected to organise what happened. It was not as professional as Steve Smith had hoped. Nevertheless he was confident his new team could be competitive as it contained his three ex-Portsmouth compatriots of Cunliffe, Warrington and Lee.

The weather was boiling and described as 'almost too hot for cricket', never mind football. The first half saw a tight game and an evenly fought contest, with New Brompton having slightly better of the exchanges. Of the two goalkeepers on show, 'Cartledge (Bristol) had more to do than Martin, but most of the shots came straight to hand'. At half-time Smith was pretty satisfied with how his team were going about things and they came out for the second half in a confident mood.

New Brompton laid siege to the Rovers goal in the second half and their 'front line repeatedly tested Cartledge and half a dozen shots missed by inches only'. Ten minutes from the end of the game the New Brompton backs stopped as Clark, the Rovers left winger, appeared to be clearly offside, he motored on and crossed for Owens to head a winning goal. Defeat was indeed hard to take after such a good performance but New Brompton were praised lavishly in the press:

> The Kentish team gave much satisfaction. The forward line is undoubtedly stronger than last season, and as the four ex-Portsmouth men have a capital understanding, there are good hopes for future successes. Smith and Lee were the pick of the bunch.

Stephen had expected the season to be a struggle and defeat was not the end of the world. But in this new challenge, which would probably be his last as a player, he saw enough to suggest his albeit limited new team could improve on the disastrous previous season and have a year free of relegation or re-election worries.

The key problems for New Brompton were in defence, they lost again in their second game 2-1 at Plymouth Argyle. Martin, the Brompton goalkeeper, kept the score down:

> The performance of the little Brompton custodian was the feature of the match, one particularly fine save at full length from Briercliffe being loudly cheered. The Brompton half-backs and backs were badly beaten in the first half and after McLaughlin had scored the first goal and McKenzie a second after twenty minutes, Argyle looked like piling up a heavy score, Martin alone prevented other goals from being scored.

In attack things were better but the forwards could not avert a second straight defeat to start the season. Danny Cunliffe pulled a goal back with twenty minutes to go and Smith was described as the best of the Brompton forwards, but it was all, too little, too late. Just like last season, New Brompton were once more at the foot of the table.

The men signed from Portsmouth, Smith, Cunliffe, Lee and Warrington started to try and make training a bit more organised. The New Brompton players respected them as they had played for such a successful Southern League club. They listened most of all, of course, to ex-England internationals Cunliffe and Smith, but especially Smith. He had done everything in the game and when the quiet man spoke, people listened. Stephen thought that his new teammates were good going forward but worried immensely about the lack of quality defensively. His assessment of his side seemed very fair after their next game, at home to Brighton. In the previous season New Brompton had finished second bottom and Brighton third from bottom. If either side hoped for a better season this time around they would need a win in a game like this.

There was another decent crowd at Priestfield of around 5,000 spectators for the visit of Brighton in a game that was described as giving those watching, 'full value for money'. Early in the first half Stephen received the ball on the left edge of the area and put New Brompton ahead with a 'fine drive', and after half an hour Marriot scored a carbon copy goal to put the men from Kent 2-0 up. Steve was elated at notching his first goal for his new club but also ecstatic at his team's dominance in the first third of the game.

The second half began with Brompton in the ascendancy but within fifteen minutes it was 2-2, as poor marking and a needlessly conceded penalty had ruined all their good work. Smith was seething, he was not used to playing with players who were used to losing and it infuriated him. Cunliffe put Brompton back in front before reckless defending led to another equaliser being conceded. Just when it seemed like it would be a third game in a row where New Brompton failed to win, Danny Cunliffe hooked a shot back from the by-line and it somehow went over the opposition goal-keeper and into the net. Jubilant scenes followed at the final whistle and Smith was in high spirits. A goal and a victory was very satisfying, especially after the start New Brompton had had. Smith was keen to make a success of his move to Kent. He didn't want to be seen as just another old veteran winding down his career and taking his wages whilst eking out his career for as long as possible. He wanted this move to be like all the others in his career – a success.

In the Napier Arms after the match, club secretary William Ironside Groombridge, his fellow directors and Groombridge's uncle the pub landlord, Thomas Saxton, drank to the players' good health. The ales flowed and Stephen felt like he was back in the Crown and Cushion in Perry Barr. Danny Cunliffe was the man of the hour and was bought many a round of drinks by gleeful supporters and on the walk home at the end of the night, with his usually polite jaw slackened by alcohol, blurted out to Smith what Stephen already knew, 'we can't defend Tich'.

In training the Pompey quartet decided the team should focus on attack rather than defence and try and outscore opponents. It led to mixed results. Reading was the next game and Brompton were thrashed 3-0, but three wins followed with Cunliffe netting in all three victories. After seven games the team now had four wins and three losses. They were ninth in a twenty-team league after finishing second bottom, after a sticky start, things were going okay. Much better than most would have expected. Ridiculously, even though it was very early on in the season the club were just four points off top spot.

The early season optimism was unfortunately a tad premature. The club then went on a six-game winless streak, they lost five out of six matches, drawing the other scoring just two goals. New Brompton's latest defeat, 1-0 home to Norwich had seen Smith's new side fall to 19th place. They were now second from bottom. All the old failings were coming out in the team's performances, things seemed as bad as they had always been for New Brompton.[10]

Relegation would be a financial disaster and it had not gone unnoticed by the directors that against Norwich the attendance had dipped below 4,000. William Ironside Groombridge and the New Brompton directors called a meeting with the club's players. Groombridge was not happy with the team's league position after the summer's investment in player recruitment. The Portsmouth quartet were asked how things were different at Portsmouth. Why were they successful? Smith and Cunliffe explained they had organised training sessions, trainers and a manager. One man, who with the help of the trainer and senior players, drilled the team in terms of fitness and tactics, and made the final decision on who played in the first eleven.

Stephen Smith explained how things had worked with George Ramsay, Fred Rinder and Joe Grierson at Aston Villa. 'Here, you seem to have to do it all, and the other directors do bits and pieces when they can, but there are no specific roles,' explained Stephen calmly and intelligently. If anyone knew how a successful team was run it was Smith. Groombridge was impressed with how Cunliffe, Smith, Warrington and Lee had spoken. He paused for thought and conferred with his fellow directors then asked, 'Where do we get a manager from then?' ventured the club secretary, 'We have never had a full-time manager before, it's not something we have ever done before.'

'We already have a manager, a player manager we can appoint,' said Danny Cunliffe. 'No one has more experience than him. He has played for England and the best football club in the world, he's won everything, done everything in the game,' Cunliffe continued. The directors conferred and discussed the situation again, as quietly as possible in front of the New Brompton squad. This muffled debate lasted longer than the previous conference. This was the direction football clubs were now starting to move toward. One man, an ex-player with plenty of footballing experience who could lead the team in his own way, who would take sole responsibility for team managers. Bob Blyth at Portsmouth had been a player-manager, George Ramsay at Villa an ex-player. Both Ramsay and Blyth had played for the club that they went on to manage.

The modern football manager is almost always an ex-professional footballer, if not always at the top level, and often appointed due to links that the ex-professional had with the club at one time during that player's career. Player-managers are more of a rarity in the twenty-first century but they were prevalent throughout the twentieth century from Blyth at Portsmouth in 1901 to Kenny Dalglish at Liverpool in the mid-1980s. But the modern football manager that we know now, that we expect to see in charge of team affairs and at the side of the touchline of match days, began in the Edwardian Era and in the time of Stephen Smith.

After discussing what Cunliffe had said with his fellow directors, and then gauging the views of the players in the New Brompton squad, William Ironside Groombridge, having asked him if he would agree to taking the job, shook the hand of Stephen Smith and appointed him as the first ever manager of New Brompton Football Club. The club that would be renamed Gillingham FC now had a modern management structure like many clubs in England at this time. Stephen Smith had once again made his mark in history.

With the help of his ex-Portsmouth colleagues, Smith could now run training and pick the team and scout for potential signings without interference from the board and make quick, unilateral decisions to take the team forward. He could do it without endless meetings and discussions with people who knew nothing about playing and running a football team, and who quite frankly had not played the game since they were children and never at the sort of level that could be considered anywhere close to first class. Certainly no one else in the Brompton ranks had scored a goal that had secured victory over Scotland and an international championship title in one fell swoop, that was for sure. It was only Stephen Smith's modesty that had prevented his much-needed appointment as manager happening earlier in the season.

There was no pre-match manager press conference as there is in modern times. No announcement in the press that a new manager had been appointed. Not until the day of Smith's first game in charge did the newsmen realise he was New Brompton's first ever manager, and player-manager to boot. Thus, there is no mention of Smith's appointment until Monday, 3 December 1906 in the *Athletic News*:

> Stephen Smith has been appointed manager of the New Brompton club. For a season or two Steve Smith and his brother William have formed the Portsmouth left wing, but Stephen will perhaps be best known for being a member of Aston Villa who acquired him from Hednesford Town in 1893, so he has completed 13 years in first-class football. Smith played in one International match. He was introduced as a surprise against Scotland at Everton in 1895, and he played such a game at outside-left that has rarely been surpassed. R.C. Gosling, one of many Etonian football brothers was England's captain and Smith's partner on the occasion. The tall and shapely amateur on the inside seemed to play only for Smith, whose sudden sprints quite entangled the Scotch defence. Dan Doyle [Scotland full back that day] will ever remember him.
>
> Unfortunately, Smith was troubled with injuries hence he is not generally referred to amongst the many great Villans. Smith, who is a native of Hednesford, where he was born in 1874 [this is incorrect, of course], 5ft 5in and 11st 6lb, when

well trained. He is possessed of a disposition which should fit him to the position to which he has been appointed.

The excerpt shows that at just 11st 6lb, Smith was still light and lean into his veteran years, and that his calm and quiet persona, sensible, with a desire to lead by example rather than rant and rave, would inspire his players and instil in them confidence to play their natural game due to his calmness under pressure in all aspects of the game. His career and general footballing skill and prowess made him a player footballers wanted to emulate whether young or old.

New Brompton travelled to Luton Town on 1 December having made a couple of changes to the previous match day line-up. They had never won at Luton before and were in terrible form. One player who always played when fit was Danny Cunliffe. Smith knew his ex-Portsmouth teammate was a proven match winner and had also like Smith gained international honours. As Smith took his first tentative steps into management he needed players he could rely on and Cunliffe fitted that bill.

It was not just the New Brompton players who were not looking forward to their trip to Luton. The Luton supporters were not desperate to see them according to the press report. It stated that, 'Brompton usually provide Luton with the smallest gate of the season, and on Saturday under four thousand spectators were present, whilst the takings reached only just over £70'. Stephen and Danny Cunliffe were going all out to gain the victory for their team. Smith's relationship was on the line now as team manager and to a lesser extent so was Cunliffe's, he having vouched for Smith in the meeting with the directors.

New Brompton piled on the pressure in the first half, 'the Kent men had a threatening attitude, Steve Smith continually dropping across centres, and Cunliffe being ever eager to turn them to account'. Despite all the New Brompton pressure it was Luton who scored first, 'Barnes netted smartly, but he was correctly ruled offside'. Steve Smith had never been so relieved to see a goal disallowed. He was now not just responsible for his own performance on a football field but an entire team's as well.

Relief soon turned to joy as the player-manager took it upon himself to once again lead by example. Smith danced down the left wing and crossed the ball into the box for Cunliffe to head home. They were ahead, and Smith was elated, he could see the confidence in his players rise and as ever, he was truly thankful for the ever-reliable Danny Cunliffe in his corner. New Brompton struggling at the foot of the table needed a win. Steve Smith as a new manager needed a win to inspire confidence that he was the right man to lead the club to safety. The second half of this football match was of huge importance for all concerned. As the second half edged into its later stages, New Brompton, understandably started to sink back and defend what they had. Luton's Fitzpatrick 'just missed heading through from a corner', and 'it looked as though Luton would equalise'. In the end the footballing gods were on Brompton and Smith's side that day.

Luton's momentum was checked by losing their player Gallagher for the remainder of the contest, 'he cut his knee so badly he had to retire altogether and directly afterwards, off a well-placed corner by Warrington, Cunliffe headed a second goal for the visitors'.

In front of a tiny crowd, with virtually no one from the Gillingham area in attendance to see it, Stephen Smith's reign as New Brompton manager was off to a victorious start. The obscure nature of the win mattered not. Goals and victories galvanise teams and this was certainly the case for Steve Smith's New Brompton. The match report explained Smith's instant effect on his team, not just in performance but in the league standings, 'Steve Smith and Cunliffe are still too very forwards to meet', Brompton leapt from 19th to 16th, two points clear of the bottom two, the two places where the ignominy of relegation or re-election could apply, thus affecting revenue and prestige with devastating effect.

The goals of Danny Cunliffe continued to flow as New Brompton continued to consolidate their position clear of the bottom places. Cunliffe was on target in a 2-2 draw with seventh placed West Ham in Smith's first home game as manager, and after a defeat at Brentford, Cunliffe scored two more goals to beat Millwall. Two wins and a draw had come from Smith's first month in charge. The directors and supporters couldn't be happier; the directors in particular congratulated themselves on their appointment.

Christmas Day 1906. Footballers today often feel hard done by having to play on Boxing Day, but for many years players accepted that Christmas Day was a holiday where people expected to be entertained. They were the entertainment. This holy day, Stephen Smith was going home, to his second home since he travelled down from Birmingham to play in the Southern League. He was taking his new team back to Fratton Park to play Portsmouth. That he was one of a handful of Pompey heroes who had ever won the Southern League title meant that just like his return to Villa Park he was welcomed warmly and with open arms.

Injury deprived William Smith of playing in this match. But this was probably just as well, thought Stephen, remembering how heated things could get when they played for Villa and Wolves in the 1890s. The scene was set for a great game between former greats and their old employees in front of a large crowd of fans who appreciated them greatly. The match report detailed the build up to this eagerly awaited contest as Portsmouth battled it out at the top of the table with Fulham:

> Yesterday was the first Christmas Day on which Portsmouth have ever played at home, and a typical holiday crowd, numbering 15,000, turned out on a seasonable Christmas morning to see the match. Additional interest was leant to the fixture by reason of the fact that the opposition New Brompton, included four old Pompey players – Steve Smith, Cunliffe, Leeand Warrington – in their ranks. The ground was covered with snow when the players lined out, but it was a delightful morning, and it was soon evident that the rapid thaw which had set in was going to render the ground exceedingly soft and treacherous.[11]

Smith, with so many ex-Pompey players in his ranks, did not need to motivate his team at all. He himself had not chosen to leave Fratton Park, they had decided he was past his sell by date. Unlike his return to Villa Park for a friendly game against a team that had tried their best to keep him, this match was a chance to prove a point. That point being that he and his fellow former Pompey teammates should not have been moved on so quickly.

It was good to be back in front of the Portsmouth crowd whatever the circumstances and mixture of emotions in his heart. Brompton began well, 'the crisp and pretty movements of the New Brompton front rank caused some surprise, it was some minutes before the home half-backs fairly took their measure'. It was clear that Smith and company had a point to prove as they attacked with pace and verve and accurate passing. From a corner, the crowd held its collective breath as Cunliffe headed just wide.

New Brompton were always effective going forward but the old failings persisted at the back and two goals ten minutes apart from Hunter and Elston, Stephen Smith's replacement on the left wing, devastated the men from Kent. That Elston's strike was called 'one of the prettiest goals seen on the ground for a long time' would have no doubt irritated the man he had replaced and yet New Brompton continued to go toe to toe with the superior opposition that they faced, 'Portsmouth by no means monopolised the play, Cunliffe and Lee being specially busy for the visitors and Phillips having several capital shots to save'.

New Brompton continued to have more of the game in the second half, but lost the services of Walker for some minutes, this serving to disorganise them. In the 67th minute the game was up for New Brompton. Elston, Smith's nemesis made it 3-0, and although Portsmouth pulled a goal back soon after when Lee tapped in after Cunliffe's initial shot was blocked it was all over.

New Brompton had battled manfully against the second placed team in the league. Praise was effusive for Lee and Cunliffe, being described as 'at the top of their form'. The press acknowledged what Smith had to work with explaining that, 'the Kentish defence is not quite so good as the attack' but also pointed out the respect that was still there for Steve Smith as Portsmouth put two men on him. The match report explained that, 'Thomson watched the wily Steve (again being referred to just by his first name due to his fame) like a cat watching a mouse, and Digweed, knowing the old Villans tricks gave him no peace'.

Despite the esteem in which Smith was obviously still held it was obvious to all that two goal match winner Elston was the 'best wing on the field'. Like life, football moves on quickly after a change occurs, and however much of a wrench that change first appears to be, nothing lasts forever. It certainly felt that day at Fratton Park that like a 'the king is dead, long live the king' moment had been evident and Smith and the rest of his ex-Pompey faction just had to accept it.

Over the course of the rest of the Christmas and New Year period results were not great. In the League they lost their next three without scoring a single goal and conceding ten into the bargain. They did however take Football League Second Division side Burton United to a third replay in the FA Cup after two 0-0 draws and the second replay was played on neutral ground at Fulham. Smith, an FA Cup winner with Villa and giant-killer with Pompey, was always up for these encounters, he knew it was a great test for his club and due to the national interest generated by the competition it was a chance for his New Brompton side to gain some much-needed glory and acclaim.

Smith himself, now at the grand old age of 33, was still hungry to grab some of that acclaim for himself. Against Burton at Craven Cottage in front of 5,000 spectators, he did just that. Despite Burton having three ex-Fulham men in their ranks the reporter was not impressed with their contribution, stating that, 'there were three old Fulham men in the United team, Bradshaw, Hunt and Gray, but only the first named did anything worthy of his reputation'.

Steve Smith's performance in this match was so dominant that the match reporter was of the opinion that, 'the old Villa man was the best forward on the field and had his efforts received better support the Southern Leaguers would have gained a much more pronounced victory'. Smith kept whipping crosses into the box but the New Brompton players could not take advantage of them, 'New Brompton had nearly all the game in the first half, but were exceedingly weak in front of goal, centre after centre from Smith going a begging, while Hartley shot straight at the goalkeeper from close range'.

Smith, though, was pleased with his team's effort and explained to his men at half-time that victory would come eventually. As ever Smith led by example in order to attain that victory. With half an hour to go Smith picked up the ball for the umpteenth time on the left and set off down the flank, his devilish cross whipped across the face of goal towards the intended target of teammate Hartley, Wood the Burton defender, in trying to avert the danger put through his own net. The crowd were virtually all spectators from Kent and they cheered with delight as the players celebrated with Smith, the gaffer, the engineer of the crucial breakthrough. And as Smith predicted victory was to be New Brompton's. Five minutes later Smith smashed a trademark cross shot goalwards and the keeper could only parry it to Hartley for a tap in.

New Brompton were in the second round of the cup thanks to the genius of their player-manager. The result was noted in the national press. Smith and his players were feted back in Gillingham and despite results in the league not being as good as the directors would have liked, victory had assured an away tie in the next round against Bury of the Football League First Division. This would mean half the gate money from a 10,000 plus crowd would be New Brompton's. The directors were delighted. The top brass at the club knew what lifeline this was for a club who could attract gates of around 5,000 at best most weeks. The immediate financial future of the club had been made secure by the footballing brilliance of its player manager. Things were going very well for Stephen Smith.

After a 0-0 draw in the league with Reading, New Brompton travelled to Gigg Lane, the home of Bury FC in the second round of the cup. Bury were FA Cup royalty in this era, they had won the cup in 1900 and 1903. They had set record margin victories for the final by beating Southampton 4-0 and then Derby 6-0. Little New Brompton had never been past the second round. Steve Smith was the only player in his side who knew how it felt to win the FA Cup. As ever his men looked to him to lead by example in this classic David versus Goliath encounter.

The directors did not even care what the score was going to be. They knew that the gate receipts would be around £300 of which half would be New Brompton's. £150 was the equivalent of around £18,000 today, a very tidy sum indeed.[12] But Smith and his men weren't just there for the day out, just like they hadn't beaten Burton just to swell the club coffers. New Brompton,[13] despite being huge underdogs, took the game to Bury and battled hard in a very tight first half. The 10,000 strong Bury crowd bristled with anxiety as the Southern League team held their own comfortably. Cunliffe and Smith were whipping dangerous crosses into the Bury box with gay abandon but their 'many fine centres were undeveloped'.

Bury were rocking back on their heels as Brompton attacked at will. Smith, Marriott and Hartley all went very close, but there was a feeling at half-time that they had wasted some excellent opportunities. There was also immense pride in Smith's heart at the way his players were matching a topflight side from the best league in the world. It was a huge achievement. But as Smith had already explained to his men, they were there not to play for the directors but for the glory of the game.

The game was even tighter in the second half with only one real chance of note for either team as Smith 'put in one shot which Raeside [the Bury keeper] had much difficulty in negotiating'. As the press report described, 'there was a lack of sting in the attack of the Bury players, while on the other hand New Brompton played pluckily'. The game was heading for a draw and a replay, the New Brompton directors were doubtless rubbing their hands in the grandstand at the thought of a second big pay day.

Towards the close 'there was a tameness about the proceedings' as minds wandered to what might happen in the replay. Spectators were making for the exits as Bury back Lindsay hoisted a ball into the Brompton area, Gildea helped the ball on and somehow it skimmed past every other player in the penalty box melee that followed and nestled into the New Brompton net. Gigg Lane erupted in celebration, New Brompton players sank to their knees and then the referee blew the final whistle. New Brompton retired beaten by a goal, scored with absolutely the last kick of the game.

The Bury players sheepishly took the acclaim of the crowd but in reality the applause was for the New Brompton men. Steve Smith beamed at his players, crestfallen in the dressing room. He explained that football was not always about money, or winning but it was always about the way you perform and they had beaten one Football League team and matched a First Division Football League team on their cup run. They had kept the club financially secure through their exploits and they should be proud of themselves. It was then time for a smoke and a drink.

The money from the cup run would be vital for the running of the club, in New Brompton's next two home games only a combined 4,000 people watched the 3-1 win (in which Smith scored) over Northampton and the 2-1 defeat to Leyton Orient. They were then thumped 3-0 at QPR as the cup hangover continued. Stephen Smith's New Brompton FC had slumped down to second from bottom, the threat of relegation or having to apply for re-election was back. A second straight season in the bottom two could spell demotion and even lower crowds which would certainly threaten the club's existence. Northampton were bottom with 15 points, New Brompton were next with 17, then Crystal Palace had 18 before a gap of three more points to fourth bottom QPR.[14]

Steve Smith was under the pressure, but that was something he had faced throughout his football career. He was used to challenges, being written off and fighting back. He was confident he could turn things round, he always did. The problem was, their next fixture was against Fulham. Fulham were top of the Southern League. This most difficult of encounters was a microcosm of New Brompton's season against the better placed teams. They battled hard and matched more illustrious opponents before being undone by late goals. Smith was, as ever, his side's most effective attacking outlet, 'getting away and crossing' for Marriott to give the Kent side an early lead. The crowd were shocked by what was happening, the second bottom side were ahead against the league leaders.

Spirits in the New Brompton ranks, in the stands and on the pitch, were high and it could, and perhaps should, have been even better. As the match report stated, 'the home forwards made a number of dashing onslaughts, and it was only the safe keeping of Fryer (the Fulham keeper) that kept them from increasing the lead'. The second half was equally one sided:

> On crossing over the play continued to run in favour of the locals, and the defenders were lucky to keep their goal intact on three occasions when bullies took place in the mouth of the goal. Fryer too, was frequently tested but he cleared all the straight shots, and he was admirably covered by the backs. Mariott and Godley, however, missed easy chances of scoring.

Therein lay the problem for New Brompton, all season they had played exciting, attacking football, but often couldn't get the second killer goal in games. They had improved a lot up front thanks to the quartet of Pompey frontmen that had been acquired in the summer. Unfortunately, the problems at the back from the previous season had continued more often than not. A tendency to switch off late on in games had cost the club many points in the league and also a longer run in the English Cup.

Late on in the game, Fulham winger Threlfall was sent through on goal and he burst past the flat-footed Brompton right back, Harvey, and silenced the home crowd with an equaliser. It seemed as though the goal had to be chalked off for offside 'but the appeal was overruled'. Smith was disconsolate, New Brompton had squandered the lead again after missing a host of chances. It was déja vu all over again.

Two more draws and a defeat followed in the next three games. The team seemed hapless and helpless in equal measure. No matter how well they played in attack they would always fail in defence. New Brompton were now just three points off the bottom of the league and it was the nadir of the season, but a late goal by the ever-reliable Danny Cunliffe rescued a 2-2 draw at Watford and another defeat was avoided. Despite the fact it was a sixth straight game without a victory they had played well again and been unfortunate to not to win. Again, Steve was convinced that if his team could just keep going, take their chances and have a bit more composure at the back, things could turn. He knew from experience that with a bit of luck and a goal at an opportune moment a team's destiny could change for the better out of all proportion. His problem was to transmit his steely confidence and belief to the rest of his squad.

Cunliffe and the rest of the ex-Pompey crew had seen it all before and knew their luck could change. For the rest of the players who knew regular defeat, it was easier said than done for them to buy into what Smith was telling them. As far as they were concerned not much had changed from the previous season in terms of their footballing fortunes.

New Brompton had attracted 5,500 supporters for the game with Fulham and their next home game after three winless away games was Swindon Town at home. Here 5,000 saw enough in the Gillingham side's performance to come back again for this encounter. As usual New Brompton scored, and played well and as usual they conceded a frustrating equaliser. The game was level at 1-1 at half time and New Brompton's luck just would not change after the break. They 'attacked repeatedly for a quarter of an hour after the change of ends, but the forwards didn't finish well and easy openings were missed by Hartley and Cunliffe'. Another draw was on the cards as the ball bobbled around by Marriot who was hugging the right hand touch line in the Swindon half of the pitch. He looped a hopeful ball into the opposition box. Everyone in the area missed the ball, everyone except Steve Smith, the ball came through to him somehow, he wasn't sure how, but the Swindon backs missed it and he didn't hesitate to smash the ball home.

The spectators threw their hats and sticks in the air, the cheers rang out and Smith was embraced by his jubilant team mates. The relief engulfed him, they were headed to only their second league win of 1907, second in eleven games and the first in two months. Mr T. Kirkham, the match referee, soon blew the whistle to end the game. Cheers rang out once more, Smith and Cunliffe embraced. It felt like a turning point, a big one, a slice of luck had gone in their favour for once. As Smith said to his men in the changing rooms after the match, it can only take one bit of luck or one goal to be scored and your outlook can look very different.

Smith had once again dragged his club through to victory. He had made a career of big goals in big games. Now in Kent at the foot of the Southern League in front of only a few thousand fans, Smith felt as good as he had at Crystal Palace in 1895. The venues might be more modest but scoring a goal and winning a football match, well the elation of that never dimmed for Stephen throughout his career. It was why he kept on playing. Football was a habit he just couldn't kick.

The victory over Swindon truly was a turning point for Steve Smith's New Brompton and their season. Including the victory over the Wiltshire club, Brompton won five and drew three of their last nine games. Thirteen points from the final eighteen available saw the club surge away from relegation and re-election danger to a final position of 15th. But that didn't tell the whole story – finishing with 33 points, they were just two behind Southampton up in 11th. The 33 point haul was the highest amount of points they had ever achieved in a single season, 11 more than the previous year and Smith's record in charge was a respectable 7 wins, 8 draws and 10 defeats. Had they matched this win rate for the whole season they would have achieved around 10/11 victories which would have seen them comfortably in mid table. The late season run included some very memorable moments indeed in Steve Smith's debut season in football management. Following the Swindon victory, New Brompton went two more games unbeaten and were now four games without defeat before the visit of Smith's old team Portsmouth. Steve's brother, William, was still with Pompey and the nearly men of the Southern League were having yet another tilt at the Championship title.

Fulham were top with 46 points from 34 games, Portsmouth had 42 points from 33 matches. This game in hand had to be won by Pompey if they were to stay in contention for the title, with just four more rounds of matches to go after this match at Priestfield Road. New Brompton had of course picked up form wise and would continue to do so, but at this time it was second placed Portsmouth versus third bottom New Brompton.

Seven thousand fans packed into the ground in what was a capacity crowd and highest gate of the season. The *Portsmouth Evening News* explained that Pompey fans thought that, 'judging from the smart game they played at Fratton Park on Christmas morning, Steve Smith and his colleagues, want a lot of stopping'. Steve and his team had been unlucky in the first game. Smith and his ex-Pompey players would always have something to prove against their old side who had decided they were surplus to requirements at the end of the previous season.

All footballers find themselves in such a situation at some point in their career. Smith was no different. He and his players wanted to be another example of when ex-players come back to haunt their old club.

At the end of the day, when your career ends, it's not how much money you earned or even the trophies you won that defines you as a footballer, but your reputation as a player. How you are remembered by the people that paid to watch you, that is how immortality is achieved. Smith and his men were determined to give the Portsmouth supporters, directors and management something to remember them by.

William Smith stared at his brother from across the pitch and smiled, he could see his older brother had something to prove against his former side. They were, of course, on opposite sides of the pitch being left-sided players, but William could see the steely look in his brother's eye. William was a Portsmouth legend in length of service alone, but it wasn't until his brother had arrived that he had become a champion. Steve Smith was a champion, and his brother and the rest of the Portsmouth team feared him and what he could do to the opposition. They had seen what he could do time and time again.

The weather was hot and fine, with no breeze, the pitch dried out and hard as this time of the season often dictated. The crowd had been swelled by supporters of Portsmouth who could be heard loudly cheering on their team as play kicked off. Steve Smith picked up the ball early on and careered at speed down the left-hand flank as sure as night follows day and crossed for Hartley who flashed a shot just wide. Steve was up for this, as was the New Brompton crowd who roared him on.

Danny Cunliffe, of course, was also let go by Portsmouth in the previous summer and he combined next with Smith. As ever the *Portsmouth Evening News* referred to Stephen Smith just as Steve. He was still a big deal at Fratton Park and held in very high regard. He was even referred to just as Steve in games when his brother William was not playing, such was the love and affection they had for a man whose arrival had changed the whole club's outlook towards how to go about winning big matches and claiming trophies. In Portsmouth everyone knew in footballing terms that there was only one 'Steve'.

The reporter stated that, 'Cunliffe was prominent with a smart pass out to Steve who shot wide'. Considering the heat and the state of the ground, which was very trying, the play was very fast, and Portsmouth forced matters, with delightful combination play between Mackenzie, Dalrymple and Kirby culminating in the latter centring straight across the goalmouth. Pompey were desperate for the victory, four points difference would be a mountain to climb with only four matches to play after this one.

Portsmouth continued to press, Kirby swung the ball to the back post where William Smith was lurking and seemed certain to score, but he just couldn't connect properly with the ball and the chance went begging. While the Smith brother in the colours of Portsmouth was missing good chances, the Brompton Smith now had two men dogging his every turn 'to nip his movement in the bud'.

New Brompton continued to have the better of the first half, 'Walker tried a cross-shot which went wide after good play by Cunliffe and Smith.' Cunliffe and Marriott also hit shots that went well wide while they were in the ascendancy. Steve Smith worried they would be made to pay for these missed chances. William Smith, annoyed at his employers for dropping his brother from the payroll, nevertheless had a job to do and a title to win. He was determined to see the job through and knew that sentiment would have to take a back seat. Portsmouth were getting back into the game as half-time approached and from one of a succession of corners, Billy Smith managed to send 'a well-judged header' towards goal, 'missing by inches'. The game was tight, nip and tuck, title challenger versus relegation battler, brother versus brother, ex-players cleared off the wage bill looking for revenge. The game had so many caveats and contexts that just added to the drama on show. But who, if anyone could gain an advantage?

William Smith continued to have an influence over proceedings even if he didn't always make the right decision in possession. The match report explained that, 'Billy Smith looked to have an easy chance close in but went out to the right wing instead of shooting and the chance was lost'. New Brompton were happy to soak up pressure as Portsmouth made the running as they went in search of the breakthrough that would keep them in the title race.

Five minutes before half time, New Brompton broke away and Stephen Smith was sent clear down the left flank. He could see fellow old warrior Danny Cunliffe racing into the Pompey box. He knew what he was going to do instantly and whipped a left cross towards Cunliffe who anticipated the ball and got ahead of his man to send a header crashing against the crossbar. Luckily Hartley was able to bundle the ball home from the rebound and New Brompton were ahead. In a quaint corner of Gillingham, nearly 7,000 supporters erupted with delight as plucky little New Brompton FC took the lead against the mighty and high-flying Portsmouth.

The *Portsmouth Evening News* reporter was unimpressed with the state of affairs, stating, 'Brompton certainly did not deserve the lead on the play', and perhaps that was a fair assessment. Brompton had started well, but as Portsmouth had got a grip on the game, the first Smith to score in the match seemed more likely to be Billy than Steve. As it was, it was Brompton who went in at half time a goal to the good. Cunliffe and Smith, surplus to requirements at Pompey last spring were now looking like they were going to derail the south coast's club this time around.

Portsmouth didn't seem to heed the warning of not marking Smith and Cunliffe more tightly as, 'upon restarting New Brompton got away on the left and from Smith's cross, Cunliffe shot wide'. Smith and his teammates knew that Portsmouth would have to chase the victory and by throwing caution to the wind in attack, there would be gaps in their defence to be exploited on the counter. 'Portsmouth swarmed down on the New Brompton goal' but the defence held firm.

Portsmouth were dominating possession but struggling to create chances on goal. As the continued heat started to sap the strength of both sets of players, Portsmouth became increasingly desperate. Dalrymple sent a shot high over the bar and 'from a rally in front of Martin's goal, Billy Smith sent wide a right foot shot'. Billy had had chances, like for Wolves against Villa all those years ago, also against his brother, and had fluffed his lines again. He was sick of the recurring theme when Steve was a direct opponent.

As the game entered its last quarter, Portsmouth continued to be frustrated and Steve Smith continued to be in thorn in their side on the counter-attack, his dribbling and crossing, relieving the pressure on the Brompton goal, if nothing else. Perhaps Portsmouth were wondering what might have been had Smith and Cunliffe been kept on. The *Portsmouth Evening News* certainly gave Smith his dues that day:

> Portsmouth struggled gamely to reduce their opponent's advantage, but their marksmanship was weak. Portsmouth played much better football without meeting with any success. Steve Smith put in several fine runs, and was the best of the home forwards, his centres being accurate. Martin saved a grounder from McKenzie and the game continued in the Brompton half, the locals defending strongly.

The one-sided match report, favouring Portsmouth notwithstanding, New Brompton were hanging on to the slenderest of leads. In the last few minutes it hardly mattered if Portsmouth equalised, they needed a win, a draw was no good. Stephen already knew his side had done enough to make a point to his ex-employer. Right on full time, Steve Smith whipped a free-kick into the Portsmouth area and Marriott headed home 2-0, almost immediately the referee blew for full time and the game was up for Pompey. 'We've stuffed up again,' Steve, said Billy as he trudged off with his older brother. The New Brompton crowd were jubilant, Priestfield Road, bursting at the seams was in full voice, the Portsmouth support slinking away into the night. Billy Smith took comfort in a family meal with his brother and their families in Gillingham Green but the damage was done.

Stephen Smith had been the architect of Portsmouth's only league title in 1902, and now in 1907, the architect of their downfall in their title battle with Fulham. It had been yet one more example of writing off Stephen Smith at your peril. There was now a 4-point gap between Fulham and Portsmouth with just four games to go. As far as other press outlets were concerned the championship was now Fulham's to lose and they were far less complimentary about Pompey's performance than the *Portsmouth Evening News*: 'Portsmouth by suffering defeat at Gillingham yesterday have practically lost all chance of wresting the Championship of the South from Fulham. The side playing in a disappointing manner. The home side quite held their own and won by two goals to love.'[15]

The defeat to New Brompton would prove incredibly costly to Portsmouth as they lost out to Fulham in the end by just two points. Steve Smith's performance that day would be forever remembered as one that cost Pompey the title, but he would always be remembered by Portsmouth fans as one of the clubs first superstar players. The directors of Portsmouth in charge in 1907 may well have remembered him with a little less affection but then it was their choice to let him go. A choice that in the end proved to be a very costly decision. Smith's New Brompton as we know, went from strength to strength at the end of the season, three wins out of four brought the footballing year to a close. Smith's goal, the fourth in a 4-2 win over Crystal Palace was the last goal they scored in a very satisfying end to 1906-07.

The Gillingham FC scrapbook summed up the improvement under Smith when comparing the 1905–06 season and that of 1906–07:

> 1905–06 was to be the club's worst season since joining the Southern League 10 years earlier. Scoring goals was proving to be a problem yet again and they only managed a paltry 10 goals at Priestfield all season. In 1906–07, ex Aston Villa and England International, Steve Smith was appointed player-manager half way through the season (he originally joined as a player in May 1906) and a decent end to the campaign ensured the team would finish well clear of the bottom two.

When you understand the context of the club that Smith had walked into, where the side had never had a 'proper' manager in the modern sense of the word before, you can see what a solid job Stephen managed to do on top of continuing to play at a consistently high level. He was 33 years of age and while his footballing powers were waning he still had enough ability and fitness left to inspire his team mates and have an effect on games, all the while overseeing tactics and the general day to day running of all the footballing aspects of the club. He was one of the first 'modern' managers that are now part and parcel of the game. It would seem strange not to have a football team led by a manager in the twenty-first century but at the start of the twentieth century this was not a given. It was seen as an oddity, a fad that probably couldn't and wouldn't work. How could one man be entrusted with so much responsibility, especially an ex-footballer, a usually uneducated member of the working class? Well, because of trailblazing individuals with tremendous ability and force of personality – men like Stephen Smith.

The 1907–08 season, Smith's second at New Brompton, began with frustration, a frustration that would under normal circumstances may have led to him not re-signing with the Gillingham club. But with Susan expecting their third child later that year the Directors explained to him that they would need to cut costs and would not be able to pay players more than they were currently earning. This presented a problem to Steve. His best players in the previous season, as the club had comfortably pulled clear of the bottom two, had been the ex-Portsmouth contingent. Centre forward Billy Lee had an offer to go back up to the Midlands and have a second stint for Chesterfield in the Football League.[16] Derbyshire was also a lot closer to his native home of West Bromwich and his friends and family than Kent. Chesterfield were prepared to up his wages, Brompton not being one of the Southern League clubs that could pay huge wages. They took gates of around 5,000 but these could dip to 3,000 at times and it was a far cry from the 15,000 plus crowds at Portsmouth FC. As a footballer who had been in a similar situation regarding wages, he accepted that Lee had to go where the money and his family were. There were no hard feelings between the two men whatsoever.

Joe Warrington followed Lee to Chesterfield on a better deal than New Brompton could offer. Again there were no hard feelings, Smith understood the economic situation for both players and the club. But there was one more mortal blow on the transfer front that Smith believed ultimately the club would be unlikely to recover from. His right-hand man, Danny Cunliffe, top scorer, the man he'd won the Southern League with at Pompey accepted a better offer at Millwall Athletic.[17] This decision stung the most. The board wouldn't stretch to match Millwall's offer. It was doubly frustrating because Millwall were direct rivals in the Southern League whereas Lee and Warrington were out of sight and out of mind. It was a decision that would come back to haunt the Gillingham based club.

Cunliffe going, also hurt because they had been close comrades during the title success with Portsmouth of 1902. They had worked well together on the training pitch after Smith had become manager as well. Smith was not as enthused by the men brought in to replace the Pompey trio and he was filled with trepidation for the new season. Despite this he was confident he could get his methods across to his squad as effectively as ever and improve on the previous season's finish.

He should not have been so confident. Only one of New Brompton's new signings really excited Smith. Charlie McGibbon was a 27-year-old centre-forward who, after being let go by Woolwich Arsenal, had played well at Eltham and accepted the more frugal contracts on offer at New Brompton much more gladly than those experienced and now departed ex-Pompey players. McGibbon scored on his debut at Bristol Rovers but New Brompton lost, 9-1. It was the prelude to a disastrous season that would see New Brompton finish rock-bottom like so many times previously after failing to invest and back Stephen Smith following the previous season's success. Despite this, in the competition that was the springboard to Smith's leap towards stardom, the FA Cup, there was one last, glorious hurrah.

A 6-0 thrashing of Shepherd's Bush in the fifth qualifying round of the FA Cup thanks to a McGibbon hat-trick meant they would play English giants Sunderland at home in the FA Cup first round proper. Steve Smith had done it again, his side had secured New Brompton's medium-term future with a guaranteed sell-out crowd in the offing and a bumper pay-day. The Priestfield Ground had been renovated to be able to house around 15,000 spectators and all those extra seats would certainly be filled for a game against one of the great sides in English football history.

Sunderland had been League Champions four times, only the Aston Villa side that Steve Smith had played for had won the title more times. Indeed New Brompton could claim to have more League Championship medals in their ranks than First Division Sunderland thanks to Smith's five awards. Sunderland had still never won the FA Cup, in fact the closest they had ever got was the semi-final of 1895. That day they had been beaten 2-1 by Aston Villa thanks to two goals by a certain Stephen Smith. That performance brought Steve Smith into the public spotlight and gained him England and Football League XI recognition.

In January 1908, Sunderland and their old nemesis had seen better days. Smith, of course, was winding down his career near the foot of the Southern League, whilst Sunderland were struggling in the First Division and would finish just two points above the relegation zone that April. The English Cup offered Sunderland respite from their league travails, and it was another shot at the one trophy that had eluded them during their glory years tussling with Villa and Smith at the turn of the last century. New Brompton was seen as a straightforward route into the second round. Cup fever abounded everywhere as was reported in the local press:

> All football lovers in the district are agog with excitement over the Association Cup tie which is to be played on the Priestfield Road ground today between New Brompton and Sunderland. It has usually been the fate of the local club to be drawn away when they have had to meet a strong team in the competition, and therefore their good fortune on this occasion is the more appreciated. The opportunity of seeing a First League team is too good to be lost and consequently there will be a large influx of visitors into the town, the

Railway Company providing special cheap facilities from various parts of the county.

In order to meet the extra demand for accommodation in the banking at the Rainham End of the ground has been further extended, no fewer than 300 loads of earth. It is now calculated that 15,000 spectators will now be able to obtain a good view of the match. The stands will accommodate 800 and there will be a steady demand for tickets. It is expected there will be very few empty seats.

Stephen Smith had learned a lot about big match preparation while at Aston Villa where he had been on many a training retreat with coastal air as a prerequisite. He organised his team preparation as to get the men as relaxed as possible for their mammoth task:

The New Brompton players have been spending the week at Herne Bay, making the Tower Hotel their headquarters. Mr J. Evans (one of the directors) is in charge of the men, who have been quietly preparing for the match. They have put in a lot of walking exercise and have also indulged in sprinting. The training, however, has not been of an arduous character, and everything has been done to cause the time to pass pleasantly. So far as can be ascertained, the players are in excellent fettle, and will turn out prepared to do their level best to learn the right to enter the second round. They recognise they will have a stiff task to face, but they are not without hopes of proving successful.

Sunderland were a team similar in style and play to New Brompton. As the statistics of the time explained the team from the North East arriving in Kent with a big squad of players to choose from, also seemed to have the same strengths and weaknesses as Smith's men: 'The Sunderland secretary has forwarded to the New Brompton club a list of 31 players from whom the team will be chosen. The players will arrive at Gillingham this morning and will put up at Beacon Court Hotel. It may be noted that the visitors possess a strong attacking line. In the 23 matches they have played in the League they have scored 41 goals and have given away 49.'

By kick-off the atmosphere had reached fever pitch inside the Priestfield Ground. The press report set the scene:

> It is not too much to say that no match that has been played on the ground has attracted so much interest as the one fought on Saturday. This is not surprising, seeing that it was the first time that a First League team had appeared at Gillingham in the national competition. The expectations that there would be a record gate were fully realised, the official returns of the attendance being given at about 12,000, while the receipts amounted to £413.

Stephen Smith had never seen so many people crammed into the Priestfield ground before. His side were in fine fettle and raring to go having arrived at the ground that morning straight from their retreat at Herne Bay. The Sunderland team were also well rested and ready for battle having 'broken their journey at London on Friday and completed it the next morning'. It showed that even back in 1908, football clubs planned their away trips and match preparations meticulously.

The 12,000 fans that had crowded into the stadium had been streaming in constantly from around Kent as the match report explained:

> The bright sunshine in the morning tempted many to make the journey from different parts of Kent to the scene of the match, whilst the residents in the neighbourhood turned up in their thousands. From one o'clock onwards there was a constant stream of pedestrians to the ground. Vehicles of all descriptions, from the up-to-date motor car to the coster's cart, were to be seen depositing their human loads. Inside, it was all bustle and excitement. The click of the turnstiles proceeded merrily, whilst a small army of checkers were engaged in receiving the tickets.
>
> By two o'clock – half-an hour before the time fixed for the match to start – there were fully 8,000 onlookers present, and this number was eventually swelled to 12,000. It was quite a sight to see the crowd of faces all-round the ground. Almost every inch of space on the banks at the main entrance end was utilised.[18]

As the two sides took to the field they were met with a wall of excited noise from the large crowd, the largest ever seen in Gillingham at the time, all thanks to a second season in a row of cup heroics from Smith and his team. Sunderland were the first to turn out and received a hearty reception. The Brompton men, headed by Steve Smith, appeared on the pitch a minute later and were cheered to the echo.

For Steve it felt like the old days at Villa. The big crowds, the big cup matches, and of course, it reminded him most of the semi-final of 1895. It was a long time ago, he was 21 back then, he was 34 now. He couldn't sprint as fast any longer, he couldn't run and run without stopping as he used too, it hurt more when he got kicked, he stayed down for longer when injured, and yet, he still loved the game as much as he ever did. He knew he would not be able to play professionally much longer. That was why he had become a manager as well to try and stay in the game for longer, to keep getting paid to be involved in the game he loved, despite all its pressure and physical and mental sacrifices.

Smith noticed that the Sunderland players had made sure that their knees were strapped up or covered by their socks. This was due to the fact that the severe frost had made the ground very hard and the action of the sun in the morning had made the pitch slippery in places. Smith was asked to call the coin toss by the referee, a Mr Gilgryst, which he won and attacked away from the main entrance end of the ground, it offered no advantage whatsoever as the wind swirled straight across the middle of the pitch and not to the back of either team.

Steve shook the Sunderland skipper's hand and watched the red and whites kick off, he was ready for this match, he wasn't sure when he would next get to play against a team of this calibre again. He wanted to savour the occasion, he did not know how many more of them he would be able to be a part of now that time was catching up with him. The ground was shaking with the excited movement and noise of the crowd as Sunderland came forward from the off. Low of Sunderland hit a long shot just wide from this early attack and it was clear for all to see that the First Division team meant business. It seemed as though New Brompton would be overwhelmed in the early exchanges. Harvey and Floyd the Brompton full backs were inundated with Sunderland attacks but defended manfully according to the reporter in attendance who wrote that, 'the visiting forwards showed rather better combination than the locals, but the opposing halves would not allow them to really settle down to their work, and whenever the middle line were beaten the backs were able to repulse the attacks. Both Harvey and Floyd played a resolute and fearless game, their tackling being very effective.'

Steve Smith saw very little ball in the first half, and it did seem like he was replaying one of those tight Villa-Sunderland games from his early days. He would have to be patient for any chance that came his way. The crowd could sense that the home team would need their support throughout and Mavin was loudly cheered stopping Sunderland's Raybould when he got close in. New Brompton were hanging on in the contest but only just. They were kicking and scrapping for dear life in the midfield area, 'always bustling their opponents'.

The volume of the crowd became louder as McGibbon, receiving from Smith, made his way into the penalty area, but whilst manoeuvring for position, he was blocked by Bonthron; it seemed that try as they might neither side could make the crucial breakthrough. It was always Sunderland though who looked the more likely. Holley, the Sunderland inside right, hit a shot that arrowed towards goal and only at the very last minute did Martin tip his drive onto the bar before Floyd cleared the rebound. All around the ground 'a sigh of relief was heard'.

As New Brompton got a rare foothold going forward, Stephen finally had a chance to get the ball down and run at his opposition, it was not quite Ewood Park in 1895 but he slalomed past one opponent after another before hitting the ball across the goalmouth, it seemed someone just had to tap the cross home, but groans rang around Priestfield Road as every Brompton player missed the ball and the chance had gone. At the end of half an hour, 'nothing had been scored, but the next two minutes saw the onlookers roused to a high pitch of excitement'. A swift move forward by the Sunderland attack led to McIntosh slamming a shot at Martin who managed to stop the ball, but the effort knocked him to his knees and as he tried to get up to collect the rebound, Holley slammed the keeper and the ball into the net. In 1906 that meant a goal not a foul. Sunderland were ahead and 'the visitors could not contain their joy at this success'. It must have been a relief for their players to go ahead, defeat to a side outside of the Football League, especially one that had been beaten 9-1 already that year, and near the foot of the Southern League, would be unthinkable and humiliating for the men from the North East.

Smith could see heads drop among the ranks of his team. But he knew that in any tight game, if you didn't capitulate and stay in the fight, success was still possible. Smith would soon be proved right. From the kick-off the ball was rushed down by the home right, and on a corner being conceded Hopkins dropped the ball in front of the goal and McGibbon headed it into the net. Straight away it was 1-1. The crowd erupted, Smith congratulated the goal scorer and the noise rang around the ground with visceral intensity, 'the spectators gave vent to their feelings in a wild outburst of cheering'.

As the first half came to a close, New Brompton now looked the more likely. Sunderland's worst fears had been realised now that the Kent side had equalised. The fans were even more ebullient, the Southern League players, once despondent and full of trepidation, now bullish, led as ever by Sunderland's seemingly eternal nemesis, Stephen Smith. In the dressing room at half time, morale was good. Smith had been in this situation many times before and was calm and explained they still had a great chance of winning the match or at least taking it to another money-spinning match away at Sunderland as they had the year previously against Bury. The home crowd, though, was baying for victory. They had got behind their team from the off and it was clear that New Brompton could mix it with the men from the First Division. As the match report detailed, 'the good show made by the Southern Leaguers led their partisans to believe that they stood an excellent chance of winning the match'.

Despite the confidence in the New Brompton ranks, it was Sunderland who came out all guns blazing at the start of the second half. McIntosh forced Martin into two saves including one which needed to be tipped round the post for a corner. The next moment in the game led to pandemonium on the terraces of the Priestfield ground.

New Brompton broke down the left with Smith, he fed the half back Robotham who drilled the ball into the area for the arriving Salter who seemed certain to score, a last-ditch challenge however forced him to touch the ball back to McGibbon who was arriving on to the scene at pace. McGibbon 'ran a few strides and drove the ball into the corner of the net with one of his express shots. It was a beautiful goal, scored six minutes from the restart, and hats and sticks were wildly flung into the air, while the crowd shouted themselves hoarse.'

Steven Smith was jubilant. The previous year they had run First Division Bury so close before succumbing to defeat with the last kick of the game. Now they stood on the precipice of victory against one of the giants of the footballing world. They just had to hold their nerve and see home the advantage they had now gained. Sunderland, of course, would not bear this humiliation lightly. They were still in the match despite being a goal down just as New Brompton had been earlier in the contest. The outcome of the contest could still go either way. Sunderland were rocking at this point. From Smith's corner the ball was headed just past the post.

After that chance Sunderland regained their composure and attacked relentlessly with an equaliser seemingly inevitable. The report explained in detail how hard-pressed New Brompton were defensively in the middle portion of the second half:

> Hartley (the Brompton forward) rendered good service by the manner in which he constantly dropped back to support Robotham. Sunderland were by no means settled, and Tait caused some anxiety with a shot that passed perilously near the upright. In dealing with a low drive from Bridgett, Martin slipped, but recovered the ball and pushed it behind as he was charged by Raybould. At first it was thought that he was badly injured, but a little attention by the trainer put matters right and he was able to resume. Nothing accrued from the corner kick and Harvey got the ball away in a scrimmage from a free-kick.

It had become a brutal battle for survival as both sets of players clattered into each other like their lives depended on it. But the result remained in the balance. Gradually New Brompton were able to break out and attack once more but the crosses of Smith and Hopkins were not utilised by the home forwards to much effect.

The game was heading into the last ten minutes and New Brompton worked the ball out to Smith on the left flank. He had been in this position so many times before in his fifteen year professional career. Once again the outcome would be as it usually was, a positive one for him and his club. In what was described as 'one of the prettiest pieces of play seen in the game', Smith careered down the left flank and bore down on Sunderland right back Bonthron, he slowed down and allowed the full back to come close to him before sending McGibbon through on goal 'where he again defeated Ward (the Sunderland keeper) with a splendidly judged shot'.

McGibbon made straight for his captain and manager and hugged Smith as the rest of the team congratulated them. The crowd 'went nearly mad at this further success'. The Sunderland players knew the game was up. Soon afterwards the whistle went. Sunderland of the Football League at that time, the second most successful club in English football history, former World Champions in 1895 had been beaten by New Brompton, sixth from bottom in the Southern League. A side, led by the very man who had once single handedly knocked them out of the FA Cup and ended their double dream, one Stephen Smith.

No sooner had the players walked from the field to the rapturous applause of the New Brompton faithful inside Priestfield Road, the pressmen began filing their reports of the momentous events that had just taken place. The local press of course were particularly effusive in their praise of the men from Gillingham:

> The good people of Gillingham have reason to be proud of their football team. The records of the club show some smart performances, but none of these will compare with the brilliant victory which was gained over Sunderland on Saturday on the Priestfield Road enclosure. In defeating the Wearsiders by such a margin as three goals to one, the locals not only surprised their own supporters but the football world generally.

The Press in the North East were equally agreed on the fact Sunderland's defeat was unexpected, but that the victory of New Brompton was justly merited:

> Great was the sorrow on Wearside on Saturday when it became known that Sunderland had been ousted from the English Cup competition. Local enthusiasts are now disposed more than ever to appreciate the triteness of the dictum that behoves us never to despise our opponents. For beyond question Sunderland were strong favourites for entry into the next round even amongst impartial critics. New Brompton's confidence proved to have some grit in it after all.[19]

The local press explained the context of how impressive the result was, even if Sunderland were not quite the team they once were:

> The Wearsiders are not one of the leading teams in the First League this season, but their name is written large in records of cup fights. It is not many years since they were known as the team of all talents, and even although their glory has somewhat departed, it must rank one of the best wins in the series of ties, second perhaps only to the fine victory, which Norwich City gained over Sheffield Wednesday, the holders of the trophy.[20]

For Stephen, it was another satisfying result in his seemingly burgeoning managerial career. Then came a disastrous end to the season for Smith as injury and influenza ravaged line-ups and they lost game after game. For Smith, who had never finished last in anything in his footballing life, it was devastating. With the chairman not prepared to let Smith bolster the squad for the following season a parting of the ways was agreed.

And just like that, in the summer of 1908, Steve had played his last professional football match (at Southampton on 4 April, 1908), scored his last first class goal (18 January, 1908) and the Smiths were on their way back to Portsmouth, looking for a business in which to invest Steve's savings. Stephen Smith, after fifteen years, international recognition, five league titles, participation in a double winning team (of which there are only eleven such sides), an FA Cup winner's medal, a Southern League championship and an appointment as New Brompton's first ever full-time manager was a professional footballer no longer.

Chapter 18

Life After Football

Stephen loved living by the sea and going back to Portsmouth, more importantly Southsea, was the perfect fit for the Smiths. They were reunited with Stephen's brother Billy and wife Helena who the brothers Smith had gone to school with back on Cannock Chase. Susan had had it tough looking after three children and a sick husband in Gillingham. Now she was back with Helena her sister-in-law on whom she could always rely. Helena also had one of her own and another one on the way. The family was all back together and teammates Billy and Steve were reunited. But playing for Portsmouth was now at an end for them both.

After 266 appearances and 85 goals over nine years, in which Billy was one of the first set of signings Portsmouth ever made when they were formed in 1899, playing in the club's first ever match, they had decided not to renew his contract. So at the age of 32, Billy signed for non-league Gosport United and went into business as a 'licensed victualler' – a pub landlord, just like Steve's good pal Charlie Athersmith. The *Hampshire Telegraph* explained that, 'Gosport United F.C. have secured the services for the coming season of W. Smith, the erstwhile Portsmouth player, who has gone into business as a licensed victualler at Portsmouth. Billy Smith will play for Gosport in the Hampshire League.'[1]

Portsmouth had finished mid-table and were looking to invest in youth. Billy was also struggling with bouts of pleurisy that would just not clear up due to his occupation as a footballer, constantly outdoors in the winter. He was convinced his bronchial problems had started during a reserve match between Portsmouth and Brighton, which began in a snow blizzard and was abandoned three minutes later as the snow continued to teem down, 'you couldn't see the other players', he recalled.[2] So he decided it was time to end his professional career and look for other opportunities to make money as he did not want to move his family from a place he loved to play football. Like Stephen he wanted to live by the water. Billy was playing fewer and fewer matches every year due to the wear and tear on his body and the bronchial problems associated with pleurisy. Professional football would have wanted more than Billy's body could give in 1908.

While Billy was embracing the life of a publican and played football part-time, Stephen invested in the perfect business for a man who loved life on the coast. Smith became a fishmonger in Southsea.[3] His eldest son, Stephen Charles Smith, worked as his assistant after he left school, whilst William, named after his uncle, resumed his schooling in Portsmouth after his brief hiatus in Kent, and Susan looked after baby Irene.

For the next few years Stephen and his family lived out their new lives without professional football looming over them as it had done for so long. The only football that was talked about was the continued non-league adventures of uncle Billy who couldn't bear to give the game up fully, not even after becoming an insurance collector where he would do his rounds in the company of his wife Helena. While the highs and lows of Portsmouth FC were always bubbling in the background in the press and when the good people of Southsea could be seen from Stephen's fishmongery boarding the trains to Fratton Park, any thoughts of Aston Villa Football Club were based on dim and distant memories. And then one sorrowful day, all the memories of his glory days came back into focus. On Monday 13 September 1910, Steve opened up the newspaper as he did every morning after collecting in the first of the day's deliveries from the local fisherman's catch.

After a while he turned to the sports section and what he read made his stomach turn: 'Charlie Athersmith, the old Aston Villa forward, is lying seriously ill at his mother's house in Oakengates, near Wellington. For some time he managed the Grimsby Town Football Club, and recently he had charge of a public-house in Evesham-street, Redditch.[4]

He'd not heard from his old friend in quite some time. It had been years since Charlie had stayed with Stephen. Athersmith had been his guest when Small Heath drew Portsmouth in the English Cup. He was still in the pub landlord game at that time and continued to dabble in that industry until like Steve he had made his way into football management. Like Smith he had met with limited success before getting back into the public house industry just as Billy Smith had on fully retiring from the world of football.

Smith was upset and worried about the news he had just read. He needed to know if his great friend was all right, but before telephones and mass production of motor cars it was very hard to contact people instantly and travel still took a very long time. Smith simply could not leave his business and family for any considerable length of time. He resolved to send a telegram inquiring about Charlie's health. He knew that if he could get that delivered he could find out exactly what was going on. In 1908 you could just simply lose touch with even the closest of friends and family, such was the remote nature of communication technology at this time. Letters and telegrams were still the most usual way of contacting someone, but replies could take weeks and months. You could not just pick up the phone or travel across the country by car or even plane as you can now. People accepted that was the way life was and that you might not hear from people in weeks, months or even years.

Steve waited a week and had no reply. His friend was on his mind constantly through that period. Exactly a week later, reading the same newspaper at the same time of the day Smith's heart broke. He read the following information in the newspaper on Monday, 19 September 1910:

DEATH OF CHARLES ATHERSMITH – FAMOUS VILLA FOOTBALL PLAYER AND ATHLETE

The death of Charles Athersmith, the once famous Aston Villa right-winger and athlete, occurred at the residence of his mother (Mrs. Hancocks) at Oakengates, Shropshire, shortly after noon on Sunday. Athersmith, who was about 40 years of age, leaves a widow and one child. In his day he was the fastest football player in the country, and won many prizes on the running track. He took part in twelve international football matches (Scotland 1897–98–99–1900, Wales 1897–98–99–1900, Ireland 1892, 97–98–99), and was at one time one of the stars of the Aston Villa team. Athersmith's illness is thought to have had its origin in a severe strain or a kick in the stomach when playing football.

On Sunday, 18 September at the house of his mother, Victoria Villas, Station Hill, Oakengates, Shifnal in Shropshire, Charlie Athersmith passed away.[5] The great Charlie Athersmith, key member of the all-conquering Aston Villa side of the Victorian era and then lately the publican at the Royal George, Evesham Street in Redditch was gone.

Steve thought of how lucky he had been to survive his bout of influenza at the end of his time at New Brompton that had wiped out not only him but three-quarters of the squad and how Albert Woolley had lost his life so prematurely, his body ravaged by disease brought on by constantly playing football in inclement weather, week in, week out. In his sadness he could not but help think about the ridiculous game against Sheffield United that both Steve and Charlie had played in. The ridiculous wind and rain and sleet, Charlie playing down the wing with an umbrella in his hand and over his head. The amount of players on both sides that went down with bouts of illness during and after that game. He thought about Charlie standing out in the cold as manager of Grimsby Town.

In his anger and despair he wondered if that had contributed to Charlie's early death, along with all the other games played in bitter conditions. Conditions that would have led to games being postponed until the advent of undersoil heating in modern times. Games that would have been postponed until the weather was better, warmer. He knew he was lucky, that Billy was lucky, his game had been called off in crazy conditions after three minutes. Steve wondered how many other games like that had not been called off over the years. Games needed to be played, fans had paid their money. Billy's game was probably only called off because it was a reserve game.

Then as now, footballers have to play in almost any conditions, at any time, whenever the pay master dictates. The game must be played. The show must go on. In 2020 the Premier League made its players play on during Covid-19. The television companies would have wanted their money back if the league had been cancelled. Money has always dictated what players will be made to do, when they will play, how they will play, how many games they must play to fit in games lost through postponement whether it be snowstorms in 1908 or Covid-19 in 2020. He who pays the piper calls the tune.

Steve felt like another chapter of his life was closing with the death of Charlie Athersmith. A bygone age, the adventures of his youth were sliding out of view as the years marched on. But when a member of Austrian royalty was shot in Bosnia, a place Stephen had never even heard of, it would change his world and the world of everyone in Britain and its Empire beyond all recognition. It would make his childhood years, kicking a ball about with his brothers and friends on Cannock Chase, seem like a beautiful, imagined dream of innocence and youth from an age that would be lost forever.

The assassination set off a rapid chain of events, as Austria-Hungary immediately blamed the Serbian government for the attack. None of this seemed of any consequence to Stephen as he read about these goings on in a dim and distant land. But the event set off a chain reaction leading to a German attempt to conquer the whole of Europe and forcing Britain to declare war on Germany on 4 August 1914. On 9 August, the British Expeditionary Force (BEF) began embarking for France to defend their allies.[6]

It was soon clear that to defend France and regain lost French and Belgian territory the British would need more men, many, many more men. Lord Kitchener, Secretary of State for War, introduced voluntary enlistment to expand the British forces. The rapid and unprecedented expansion of Britain's land forces in 1914–1915 was a gigantic act of national improvisation which helped to create, not only Britain's first-ever mass citizen army, but also the biggest single organisation in British history up to that time.

The recruitment drive called for men between the ages of 19 and 35 to join up. Stephen Smith, now a 40-year-old fishmonger, was exempt on grounds of age and profession. As someone involved in distributing food on the home front Steve would have been exempt from military service even had he been of recruitment age. His business would have undoubtedly had to close if he went to war, so on this count as well Steve would not be called up in the earliest years of the war.

Steve, though, was very worried that his eldest son Stephen Charles would be forced to join up. Stephen Charles was a fine outside left like his father and was being courted by local football clubs including Portsmouth F.C. Stephen was 18 in 1914, so just underage, but of course he could easily pass for 19 if he went to the recruitment office. His son also felt the pressure to join up.

Stephen was also worried that even though he was underage now, eventually he would be 19. March 27, 1915 would be Stephen Charles' nineteenth birthday and his father was deeply concerned about whether or not as an assistant fishmonger that would class as a 'reserved occupation' in the same way actually owning the fish business patently did. It was important due to the rising societal pressure for men to be seen to be 'doing their duty'; those remaining at home needed to adequately demonstrate they were working in the national interest and constantly validate the reasons for their being kept back. Smith hoped his son's job would entitle him to papers and a special badge to prove he was undertaking war work on the Homefront.[7]

Billy Smith at 38 years of age was also too old to enlist, and his sons were mercifully far too young to be expected to fight. Stephen's two eldest brothers, John and Charles, were far too old and his youngest brothers, Henry and William both survived the war but it is unclear if they served. The war continued into 1915 as the two sides settled down for the stalemate slaughter of the trenches.

John Smith, the eldest of the Smith brothers, was living and working in Manchester at this time and it was in Manchester that his son Samuel Smith joined up to fight in the 9th Battalion of the Rifle Brigade.[8] The 9th (Service) Battalion landed at Boulogne-sur-Mer as part of the 42nd Brigade in the 14th (Light) Division in May 1915 for service on the Western Front.[9] They took part in most of the same battles as the 7th and 8th battalions.[10] Samuel Smith survived the Second Battle of Ypres, which had begun on 22 April 1915 and the action at Hooge in July 1915 where they saw the first use of flamethrowers by the Germans.[11] By 8 August, Samuel, Stephen Smith's nephew, was dead. We can not be sure where he fell, there were no major actions in early August involving Samuel's battalion but the records state he was lost to this world in 'France and Flanders, killed in action, Western European theatre'. He had been at war for just four months.

It was another brutal loss to Stephen's older brother John who had lost his wife in 1908 and this led to him relying on their mother Elizabeth to look after John's youngest two, John and Dorothy in Hazel Slade as he continued to work in Manchester. The family was devastated by the loss of Samuel and it heightened Steve's worries over the fate of his own eldest son who by the time of Samuel's death was 19 and able to enlist. Stephen's anxieties were set to continue. The British Government introduced conscription in March 1916 because voluntary enlistment could no longer meet the army's need for recruits. Under the terms of the Military Service Act, all medically fit single men between the ages of 19 and 41 were deemed to have enlisted in the armed forces on 2 March. In May 1916 a second Government act extended conscription to married men and the age limit was lowered to 18.

Stephen and Billy found it ironic that after all Steve's angst over his son's fate, now Billy, at the age of 40, was expected to join up. In the end Stephen (despite being 42 and not required for service until April 1918 when the age limit was raised to 51) and his son were eligible for the War Service

Badge Certificate, as the fishing industry on the south coast was protected by the Royal Navy and Germany tended to focus its naval efforts around the North Sea. Much as key workers in shops and supermarkets were needed to keep food supplies up and running in 2020, the Smith fishmongery was needed to feed the people of Portsmouth and the surrounding area. Stephen Charles could still have ended up in the Army by the end of the war for a short period if only on the home front, but the evidence is inconclusive. If he did go, he returned unharmed to his father.

In the end, of Stephen's closest relatives in terms of blood and geography, it was Billy himself who was conscripted into the army in 1916 in the Royal Field Artillery. In an interview many years later Billy revealed that, 'he spent the most enjoyable and exciting days of his footballing career (in the army)'.[12] It was enjoyable because, 'he was playing soccer for the sheer joy of it – not partly from the cold hard necessity of earning a living, and exciting, because in many of the Army teams he played against, he frequently found footballers from some of the big professional clubs'. Billy would not be demobilised until 1919.

Despite his lengthy stint in the Army, Billy did not go to France. The recollections of Billy's granddaughter's husband (who never met Steve Smith) provided by his nephew Ray Stubbington, explained that:

> For a period of time he was stationed at Bordon which is an army training base just north of Waterlooville, where they were living. He remembers that Billy's son, 14-year-old William John (my uncle's father in law) used to cycle to meet Billy at Bordon with additional provisions.

At 11 o'clock on 11 November 1918 the guns fell silent on the Western Front. The Great War was over. Like nearly every family in Britain, the Smiths were wounded by the loss of a loved one in the fields of Belgium and France. The newspapers of the day mixed joy with reflection. None more so than the *Irish Independent*.

The Irish had given up many men for the British cause and its main newspaper poignantly pointed out the feelings of the majority of the victors on their headline page:

> The enemy has to go back behind the Rhine, and submit to seeing the strong places along its banks occupied by the

victorious troops of the Allies. The nations and peoples who have triumphed over the spirit of modern Germany may well exchange felicitations upon the outcome of the long and bloody struggle. Amid the popular clamour, natural though that be it cannot be forgotten that hearts are sore in many homes, for the loved ones that will never revisit them. The war-makers have inflicted wrongs which they can never redress; they have caused desolation and sorrow for which no earthly power can provide a healing balm.

Stephen Charles Smith, Steve's eldest son had survived the war. To his father that seemed like the greatest triumph of his life, never mind the war. The relief turned to pride as Stephen junior made his professional debut for Portsmouth in the spring of 1919. He then, after playing just one match in the Southern League, secured a contract in the Football League with West Ham United. He made his Football League debut at Coventry in December 1919, scoring his only goal for West Ham in a resounding 6-0 win over Bury in the FA Cup a month later.[13]

He made 31 appearances before joining Charlton Athletic in the summer of 1922 and had three seasons at The Valley, scoring 10 goals in 102 appearances before a move to Southend United in the summer of 1925. At Southend he scored 11 goals in 86 appearances over the next two seasons, joining Clapton Orient in the close season of 1927. However he only made seven appearances, scoring once, in a single season in East London, before joining Queen's Park Rangers in the summer of 1928. He had a single season at Loftus Road, scoring once in 25 appearances before finishing with professional football.

Stephen Charles Smith may never have played in England's topflight nor scaled the heights of his father, but in a career delayed by the Great War, in which he did not make his professional debut until he was 23, he was able to play over 230 professional matches. In 1929, after ten years in the game, he retired at the age of 33. He was a left-footed winger just like his proud father who loved to watch him play.

Steve Smith senior continued to live and work in Southsea running his fishmongery business. Every now and then he would once more don his football kit and put on his boots in the aid of a good cause. The *Hampshire Advertiser* of Saturday, 23 October has a picture of a still stout, stocky and athletic looking Smith, who despite a slight pot belly and greying hair, whiskers and moustache, looked at 49 years of age like a man who could still easily take on the other old internationals who played in the Veterans match at The Dell, earlier that week in aid of the Newspaper Press Fund.

As Stephen's children, Stephen Charles, William and Irene grew up and flew the nest, Smith and his wife Susan decided they wanted to live a quieter life. They decided to move to Benson, a tiny village in South Oxfordshire. Steve and Susan took over the running of The Roke Stores in Roke, a hamlet, a stone's throw from Benson. The village is about 1½ miles north of Wallingford at the foot of the Chiltern Hills and the confluence of a chalk stream and the River Thames, next to Benson Lock.

Yet again Stephen was drawn to live by the water. He was from the West Midlands, the canal capital of the world and of course he played for Aston Villa in Birmingham which has more canals than Venice. There were plenty of canals, streams and rivers near Hednesford. Hazel Slade had a brook nearby adjacent to Cannock Chase. He did then, of course, live by the coast when playing in Portsmouth. Whilst at Gillingham he lived near Chatham Docks and now he lived at Benson with its canal lock and its close proximity to the River Thames. In Stephen's time it was quite the tourist attraction particularly with boaters.

Roke Stores was a small village shop in part of a cottage in Roke which is now called The White Cottage. There was a ground floor rear extension which probably housed the stock room and a large barn at the end of the garden. It was adjacent to a farm and near to a public house called 'The Home Sweet Home'. The cottage itself was large enough to be considered a spacious, detached house. The front, facing the road, had three large windows that were segmented into 16 panes of glass divided by timber bars painted white. Each window had large blue wooden shutters either side. Instead of a window in the bottom left-hand section of the cottage frontage, there was a traditional shop front with a door into the store and a large 36-pane window in the same style of the other three windows but without shutters displaying the goods sold in the shop.

It was a beautiful country cottage and plot of land with a small, calm and manageable business for a couple in their late 50s. If this was not full retirement it was certainly partial. Stephen had everything he needed, he was able to invest some of his savings into a business that was also a beautiful place to live with his beloved wife and what was more, Steve could still live by a stretch of water as he had always aspired to do.

In the 1930s Stephen lived happily and quietly in his new Oxfordshire home. He was living in a vastly changed world to the one he entered into when he was born in Abbots Bromley, Staffordshire in 1874. Unlike the late Industrial Revolution era into which Steve was born, there was mass unemployment in the Thirties. There was already mass unemployment in the 1920s then in the early 1930s the economy was struck by The Depression.

Steve himself was lucky that he was never out of work throughout his life, but although many in the North struggled, new industries such as car and aircraft making and electronics prospered in the Midlands and the South of England where unemployment was relatively low.

Stephen had left school at just twelve years old to work down a mine. By the 1930s children were now forbidden from working in such brutal industrial conditions. Furthermore education was a totally different experience for Stephen's children compared to his schooling. In 1900 children in Britain sometimes left school when they were only 12 years old. However, in 1918 the minimum school leaving age was raised to 14. Between the wars, working-class children went to elementary schools and had the chance to go to grammar schools with their middle-class counterparts. The world had changed politically, not all men had the vote when Stephen was born, now they all had it and women finally gained the right to vote in 1929.

While democracy was evolving in the UK and the USA, it was faltering in Europe. Fascism characterized by dictatorial power, forcible suppression of opposition and strong regimentation of society and of the economy, came to prominence in early twentieth-century Europe. The first fascist movements emerged in Italy during the First World War, before spreading to other European countries.[14] The conditions of economic hardship caused by the Great Depression brought about an international surge of social unrest. In Germany, it contributed to the rise of the National Socialist German Workers Party, which resulted in the demise of the Weimar Republic and the establishment of the fascist regime, Nazi Germany, under the leadership of Adolf Hitler. With the rise of Hitler and the Nazis to power in 1933, liberal democracy was dissolved in Germany and the Nazis mobilized the country for war, with expansionist territorial aims against several countries. This was the world of the 1930s, a world in which Stephen Smith was living now as a semi-retired ex-footballer.

This was the young man who worked in a colliery at the same time as amassing medals and trophies and England and Football League caps.

The man who refused to have his wages capped in a country that prided itself on Liberal free trade internationally even if that did not always extend to its own workers' wage rights.

He was a trailblazer who left for better wages in an upstart Southern League that aimed to match and supersede the more established Football League by coaxing footballers south to enjoy unrestricted earnings in a way that would be seem as totally acceptable and in no way taboo in the twenty-first century with the Premier League, professional Rugby Union and the riches of the Indian Premier League cricket competition.

Footballers and the working class more generally, were expected to know their place in the Victorian and Edwardian era and accept the wages and role in society that was defined for them. Stephen Smith, who grew up surviving, living a hand-to-mouth existence like so many others, refused to accept this and created a better life for himself and his family. He was a symbol of a changing world, a more egalitarian, levelled-up world. There was still work to be done in breaking down the class barriers of twentieth century British society, but Stephen Smith had more than played his part.

Then on Sunday, 19 May 1935, Stephen Smith on his one day off from the week, suffered a stroke and collapsed at his home in Roke, near Benson. He was taken to the nearby Littlemore Hospital but died later that day. He slipped out of this world almost thirty years after the end of his professional career. He was still famous enough, however, that his passing was noted in newspapers the length and breadth of the land.

The *Belfast Telegraph* reported simply: 'STEVE SMITH DEAD. Steve Smith, the former Aston Villa, Portsmouth and International outside left, had a fatal stroke at his home near Oxford on Sunday'. The *Sheffield Independent* explained that, 'He was one of the best outside lefts the game ever produced'. In Portsmouth where he had helped to deliver the Southern League title they so craved the *Portsmouth Evening News* reported the event at the front of the paper not in the sports pages at the back, as follows:

STEVE SMITH – DEATH OF FORMER POMPEY FOOTBALLER

News has been received at Portsmouth that the former Aston Villa and Pompey international outside left, Steve Smith had a stroke on Sunday and died. One of the best outside-lefts the game has ever produced, he delighted onlookers by his twinkling footwork on the wing and the accuracy of his centres. After his retirement from the game he was for a number of years a fish merchant in Fawcett Road, but recently he had been residing in the neighbourhood of Oxford.

In Birmingham, where he had gained international recognition whilst at Aston Villa amongst all the other laurels won, his death was reported on the same pages of the *Birmingham Gazette* as those usually reserved for the key national and world events relating to the United Kingdom. Smith's obituary was perceived to be as noteworthy as a certain Adolf Hitler's speech on relations with Poland and France now that he had become Chancellor and what his intentions regarding German Foreign Policy would be. Next to analysis of Hitler's speech was set, the respectful reporting of Stephen Smith's passing. A dubious honour no doubt, but one that showed the esteem there still was in Birmingham for a player who had not been seen in claret and blue in 34 years.

The *Birmingham Gazette* report went as follows:

> STEVE SMITH DEAD – Former Aston Villa Player Succumbs To Stroke. Steve Smith the former Aston Villa and Portsmouth forward, has died as a result of a stroke at his home, near Oxford during the weekend.
>
> During the heyday of his career, over thirty years ago, Smith was considered one of the cleverest outside lefts in the game. He figured in many important matches for Aston Villa with his famous partners Dennis Hodgetts and Fred Wheldon.
>
> Small in stature, Smith's touchline dribbles and brilliant centres were a feature of his play. Smith was secured by Aston Villa from a Black Country club and following his service with the Aston club he went to Portsmouth. He was capped for England against Scotland in 1895.

Despite all the plaudits from a glittering football career, Stephen Smith was laid to rest in the modest surroundings of Benson cemetery situated over the road from St. Helen's church. His funeral took place on Friday,

24 May, 1935. Stephen's wife Susan, his partner since the earliest days of his footballing adventure and beyond, was comforted by Steve's sons, Stephen and William and daughter, Irene.[15]

Smith's two surviving brothers, Billy and Henry, were also present as well as his elder sister, Mary Ann. Billy was devastated. Steve was his best friend. Only they understood how each other felt about the pressures of playing football. They were teammates at Portsmouth and so close that they named their second sons after each other.

Billy and his family found solace in the huge amount of flowers in the church during the service, sent in tribute to Stephen. Smith was a quiet man, a modest man, but a much loved man by family and public alike who followed him in Birmingham and on the South Coast. He was probably quite unaware of how important he was to so many people far beyond the confines of his own friends and family.

He, as with many professional footballers, probably didn't realise that when you play for a club at any level, that your occupation is more than just a job. You are an extension of the local community that the football club represents and the player fights for the honour and reputation of that aforementioned locality. Smith gave the workers of Cannock and Rugeley Colliery, and in particular the people of Hazel Slade who provided the colliery company with the majority of its workforce, a sense of pride when he signed for Hednesford Town. That someone like them could make the grade as a footballer. He won them many trophies in local football, many victories over rival town Cannock. The people of Hednesford and Hazel Slade could walk tall at work amongst their Cannock counterparts after Steve Smith's winner vanquished the old enemy, and of course, he still walked amongst them as a haulage engineer in the mine.

It was at the coalface that Smith was signed by Fred Rinder, director of Aston Villa Football Club. He continued to be a local hero but on a bigger regional scale. His exploits on a national stage for Villa and England gave people of Birmingham pride in the glory accrued by its flagship club. It was a club followed across the Midlands and one that flew the flag for the region in the Football League as Villa became the greatest club in England, and also on the planet after dispatching the best Scottish teams of the age, as well as consistently winning the only fully professional football competition in the world at that time.

An ordinary man doing extraordinary things and still working shifts down the mine when time allowed. Smith never forgot his roots and the industrial Midlands burst to the seams with pride from the Colliery on Cannock Chase all the way across to Perry Barr and the Wellington Road ground when Smith was called to play for England against Scotland. Many people across Staffordshire and Warwickshire basked in the reflected glory of the man from Staffordshire playing for England and scoring the winning goal to take the 1895 International Championship. It was all done on the back of his form for a football club that has had its headquarters in both Staffordshire and Warwickshire. In football where you are from is important. In England where you are from is important. You can pinpoint where a person comes from in this country to within around fifteen to twenty miles based on their accent. Even when he played for Portsmouth, you knew that Stephen Smith was from the western half of the English Midlands and those people from that part of the world are intensely proud of their parochialism.

To the majority of the country if you are from South Staffordshire or North Warwickshire and Worcestershire, Rugeley, Hazel Slade, Hednesford, Cannock, Burntwood, Lichfield, Tamworth, Sutton Coldfield, Perry Barr, Wednesbury, West Bromwich, Small Heath, Bromsgrove or Wolverhampton – you must be from Birmingham. But that is simply not the case and Stephen Smith won honour for the Brummies of Perry Barr and Aston who sounded different to the people of West Bromwich and Wednesbury, who in turn sounded a little different to those from Wolverhampton and ever so slightly different to the more watered-down Midland tones of those from Lichfield or Bromsgrove.

He was a true local hero for an area obsessed with keeping its nuanced Midland identities. Victories over West Bromwich by Villa were won by players like Smith ,not Brummie bragging rights, but for Birmingham victories over the Black Country. The imaginary dividing line that cuts through Handsworth and means you are either a Brummie from Aston or Perry or Great Barr as opposed to a member of the Black Country simply yards away in West Bromwich.

Then when you add into that the national battlegrounds in which Smith often ended up gaining national glory for his Birmingham club whilst directly humiliating the clubs from the Black Country, in winning trophies for Villa and thus taking them out of the hands of Wolves, but most especially and bitterly West Bromwich Albion, as in 1895, you can see he was the epitome of a prodigal son made good on a national stage. Then on the South Coast, Stephen Smith won the Southern League with

Portsmouth at the expense of bitter local Hampshire rivals Southampton. Whether winning glory in the Football League or the Southern Championship, Smith was known to a national audience. He had fame throughout the land for his achievements. Fame that lasted for at least a generation after he retired.

His legendary feats were clutched to the bosom by the people of the districts he represented and meant that although he retired from football in 1908, his reputation saw that his death caused a great stir in the footballing world, a generation later in 1935, especially in Birmingham and Portsmouth. To the people of the Midlands and the south coast his glories won for them gave him and their football clubs national prominence and because of this to these proud communities he was truly a national and local hero.

Postscript

When researching Stephen Smith's life, I was hoping, Covid-19 restrictions permitting, to go and visit his grave site and take a photograph of his headstone for the book. For me it would have been a little bit of a personal pilgrimage to see the resting place of my subject, as it were. Due to the funeral details in the newspapers of the time it was fair to assume that as Benson only had one church, St. Helen's, that is where Stephen must have been buried. The only bone of contention was that the press reports suggested that he was buried at Benson cemetery, not at the church.

My partner, Rachel, visited Benson Library where burial records are kept and meanwhile she had contacted the Reverend Patrick Gilday at St. Helen's church. He said that the church's paperwork 'was not fulsome, but there is a record of a grave to Stephen Smith in the so-called 'New Churchyard' in Benson'. He went on to explain that: 'This is a churchyard over the road from the main church, in which some Commonwealth War Graves are also situated. The earliest burials in that churchyard took place in the late 1930s, so I would imagine that the Stephen Smith is buried there. If so, his grave is in the first row, just to the left of the lych gate.'

Rachel asked the Reverend if he could take a photo of the headstone for the book, due to the pandemic making it impossible to visit the Church at the time of our research. He replied, having had a look in the churchyard, that: 'It does not look like a memorial was ever placed to Stephen Smith, so there's no photo to give you I'm afraid!'

This was disappointing and sad; this great man, a lion of a footballer who had contributed so much to the game, was resting in an unmarked grave. It seems as though no one ever got round to placing a lasting memorial after Steve's death. None of his family lived within easy reach of Oxfordshire and by 1939 and the outbreak of war, Stephen's widow, Susan was living with her daughter, Irene, and her husband in Orpington, Kent.

Postscript

With the descendants of Stephen Smith and the nation having bigger things to think about between 1939 and 1945 than a gravestone being placed in Oxfordshire, it is no wonder that it was overlooked and eventually forgotten and so the reason for writing this book took another twist, not just to honour Stephen's memory, but perhaps to help raise funds for a permanent memorial to a footballing hero who represented England, Villa, Pompey, Gillingham and Hednesford Town with such distinction. A world champion at club and international level, a man with as many league title winning medals as Peter Schmeichel, John Terry and Wayne Rooney. A man with more league winners medals than Eric Cantona, Sergio Aguero, David Silva, Dennis Bergkamp, Frank Lampard, Cristiano Ronaldo, Thierry Henry and Alan Shearer.

Surely this man deserves a memorial, I thought, a gravestone to mark his burial site at least. It was pretty obvious it was Stephen who lay there but we needed a plot number from the records office to prove it before the campaign for a headstone could get underway. Dave Rushton who runs the Family History Clinic at Benson Library was our 'knight in shining armour' in terms of being a mine of information on Benson in general and getting us the confirmation we needed on the point of Stephen Smith lying in Benson churchyard. Although I had ancestry.co.uk I was not *au fait* with the finer points of all the searches. Dave pointed out that on Ancestry there was already a family tree on Stephen – the Holcroft tree – where descendants have put on information about relatives. Another check showed he was buried in St Helen's Church Benson on 24 May 1935 and that there is no stone at all. My aim is to get some sort of headstone or memorial placed – somehow with permission from Stephen's family.

Through Ancestry we were able to locate three people who included Stephen Smith in their family tree and one of them, Sue Jones, explained that: 'Stephen was the husband of my third cousin so no blood relation. It looks to me that all his children didn't have grandchildren, but I could be wrong. Susannah (Steve's wife) was a general servant in Birmingham just before she married Stephen. I have no objection whatsoever in a headstone being erected in his honour. As you say he deserves better. Stephen's son, Stephen Charles Smith called Stephen C.W. Smith (born 1924 died 1988). He and his wife didn't have any children.'

Thanks to Sue I was able to ascertain that Stephen Smith's direct descendent line had now unfortunately died out. Michele Holcroft was also very helpful in locating family members and photos of Stephen Smith in the family. Nicola Theobald got in touch with a photo and newspaper cutting of Stephen Smith playing football for Portsmouth, also a picture of Billy Smith in later life standing with General Montgomery at Portsmouth and a photo of him with his wife when they were much younger.

It seemed that no one had any objection to the erection of a headstone for Stephen, so then I went cap in hand to the football clubs he served hoping perhaps for assistance with fundraising and also to see if there was anyone else the football clubs knew who was related to Stephen and who I could ask for permission from to erect his headstone. The Football Association replied negatively and the Football League didn't reply at all. It was ironic that their lack of interest mirrored the lack of interest in footballers' welfare back in the early 1900s that led to Smith's departure down south. Hednesford Town and Gillingham also neglected to respond, but in a worldwide pandemic it is understandable that clubs the size of these with resources stretched to the maximum would not have the manpower and resources to reply to every email sent to them. Despite the best efforts of Marion Stringer, former Aston Villa Club Secretary, no one from Villa Park got back to me regarding Stephen either.

Of all Stephen's former clubs, Portsmouth FC were really helpful right from the start. I sent an email to Portsmouth on 30 November 2020 and had a reply from Colin Farmery on the same day: 'I am chair of the Pompey History Society, which is a charitable organisation responsible for managing the club's archive. I have copied in Paul Boynton and Graham Dubber from the society who between them will be able to see what we have on record about Stephen. We would certainly want to be kept in the loop about your project.'

Paul Boynton then contacted me: 'If you are looking for any particular information during his time at Portsmouth, let us know. If I remember rightly, I did provide some information for a relative of his brother Billy three or four years ago. I'd be very interested in a copy of the book when it becomes available.' Paul was able to put me in contact with Ray Stubbington, whose uncle was married to Billy Smith's granddaughter. Ray proved to be a mine of information about Stephen and Billy, all of which is covered in this book.

Dave Rushton came back to me with more information on the same day as the Pompey History Society got in touch. The current owners of the old Roke Stores provided information and a little background on the shop and a picture of the building in the early 90s showing the old shop window. They also passed on an invitation to visit the old shop, their home, while the village magazine – *The Benson Bulletin* – would mention the book and the plan for a headstone.

From Ancestry.co.uk I was able to find out the fate of the rest of the Smith family after Stephen's death. Stephen's brother Billy died in 1955 and his three sons have all since died. Stephen's second son William was a Cooper Bus Conductor in Portsmouth and died in 1973. His daughter died aged just 39 in 1970, three years before her father. Stephen's youngest child, Irene, took Susan to live with her in Kent and as the last surviving member of the family, died childless at the age of 93 in 2001. Susan and Irene would have been well cared for as Smith left an estate worth £592, the equivalent of over £42,000 in today's money, a sizeable sum to help support his daughter's family and his widow.

Three things leapt out at me after all this. Firstly, the enormous local and family pride that Stephen engendered in all the people who have so willingly given their time and help, despite his passing eighty-five years ago. Secondly, that football has and always will be a universal language and conductor of community that leads to comradeship, a desire to help others and a longing to work for a common goal. The third conclusion is that there is a limit to how much you can expect people to do if you don't have something tangible to bring to the table yourself, the ultimate piece of publicity in getting Stephen Smith a headstone was to get my book finished and published. Only by that would Smith's name be in the public eye in a manner that would make people sit up and take notice of the cause. Otherwise, the campaign to get the headstone erected was just about a bloke with a collection of information about a Victorian footballer claiming he was going to write a book about someone who may or may not be famous.

People needed to be able to make their judgement on whether or not Smith deserved to be remembered with a headstone. Until his exploits had been written down for posterity, the case for my claim that Stephen Smith's life deserved a greater physical commemoration than he already had, and that it was right the football clubs that he served so well would help in bringing that about, could not be made. I decided to worry about the headstone later and resolved myself to the fact that I needed to finish the book.

Addendum

As I dotted the I's and crossed the T's on this book, Cannock Chase Museum got in touch with me about a photograph copyright request I made. Yvonne Cooper, the curator explained they had, 'an athletics trophy in the name of Stephen Smith in the museum collections'. On 25 October 2021, Yvonne invited me in to see the trophy. It was a small silver cup about 15 centimetres high with the engraving, 'presented to S. Smith of *The Athletic Sports*, HAZELSLADE, AUG.1, 1891'.

The 130-year-old trophy, presented to Smith a month after he'd won the Wednesbury Charity Cup with Hednesford, was given to the museum in 2019 by a Mrs Glynis Tingay, the great-granddaughter of Stephen Smith. Stephen's grandson Stephen C.W. Smith did have a child after all, and it was Glynis! Yvonne and her assistant Ray Smith had her contact details and at last a direct blood link to the man himself had been found.

Stephen Smith then, at just 17 years of age, whilst playing football for Hednesford Town was also winning trophies for Hazelslade Athletics Club. Ray at the museum said it was likely he was also a cricketer as well but further investigation was needed. Whatever the outcome, it was clear that Smith was a very gifted sportsman in more than one discipline. It was also clear that from speaking to Glynis that Stephen was not only a man of many talents but also a man of the people. Glynis sent me an auction catalogue of all Smith's football medals that had been sold. Many of his medals for winning the Birmingham and Staffordshire Cups were missing as they had been given to friends who were in financial difficulty, either to get cash or to be used as security in pawn shops to obtain a loan. It seem despite his stardom Steve never forgot his friends.

Glynis had a wealth of personal recollections that were of great interest. She had met Stephen's wife Susan in her later years, by this time confined to a wheel chair, and thought perhaps Stephen Charles Smith had not avoided the Great War after all but couldn't be sure. Glynis had worn Smith's England cap and explained how small it was on her head being for decoration only. Most importantly Glynis was able to corroborate much of what had already been detailed in the book which to a historian is comforting when you have extra evidence to cross-reference your claims. Stephen Smith had been performing sporting feats and winning trophies from the start of his career over 130 years ago. Now, myself and Glynis, the link to the past I thought I would never gain, put our heads together to see how we could best honour one of football's first superstars.

Endnotes

Introduction

1. Edgar in *The Times*, Why England's ten biggest clubs are still the same ones as 100 years ago', 11/12/2018.
2. Allman and Shaw, 100 years of soccer: Hednesford Town Football Club, 1980.
3. *Sports Argus*, Saturday 1 January 1949.
4. Matthews, *Aston Villa: A complete record 1874–1988*, 1988.
5. Page, 1997 Pinnacle of the Perry Barr Pets, p.10.
6. Bishop and Holt, 2010, Aston Villa: The Complete Record, p.338.
7. *The Aston Villa News and Record*, 1/9/ 1906.
8. http://www.coachesvoice.com.
9. William McGregor in *Sports Argus*, 20 February 1909.

Chapter 1 – Abbots Bromley

1. Wilson, Fularton and co, 1870–72, *The Imperial Gazetteer of England and Wales*.
2. Dugdale and Burnett, 1835, England and Wales delineated.
3. Hutton, R. (2001). The stations of the sun: a history of the ritual year in Britain.
4. See 2.
5. Malham; 1807, *Complete Pocket Gazetteer of England and Wales*.
6. Staffordshire Past Track Website – Abbots Bromley.
7. Abbots Bromley Conservation Area Appraisal, 2015, p16.
8. *The Cornhill Magazine*, Vol. 29 (1874): 686-697.
9. Kitchener, M. *The Rural Community: A case study of two regions of Staffordshire 1750–1900* (1987).
10. www.abbotsbromley.com.
11. *The Cornhill Magazine*, Vol. 29 (1874): 686–697.

Endnotes

12. www.ccmhs.co.uk.
13. Fasanaro L. (2008) Franco-German Relations and the Coal Problem in the Aftermath of the First and Second World Wars. In: *A History of Franco-German Relations in Europe*. Palgrave Macmillan, New York, p.89.

Chapter 2 – Hazel Slade

1. www.yeoldeduncow.com.
2. whatpub.com.
3. In 1870–72, John Marius Wilson's Imperial Gazetteer of England and Wales described Rugeley.
4. hazelslade.org.uk.
5. British Newspaper Archive.
6. www.parliament.uk.
7. www.mylearning.org.
8. *The Cornhill Magazine*, Vol. 29 (1874): 686–697.
9. www.mylearning.org.
10. 1881 census.
11. British Newspaper Archive.
12. Bradbury, 2013, *Lost Teams of the Midlands*. p211.
13. Page, 1997, Perry Barr Pets, p.52.
14. The Aston Villa Chronicles 1874-1924 (and After), John Lerwill, 2010, p.222.
15. *Aston Villa: The Complete Record*.
16. *The Villa News and Record*, 1 Sept. 1906.
17. *Aston Villa: The Complete Record*.
18. *Aston Villa: The Complete Record*.

Chapter 3 – Hednesford

1. 1891 census.
2. http://www.hazelslade.org.uk.
3. https://spartacus-educational.com.
4. Ibid.
5. Bradbury, 2013, *Lost Teams of the Midlands*. p.211.
6. https://www.nonleaguematters.co.uk.
7. *Birmingham Daily Post*, April 21, 1890.
8. *Walsall Advertiser*, May 17, 1890.

9. *Birmingham Daily Post* – Wednesday, 3 September 1890.
10. *Birmingham Daily Post* – Monday, 2 March 1891.
11. www.hazelslade.org.uk.
12. *Birmingham Daily Post*, April 1, 1891.
13. *Lichfield Mercury* – Friday, 24 April 1891.
14. *Birmingham Daily Post* – Wednesday, 22 April 1891.
15. *Staffordshire Advertiser* – Saturday, 16 May 1891.
16. *Birmingham Daily Post*, Monday, 11 May 1891.
17. *Coventry Evening Telegraph* – Friday, 9 October 1891.
18. *Coventry Evening Telegraph* – Friday, 20 November 1891.
19. *Lichfield Mercury* – Friday, 8 January 1892.
20. *Coventry Evening Telegraph* – Friday 15 July 1892.
21. *Birmingham Daily Post* – Tuesday, 30 August 1892.
22. *Lichfield Mercury* – Friday, 13 January 1893.
23. www.hazelslade.org.uk.
24. www.cannockchasedc.gov.uk.
25. P153, Bradbury, M. *Lost Teams of the Midlands*.
26. P153, Bradbury, M. *Lost Teams of the Midlands*.
27. *Lichfield Mercury*, Friday 20 January 1893.
28. *Lichfield Mercury*, Friday 27 January 1893.
29. www.hazelslade.org.
30. *The Little Book of Aston Villa* – Dave Woodhall – page 13.
31. *Lichfield Mercury* – Friday, 24 February 1893.
32. *Birmingham Daily Post*, Monday 27 March 1893.
33. *Wellington Journal*, Saturday 4 March 1893.
34. *Birmingham Daily Post*, Thursday 6 April 1893.
35. www.historywebsite.com.
36. T. Matthews, *Who's Who of Aston Villa*, 2004.
37. *Birmingham Daily Post* – Thursday 06 April 1893.
38. Goldstein, Dan (1999). *The Rough Guide to English Football*.
39. Page, *Perry Barr Pets*.
40. Page, *Perry Barr Pets*, p80.
41. *Lichfield Mercury,* Friday 19 May 1893.
42. PB Pets p.43.
43. *Athletic News*, March 1893 in Lerwill.
44. *Lichfield Mercury*, Friday 7 July 1893.
45. *Athletic News*, 1928.
46. PBP P52.
47. spartacus-educational.com.

Chapter 4 – Perry Barr

1. spartacus-educational.com.
2. www.birmingham.gov.uk.
3. www.localhistories.org.
4. Berg, Maxine (1991). 'Commerce and Creativity in Eighteenth-Century Birmingham'.
5. Hartnell, Roy (1995). Urban History. 22 (2): 229–237.
6. Matthews, *The Complete Record*.
7. PBP – Page – p.83.
8. *The Sporting Mail*, 10 Feb 1906.
9. PBP – P.63.
10. Avfc The Complete Record p331.
11. www.englandfootballonline.com.
12. Lerwill p.495.
13. Complete Record p.186.
14. www.englandfootballonline.com.
15. Complete Record p.329.
16. Lerwill p.183.
17. Complete Record p.231.
18. PBP – p.88.
19. www.footballhistory.org.
20. Lerwill p.335.
21. *Athletic News* 5 June 1893.
22. PBP p.26.
23. PBP p.27.
24. Lerwill p.488.
25. 50 PBP.
26. COMPLETE RECORD p.334.
27. *Birmingham Daily Post*, Monday 28 August 1893.

Chapter 5 – Culture Shock

1. www.11v11.com.
2. Lerwill p.335.
3. *Athletic News*, Monday 4 September 1893.
4. Lerwill p.335.
5. *Athletic News*, Monday, 4 September 1893.

6. *Sheffield Daily Telegraph*, Monday, 4 September 1893.
7. *Birmingham Daily Post*. Monday 4 September 1893.
8. Lerwill p.335.
9. Lerwill p.335/6.
10. *Sheffield Daily Telegraph*, Monday, 4 September 1893.
11. *Athletic News*, Monday 4 September 1893.
12. Complete Record p.332 – 334.
13. Lerwill p.336.
14. Complete Record p.334.
15. Lerwill p.337.
16. Complete Record p.334.
17. *Sheffield Daily Telegraph*, Tuesday, 17 October 1893.
18. *Birmingham Daily Post*, Monday, 23 October 1893.
19. *Athletic News* in Lerwill p338.
20. *Birmingham Daily Post*, Monday, 23 October 1893.
21. Complete Record p.334.
22. *Leicester Daily Post*, Monday, 23 October 1893.
23. Complete Record p.332.
24. *Derby Daily Telegraph*, Monday, 10 February 1896.
25. *Athletic News*, 30 October, 1893.
26. *Lloyd's Weekly Newspaper*, Sunday, 29 October 1893.
27. *Birmingham Daily Post*, Monday, 30 October 1893.
28. AVFC Complete Record, p341.
29. *Lloyds' Weekly Newspaper,* Sunday, 29 October 1893.
30. *Athletic News*, Monday, 30 October 1893.
31. *Birmingham Daily Post*, Monday, 30 October 1893.
32. *Birmingham Daily Post*, Tuesday, 31 October 1893.

Chapter 6 – The Team of All Talents

1. *Birmingham Daily Post*, Monday, 6 November 1893.
2. *Lincolnshire Echo*, 7 November 1893.
3. Paul Days; John Hudson; Bernard Callaghan (1 December 1999). Sunderland AFC: The Official History 1879–2000.
4. www.11v11.com.
5. *Birmingham Daily Post*, Monday, 13 November 1893.
6. www.11v11.com.

7. Lerwill p.341.
8. Complete Record p.334.
9. *Sunderland Daily Echo and Shipping Gazette*, Monday, 13 November 1893.
10. *Birmingham Daily Post* , Monday, 13 November 1893.
11. Villa complete record p.334.
12. Lerwill p.341.
13. *Birmingham Daily Post*, Monday, 18 December 1893.
14. Lerwill p.341.
15. Complete Record p.334.
16. *Birmingham Daily Post*, December 1893.
17. *Burnley Express*, Wednesday, 27 December 1893.

Chapter 7 – On the Sidelines

1. *Birmingham Daily Post*, Monday, 8 January 1894.
2. Complete Record p.334.
3. *Birmingham Daily Post*, Monday, 5 February 1894.
4. Lerwill p.344.
5. Complete Record p.334.
6. Lerwill p.344/345.
7. *Birmingham Daily Post*, Monday, 26 February 1894.

Chapter 8 – English Champion

1. *Athletic News*, Monday, 5 March 1894.
2. 1901 census.
3. *Birmingham Daily Post*, Monday, 5 March 1894.
4. Lerwill p.345.
5. Complete Record p.334.
6. *Birmingham Daily Post*, Monday, 26 March 1894.
7. *Birmingham Daily Post*, Monday, 26 March 1894.
8. *Birmingham Daily Post*, Tuesday 27 March 1894.
9. *Birmingham Daily Post*, Wednesday, 28 March 1894.
10. Complete Record p.334.
11. *Athletic News*, Monday 9 April 1894.

12. *Birmingham Daily Post,* 9 April 1894.
13. *Athletic News*, Monday, 9 April 1894.
14. *Birmingham Daily Post*, Monday 9 April 1894.
15. *Birmingham Daily Post*, Tuesday 10 April 1894.

Chapter 9 – Apotheosis

1. *Birmingham Daily Post*, Monday, 16 April 1894.
2. *Athletic News*, Monday, 16 April 1894.
3. *Birmingham Daily Post*, Monday, 30 April 1894.
4. Complete Record p.21.
5. *Sheffield Daily Telegraph*, Tuesday, 4 February 1896 & *Derby Daily Telegraph*, Monday, 10 February 1896.
6. Complete Record p.337.
7. *Birmingham Daily Post*, Monday, 3 September 1894.
8. *Athletic News* in Lerwill p.352.
9. Lerwill, cover page.
10. *Atheltic News* in Lerwill p.352.
11. *Scottish Referee*, Monday, 17 September 1894.
12. Lerwill p.353.
13. *Athletic News* in Lerwill p.353.
14. *Birmingham Daily Post*, Monday, 1 October 1894.
15. Lerwill p.354.
16. *Birmingham Daily Post*, Monday, 29 October 1894.
17. *Athletic News,* Monday, 29 October 1894.
18. Complete Record p.336.
19. *Birmingham Daily Post*, Monday, 12 November 1894.
20. *Sheffield Daily Telegraph*, Tuesday, 13 November 1894.
21. Lerwill p.357.
22. *Athletic News* in Lerwill p.357.
23. Complete Record 336.
24. *Birmingham Daily Post*, Monday, 26 November 1894.
25. *https://spartacus-educational.com/ASTONhunterA.htm.*
26. Lerwill p.358.
27. *Birmingham Daily Post*, Monday, 3 December 1894.
28. *The Essential Aston Villa*, Adam Ward and Jeremy Griffin.
29. *Athletic Ne*ws, Monday, 3 December 1894.

30. Lerwill p.359/60.
31. Complete Record p.334-p337.
32. Matthews p.214 – A complete record.
33. hazelslade.org.
34. vintage footballers.com.
35. angel-pig.net.
36. *Birmingham Daily Post*, Monday 4 February 1895.
37. *Athletic News*, Monday, 4 February 1895.
38. Lerwill p363.
39. *Birmingham Daily Post,* Monday, 18 February 1895.
40. *Birmingham Daily Post*, Monday, 4 March 1895.
41. *Athletic News*, Monday, 4 March 1895.
42. *Morning Post*, Monday, 18 March 1895.
43. *Birmingham Daily Post*, Monday, 18 March 1895.
44. *Athletic News*, Monday, 18 March 1895.
45. Referee of the match overheard conversation and recounted it in *Sporting Mail* 21 Jan 1911.
46. *Athletic News*, Monday, 18 March 1895.
47. McGregor, *Sports Argus,* 20 Feb 1909.
48. *Birmingham Daily Post*, Monday, 18 March 1895.
49. McGregor.
50. *Birmingham Daily Post,* Monday, 18 March 1895.

Chapter 10 – World Champion

1. *Pearson's Weekly*, Saturday, 13 April 1895.
2. *Scottish Referee*, Monday, 1 April 1895.
3. *Manchester Courier and Lancashire General Advertiser*, Saturday 6 April 1895.
4. *Athletic News*, Monday, 8 April 1895.
5. Jonathan Wilson (2020-04-25). 'Sunderland's Victorian all-stars blazed trail for money's rule of football'.
6. *Scottish Referee*, Friday, 5 April 1895.
7. *Scottish Referee*, Monday, 8 April 1895.
8. Grayson, Edward (1996 edition of 1955 original). Corinthians and Cricketers and Towards a New Sporting Era.
9. *Athletic News*, Monday, 8 April 1895.

10. *Scottish Referee*, Monday, 8 April 1895.
11. www.lancashiretelegraph.co.uk.
12. *Athletic News*, Monday, 8 April 1895.
13. *Scottish Referee*, Monday, 15 April 1895.
14. *Athletic News*, Monday, 15 April 1895.

Chapter 11 – 'For Archie'

1. *The Sportsman*, Saturday, 13 April 1895.
2. *Maidstone Journal and Kentish Advertiser*, Thursday, 18 April 1895.
3. *Manchester Evening News*, Friday, 19 April 1895.
4. *Scottish Referee*, Friday, 19 April 1895.
5. James Harrison, ed. (1996). *Imperial Britain*. Children's Encyclopaedia of British History.
6. https://londonist.com/2015/05/when-fa-cup-finals-were-a-picnic-in-crystal-palace-park.
7. *Penny Illustrated Paper*, Saturday, 20 April 1895.
8. *Reynold's Newspaper*, Sunday, 21 April 1895.
9. *Athletic News*, Monday, 22 April 1895.
10. *Birmingham Daily Post*, Monday, 22 April 1895.
11. *Sporting Life*, Monday, 22 April 1895.
12. John Devey in the *Sporting Mail,* 20 Jan 1906.
13. *Athletic News*, Monday, 22 April 1895.
14. *Birmingham Daily Post*, Monday, 22 April 1895.
15. *Athletic News*, Monday, 22 April 1895.
16. 1895 FA Cup – fa-cupfinals.co.uk. Archived from the original on 19 April 2012.
17. Devey in McGregor's column in *Sports Argus* 16 Jan 1909.
18. *Athletic News*, Monday, 22 April 1895 & *Sporting Life*, Monday, 22 April 1895.
19. *Sporting Life*, Monday, 22 April 1895.
20. *Birmingham Daily Post*, Monday, 22 April 1895.
21. *Sporting Life*, Monday, 22 April 1895.
22. *Birmingham Daily Post*, Monday, 22 April 1895.
23. *Birmingham Daily Post*, Monday, 22 April 1895.
24. *Sporting Life*, Monday, 22 April 1895.
25. *Athletic News*, Monday, 22 April 1895.

26. 1901 census.
27. *Birmingham Daily Post*, Tuesday, 23 April 1895.

Chapter 12 – William Smith

1. *Worcestershire Chronicle*, Saturday, 15 June 1895.
2. *Athletic News* in Lerwill p.372, Lerwill p.384.
3. *Athletic News*, Monday, 23 November 1896.
4. Centenary Wolves 1877- 1977, Percy M. Young, 1976.
5. PBP P20 & 34.
6. *Athletic News*, Monday, 2 November 1896.
7. Lerwill p.396.
8. COMPLETE RECORD p.340.
9. *Daily Telegraph & Courier* (London), Saturday, 26 December 1896.
10. *Athletic News*, Monday, 28 December 1896.
11. PBP P34.

Chapter 13 – Celebrity, Superstar, 'Double Winner'

1. PBP 48.

Chapter 14 – Champion Again

1. Club Minutes 13 April 1897 in Lerwill p.417.
2. Lerwill p.435.
3. Bob Crampsey (1990). The First 100 Years. Scottish Football League.
4. https://spartacus-educational.com.
5. *Scottish Referee*, Friday, 27 December 1901.
6. *Sheffield Daily Telegraph*, Monday, 11 April 1898.
7. Lerwill p.438/9.
8. Complete Record p.342.
9. Lerwill p.456/457.
10. *Athletic News*, Monday, 1 May 1899.
11. The Complete Record p.344-348.
12. Paul Boynton, Pompey History Assoc.

13. *Athletic News*, Monday 11 September 1899.
14. *Athletic News*, Monday, 4 December 1899.
15. Argus in Lerwill p.469.
16. Villa club minutes in Lerwill p.479.
17. Complete Record p.351.

Chapter 15 – Portsmouth

1. spartacus-educational.com.
2. rsssf.com.
3. *Derby Daily Telegraph*, Wednesday, 8 May 1901.
4. www.portsmouthfc.co.uk.
5. *Bournemouth Guardian*, Saturday, 18 May 1901.
6. www.thebeachguide.co.uk.
7. *Birmingham Mail*, Thursday, 2 May 1901.
8. *spartacus-educational.com.*
9. *Portsmouth Evening News*, Tuesday, 3 September 1901.
10. https://www.vintagefootballers.com.
11. *Portsmouth Evening News*, Thursday 5 September 1901.
12. www.vintagefootballers.com.
13. *Bournemouth Daily Echo*, Thursday, 12 September 1901.
14. https://www.portsmouthfc.co.uk/news/2020/august/pompeys-title-triumphs-190102.
15. *Hampshire Advertiser*, Saturday. 14 September 1901.
16. *Lloyds Weekly Newspaper*, Sunday, 8 September 1901.
17. *Portsmouth Evening News*, Monday, 14 October 1901.
18. *Bournemouth Daily Echo*, Monday, 4 November 1901.
19. International Cricket Council. Retrieved 21 June 2018.
20. Wilton, Iain (June 2004) Charles Fry – Up with the Gods. Ellis, Clive (1984). C.B.: The Life of Charles Burgess Fry. J. M. Dent & Sons; 1st edition. C.B. Fry. Player Profiles. Corinthian Casuals. Archived from the original on 20 October 2012.
21. Ellis 1984, pp. 137–139.
22. *Bournemouth Daily Echo*, Monday, 4 November 1901.
23. *www.11v11.com.*
24. Sporting Life – Thursday 26 December 1901 118 Sporting Life – Thursday 26 December 1901.

25. en.wikipedia.org/wiki/1901/02_FA_Cup.
26. *Portsmouth Evening News*, Monday, 16 December.
27. www.stadiumguide.com.
28. *Bournemouth Daily Echo*, Monday, 3 March 1902.
29. *Nottingham Evening Post*, Saturday, 8 March 1902.
30. *Scottish Referee*, Friday, 27 December 1901.
31. *Portsmouth Evening News*, Saturday, 29 March 1902.
32. *London Daily News*. Tuesday, 1 April 1902.
33. rsssf.com.
34. *Bournemouth Daily Echo*, Wednesday, 2 April 1902.
35. *Bournemouth Daily Echo*, Monday, 7 April 1902.
36. *Middlesex Independent*, Wednesday, 23 April 1902.
37. http://www.rsssf.com.
38. *Leeds Mercury*, Monday, 7 April 1902.

Chapter 16 – The Old Warrior's Return

1. *Birmingham Daily Gazette*, Monday, 6 February 1905.
2. 11v11.com.
3. Old Town Plan of Birmingham 1883.
4. The Encyclopaedia of Birmingham City Football Club 1875–2000.
5. *Bournemouth Daily Echo*, Monday, 6 February 1905.
6. *The Sportsman*, Monday, 6 February 1905.
7. *Portsmouth Evening News*, Monday, 30 April 1906 Gillingham.

Chapter 17 – Gillingham

1. *Portsmouth Evening News*, Friday, 4 May 1906.
2. rsssf.com.
3. www.englandfootballonline.com.
4. www Triggs. Gillingham Football Club, p. 8.
5. Davies, Hunter (2003). The History of Spectators Boots, Balls and Haircuts p. 85.
6. Triggs. Gillingham Football Club: A Chronology 1893–1984. p. 4.
7. Local history: Gillingham Football Club;. Medway Council.

8. Inglis, Simon (1983). *The Football Grounds of England and Wales.* pp. 243–245.
9. gillinghamfcscrapbook.co.uk.
10. gillinghamfcscrapbook.co.uk.
11. gillinghamfcscrapbook.co.uk.
12. www.in2013dollars.com.
13. Gillingham scrapbook.
14. *Athletic News*, Monday, 18 February 1907.
15. Gillingham scrapbook.
16. www.vintagefootballers.com.
17. Brown, Tony (2003). *The Definitive Gillingham F.C.*
18. Gillingham scrapbook.
19. *Newcastle Daily Chronicle*, Monday, 13 January 1908.
20. Gillingham scrapbook.

Chapter 18 – Life After Football

1. *Hampshire Telegraph*, Saturday, 29 August 1908.
2. Ray Stubbington e-mail.
3. 1911 census.
4. *Hull Daily Mail/Aberdeen Express*, Monday, 13 September 1910.
5. www.englandfootballonline.com.
6. George Stuart Gordon, The Retreat from Mons, p. 12.
7. www.royalcornwallmuseum.org.uk.
8. WWI service records.
9. The Rifle Brigade; The Long, Long Trail.
10. 9th Battalion Rifle Brigade; Wartime Memories Project. Retrieved 19 June 2016.
11. *With the British Army in Flanders: Hooge Crater*; The Big Note.
12. Stubbington email – newspaper clip.
13. https://www.vintagefootballers.com.
14. Davies, Peter; Lynch, Derek (2002). *The Routledge Companion to Fascism and the Far Right. Routledge.* pp. 1–5.
15. *Berks and Oxon Advertiser*, Friday, 31 May 1935.